Understanding
the Pipe Organ

D1548446

Understanding the Pipe Organ

A Guide for Students, Teachers and Lovers of the Instrument

JOHN R. SHANNON

McFarland & Company, Inc., Publishers
Jefferson, North Carolina, and London

LIBRARY OF CONGRESS CATALOGUING-IN-PUBLICATION DATA

Shannon, John R.
Understanding the pipe organ : a guide for students, teachers
and lovers of the instrument / John R. Shannon.
p.   cm.
Includes bibliographical references and index.

ISBN 978-0-7864-3998-0
softcover : 50# alkaline paper ∞

1. Organ (Musical instrument)—Construction.   I. Title.
ML552.S43   2009   786.5'192—dc22   2008055195

British Library cataloguing data are available

Cover photograph: Organ 1800 by the American builder David
Tannenburg (1728–1804); originally in the Home Moravian Church,
Salem, North Carolina, restored in 2003–2004 by Taylor and Boody
Organ Builders, now in the Visitors' Center, Old Salem, North Carolina.

Manufactured in the United States of America

*McFarland & Company, Inc., Publishers
Box 611, Jefferson, North Carolina 28640
www.mcfarlandpub.com*

To my wife, Sylvia

Table of Contents

List of Figures

Introduction

The purpose of this book is a simple one: to lead more persons, both inside and outside the professional world of music, to understand more about the pipe organ and the ways the instrument works. The pipe organ often fascinates and baffles the layman, who many times will ask rudimentary questions about it. An understanding of the pipe organ among otherwise knowledgeable musicians is often equally slight, and such confusion may even extend to many who play the instrument regularly. The history of organ building is a microhistory of western technology. It spans, over a thousand years, a range from simple mechanics to solid-state electronics. As long as a technology is mysterious to us, it holds control over us. It's hoped that an understanding of the pipe organ's technological basis will aid readers in appreciation of this most wonderful of musical instruments.

The author intends his audience to include both professionals and laymen. He certainly has in mind players, students, and their teachers, who need this knowledge almost daily. There are those (the author is certainly one) for whom mechanical gadgetry is fascinating in its own right. I hope those who approach the pipe organ from this point of view will find this book a guide. Many persons who first encountered the organ as an interesting mechanical object have found themselves caught up in its music. If this book can encourage this process, all the better. Often laymen are called on to have an understanding of the instrument. For no other group is the material contained here more important than for those who serve their churches on organ committees. Such committees are very often vested with spending six-digit amounts (or more!) for an instrument that is as mysterious as a nuclear reactor. Hopefully this book will throw light on the darkness that often clouds the discussions of these committees.

Webster defines *instrument* first as "that by which something is performed or effected, a means," but then the definition continues: "a tool, an implement." We speak of surgical and dental instruments and take it for granted that the professionals who employ them understand their operation, construction, capabilities, and limitations. It is rare that musical instruments are thought of in this light, as merely the physical means by which we accomplish musical tasks. Nonetheless, musical instruments are merely tools, highly sophisticated ones to be sure, but nonetheless tools. Good tools are, in their own right, works of art, visually and tactilely beautiful. To understand the art in the tool that is the organ is to understand more of the art of music, both in its production and in its consumption.

Two volumes I encountered in the early seventies have served as successful models for initiating the layman into the complexities of machinery: *The Way Things Work: An Illustrated Encyclopedia of Technology* (New York: Simon and Schuster, 1967, 1971. Originally

1

published in German as *Wie funktioniert das?*). Much more recently another volume in the same vein has been most helpful: *Scientific American—How Things Work Today* (edited by Michael Wright and Mukul Patel, New York: Crown Publishers, 2000). Although the present book is written for the mechanically unlettered, it is hoped that those with mechanical knowledge still find fascination.

This book does not propose to be a manual on the art of organ building; I do not intend to describe how the instrument is built, only how it functions. I have neither the inclination nor the expertise to attempt a book on organ building, and those who seek such material will be disappointed here. Many times in the drawings, as well as in the text, I have simplified and reduced mechanisms to that which are absolutely necessary. To attempt to build from these drawings and explanations would be ludicrous.

There is no intention to recommend or to advocate the building of any particular type of pipe organ. I've attempted to describe each of the various types of organ actions in equal detail. Equal detail does not demand equal space. Mechanical action is much easier to describe and will require much less space than will various types of electric actions.

As I began this book, no question plagued me more deeply than what it should contain in regard to the electronic organ. The ubiquity of these instruments is certainly obvious, and those who play electronic organs need this type of material also. My final decision to omit discussion of electronic instruments is based neither on a failure to recognize this need nor on any qualitative judgments of the value of these instruments. Instead it is based on two facts: first, the electronic organ belongs to an entirely different class of musical instruments than does the pipe organ, and, secondly, my knowledge about electronic instruments is far too limited. Although there are external similarities between the pipe and electronic organs, in actuality there is as much difference between the two is there is between the piano and the pipe organ.

Essential to categorizing musical instruments, as the lengthy tomes on the subject will attest, is the manner in which each produces its sound. The pipe organ produces its sound by wind which causes either the air molecules or a reed in organ pipes to oscillate. The electronic organ produces electronic oscillations, which in turn are amplified and then sent into the open by transducers which we call speakers. The pipe organ is a wind instrument; the electronic organ is an electronic synthesizer. I hope, as much for myself as for others, that someone will soon write a similar book devoted to all electronic instruments but particularly to the electronic organ. It is sorely needed by all of us in the twenty-first century musical world.

One final goal of this book is the hope that it will stimulate a "do it yourself" attitude toward limited organ maintenance. The professional technician will always have a very important place in the organ world. But in a day in which problems of economics, lack of good technicians, and the high cost of travel abound, it will become increasingly necessary for each of us to make minor repairs on the instruments we play. Most day-to-day mechanical difficulties encountered by organists: the cipher, the stuck key, the blown rectifier fuse, the dirty pipe, or the slipped sliding tuner, can be easily repaired by a knowledgeable layman. To aid the lay repairman, the last chapter of the book will be devoted to trouble shooting. As we go along, it will help the reader to arm himself or herself with common hand tools, with permission to enter organ chambers, and carefully take components apart. Before undertaking this, be certain to read carefully and follow the caveat which introduces Chapter 11.

As one begins to understand any mechanical device, he or she must first become conversant in the language which applies to it. A student in a high school course in automotive mechanics must quickly learn the technological meanings of clutch, tie rods, valves, pistons, MacPherson struts, lug nuts, disc brakes, fuel injection, and the like. The same is true here. My daughter pointed out to me, for instance, that the word *sticker,* which I had casually used in an early draft of this book, meant to most persons a label to be attached to a piece of paper. In organ technology, a sticker is a rod which transmits energy by being pushed. So important is the meaning of words in these pages, that a glossary becomes a mandatory tool. Words with particular technological meanings will appear early in the text in italics. These words are in the glossary. The reader is urged to consult it at each occasion. The term "organ" in the text of this book will refer to the pipe organ alone. This decision is in no way pejorative. I've adopted this procedure merely to avoid having to modify the word each time it appears.

This book has been long in the making. Its roots lie in the mid–1980s before my early retirement from the faculty of Sweet Briar College. It was first suggested to me in conversations with Fenner Douglass, professor emeritus of Duke University. Early work on the book was done at that time. Sweet Briar College provided some financial assistance. I must thank both Oberlin College and Duke University for access to their various organs. The project was put aside for two decades, and I have returned to it after my second retirement. Traces of the earlier work are still visible in the final text.

My daughter, Cynthia Shannon, has been of immeasurable help throughout this work. She has read sections of the manuscript, made numerous suggestions, and given me computer assistance and hours of unpaid labor. Her husband and my son-in-law, Don Williams, has been equally helpful. He has approached the manuscript as one largely ignorant of the organ but as a trained engineer, knowledgeable in mechanics, electrical circuitry, electronics, and computers. His unique orientation to the text has resulted in many suggestions and corrections.

Portions of the text have been read by John (Jack) Mitchener, associate professor of Organ, Oberlin Conservatory. For his work I am grateful. Finally, last but assuredly not least, the many suggestions and hours of instruction provided me by John Allen Farmer of J. Allen Farmer, Organ Builders, have been simply invaluable. At times he directed me through complex problems that I could not have solved alone. He and his wife, Kristin, have read the manuscript and made numerous suggestions. Each of these has improved the text. The book could probably not have come to fruition had I not had a professional organ builder and a professional organist giving me support, information, and guidance.

Designations such as eight foot, sixteen foot, four foot, etc., will appear as 16', 8', 4' etc. The notation of pitch adheres to the following accepted convention:

Octave Designations

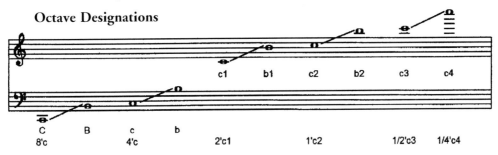

32' octave: CCC to BBB; 16' octave: CC to BB

There is a time-honored convention in the world of organ builders and technicians to designate pipes using only sharp designations. Flat spelling is not used. Hence the chromatic octave is always spelled:

$$C \; C^\sharp \; D \; D^\sharp \; E \; F \; F^\sharp \; G \; G^\sharp \; A \; A^\sharp \; B$$

Even though to others in the musical world it may seem incongruous, a minor third above C is spelled C to D$^\sharp$, not C to E$^\flat$. This convention will be used from time to time in this book.

CHAPTER 1

The Principal Components of the Organ

To define the pipe organ is no easy matter either for the professional or the layman. Individual examples of violins, flutes, pianos, clarinets, or trombones are remarkably similar in outward appearance, and even a novice can easily identify each of them. The outward appearance of two violins, for instance, is essentially the same, and although a professional may find worlds of difference between two of them, there is little doubt that both are indeed violins. The situation is very different when a novice meets the organ. If he tours various churches to see their organs, at one place he may be shown a large console with as many as five sets of keys to be played with the hands and another to be played with the feet. There might be enough additional apparatus to fly a 747 jet, but he may see no pipes at all. At another site he may see a striking display of pipes reflecting a close connection to contemporary architecture and a sleek console with limited accoutrement. Again he might encounter an ornate piece of furniture obviously influenced by eighteenth century cabinetry, displaying a single set of keys, a few knobs with writing on them, and a single row of elaborately embossed pipes. In each situation he is assured that what he is seeing is a pipe organ, yet the instruments he has seen seem to him largely disparate. His confusion is understandable.

But the confusion is not limited to the layman. I've known students trained on the best organs in the classic tradition who had little knowledge of, or sympathy for, *combination actions*, *crescendo pedals*, *swell pedals*, or *octave couplers*. Some organists would not consider playing on a straight *pedalboard* and others will play on no other. Some organists are lost without a *swell box* and others consider them to be abominations. Organs simply differ and they differ extravagantly.

My purpose at this point, however, is not to stress the variety one encounters in organ building, but to attempt to identify elements which all organs have in common, no matter what their overall designs might be. These elements, the principal systems of the organ, are:

- a means of raising wind pressure, of regulating that wind pressure, and then wind lines to transmit wind to various portions of the organ;
- a selection mechanism containing both the *keyboards* and the *stop* controls, known as the *console* or *playing desk*, by which a player may select those pipes he wishes to sound at a particular moment;

- a means, known as the organ *action*, of connecting the keyboard and stop controls to the chests upon which the pipes are mounted;
- wooden *chests* which support the pipes, contain the wind under pressure, and house the valves which allow wind to enter selected pipes; and
- the pipework itself.

Every organ, no matter what its design or size, contains these elements. To these mandatory systems may be added others: swell boxes, elegant *cases*, registration assists, and the like.

Although in the following chapters each of these systems will be discussed in detail, some general comments on each are appropriate here. In earlier times, wind was raised by use of one or more manually operated *diagonal (cuneiform) bellows* similar in principle, if not in size, to the small fireplace bellows found in many homes. Today the source of organ wind is usually an enclosed fan, known as a *centrifugal* or *squirrel cage blower*, activated by an electric motor. Since such blowers generally produce wind at higher pressure and greater volume than organs require, a valve mechanism is necessary to admit into the ducts only the wind which is necessary at a particular moment. The pressure of the wind is then kept constant by bellows which expand against the consistent pressure of weights or springs. From that main bellows the wind is led to the various components of the organ, requiring pneumatic pressure. The wind is carried to various parts of the organ by wind lines or wind trunks. These closely resemble the ducts found in home hot air and cooling systems. In many organs various components use wind at varying pressures. Hence it is necessary to re-regulate wind wherever there is a necessary pressure change.

The mechanism for key and stop selection takes place at the console of the organ, which contains both the keyboards used in key selection and the stop controls used for stop selection. Consoles may be built into the front of the organ case, where they are hardly obtrusive, or they may be detached from the pipes, cases, and chests. Some can be so massive that a layman may think that the console itself is the organ. This misconception often occurs when the pipework is hidden.

The keyboards are similar to those used in other keyboard instruments. Although there are organs with a single keyboard, most have multiple sets of keys to be played with the hands. These are known as *manuals* or *claviers*. There is also a set to be played by the feet, the *pedalboard*. The manual keyboards are stacked in stair-step fashion, one atop the other. They are always set so that the keys for the same note on two manuals are precisely in alignment. A single keyboard normally controls its own set of pipes, known as a *division*. Somewhat more confusing is the fact that each division is sometimes referred to as itself an organ. Thus the most important manual on a three-manual organ, known as the *great* organ, controls pipes on the great chest. Auxiliary manuals on a three manual organ might control the swell organ and the *positive organ*. Each manual is connected to its own pipework mounted on its own chest or division of the organ. Each of these organs within an organ has its own musical integrity and differs from other manuals by the quality and intensity of its stops.

Almost all multi-manual organs have a means by which one or more manuals may be played together by means of a *coupler*. Thus it is generally possible to play the swell organ on the great manual, the positive organ of the great manual, and the swell and the positive together on one manual or the other. Coupling allows the player a greater number of dynamic levels than the uncoupled manuals alone would provide. On a three manual organ the organist would have the following possibilities: great alone, swell alone, positiv alone, great + swell, great + positiv, positiv + swell, and great + swell + positiv. Normally all manuals can be coupled to the pedal. Although many organs have complete *pedal organs*, others do not. These depend on coupling to fill out the limited number of stops which the pedal independently possesses.

Stops are normally controlled by means of knobs which are drawn outward if the stop is on or by *stop tabs*, which are nothing more than simple electrical switches. Stop controls are arranged either to the right and left of the player or directly in front of him above the keyboards. Stops are conveniently arranged so that those controlled by a single manual are grouped together and in an order in which the player is likely to use them.

Many organs have extensive systems by which the player can pre-set combinations of stops. Older *combination actions* required considerable space within the console. This often led to consoles of imposing size and complexity. Combination action is a practical impossibility on organs with *mechanical stop action* (see below), but with *electric action* it is extremely practical. The introduction of electronic switching in recent years has diminished the size of combination actions to small computers with almost infinite possibilities for various combinations. The player usually selects combinations by pressing buttons (commonly called *pistons*) which are directly below each keyboard and often duplicated by toe studs to be activated by the feet. Finally, one often finds two (and sometimes more) large pedals mounted above and in front of the pedal board. The one of the left opens and closes the shades of the swell box. The other, called the *crescendo pedal*, controls a set of combinations moving from soft to very loud. As the player pushes the pedal, one combination after another comes into play producing the illusion of a crescendo. The crescendo pedal is preset and cannot normally be altered.

By the action of the organ, we mean the method used to transfer the actions taken by the player at the console to the mechanism which actually activates stops and individual pipes. The type of action an organ will have largely determines its nature. Each of these actions will be discussed in some detail in following chapters. Nevertheless it is important that each be briefly defined below. There are six possibilities: (1) *mechanical*, (2) *pneumatic*, (3) *mechanical pneumatic*, (4) *direct electric*, (5) *electro-mechanical*, and (6) *electro-pneumatic*.

As we briefly discuss each of these actions, there will be a diagram to aid in understanding. These diagrams are not intended to be more than a sketch to introduce the reader to the more detailed discussion of each action in later chapters. Each diagram deals only with key and not with stop action.

In mechanical action the connections between key and pipe and between stop knob and stop action is accomplished completely by mechanical linkages. When the player depresses a key, a series of levers and other hardware opens a valve inside the chest and below the selected pipe. This admits air into that pipe. The hardware used in the drawing on page eight has the following elements:

- Key lever: The front portion of the lever is covered with some material such as ivory and is visible. The rear section lies hidden within the console and is a simple first class lever.
- Sticker: A dowel generally about the diameter of a lead pencil which transfers motion in compression (by pushing).

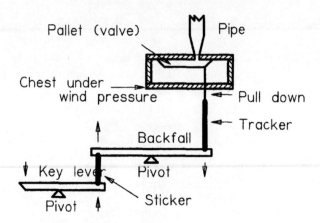

Figure 1.1 Mechanical Action

- Backfall: A relatively long first class lever which transfers motion horizontally.
- Tracker: Thin strips, generally of wood, which transfer motion in tension (by pulling). They are so common in mechanical action that this action is sometimes called tracker action.
- Pull down: A wire running from the tracker through the bottom of the chest and connected to the pallet.
- Chest: The box on which the pipes are mounted that contains the organ action and is charged with wind pressure.
- Pallet: A rectangular shaped valve, hinged in the rear and pulled down at the front. It is spring loaded (not shown). The action of the player's fingers is transferred via the key lever to the sticker, then to the backfall, the tracker, the pull down, and finally to the pallet. Wind is then admitted to the pipe.

When a stop is pulled, similar, although more massive, linkages are connected to the stop mechanism in the chest. The principal advantage of mechanical action, and it is an important one, is that the player can feel a close contact with the wind entering the pipe. Since there are severe limitations of the distance the keyboards may be from their respective chests, there are also severe limitations on the overall design of the organ. Combination action rarely exists in completely mechanical instruments, and, even if it does, it consists of one or two rudimentary *machine stops*, pre-set by the builder and operating certain frequently used combinations.

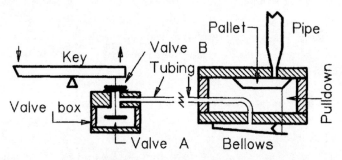

Figure 1.2 Tubular Pneumatic Action

In the latter part of the nineteenth century, builders sought a more flexible means of action than simple mechanics allowed. This they first found in air itself. In pneumatic action, when a player depresses a key, it allows a small puff of air (or in some versions an exhaust of air) to move through one of the many tiny tubes which lead from the key action to small bellows (called *pneumatics*) below the pipe valves. This air causes the appropriate bellows to inflate (or in some cases deflate) and, by mechanical linkages between the bellows and pipe valve, cause the pipe valve to open. The drawing above makes the mechanism clear. Stop action is accomplished in a similar manner. Since the leaden tubes are the most obvious component of this action, it came to be called tubular pneumatic action.

Pneumatic action is now obsolete. The tubes were generally of lead and were fragile. A misstep by an organ tuner and these tubes could be easily smashed. When seriously damaged, they were almost impossible to repair. Pneumatic action was often sluggish and would not repeat notes quickly. Today one occasionally finds pneumatic action actuating single pedal stops, particularly in historical restorations.

Mechanical action had another liability which builders sought to avoid. There is a limit to the amount of energy the player's fingers can be expected to exert. In the nineteenth century, taste moved to larger and larger organs with higher and higher wind pressure. The combination of many stops and higher wind pressures placed undue stress on the player's fingers. Mechanical actions to actuate such organs became impractical. Some builders moved to mechanical-pneumatic action. In this action the transmission from key to chest remains mechanical. The mechanical action, however, opens small bellows attached to the valves under each key valve. When a key is depressed, a bellows deflates (sometimes inflates) and that opens the pallet.

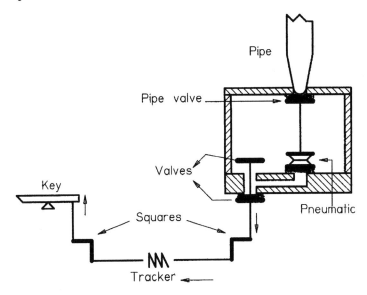

Figure 1.3 Mechanical Pneumatic Action

A variety of this type of action allows mechanical connection to the pallet to remain intact and, at the same time, assist this motion pneumatically. This device is known as the *Barker lever* after one of those who perfected it. A similar system, operating hydraulically, assists the driver in a modern automobile power steering mechanism.

The problems of inflexibility of design and the limitation of the player's fingers are both avoided in the several types of electric action. In electric action the mechanical connections between console and chest are replaced by low voltage electric circuits. These are similar to the circuits used in model trains and home doorbells. Cables made of hundreds of small wires could now replace the inflexibility of mechanical and pneumatic actions. Recently these wire cables have been superseded to fiberglass ones. When the player depresses a key or pulls a stop in electric action, he merely activates appropriate circuits. His actions become that of an electrical switch maker or breaker. Since electricity travels at the speed of light (c. 186,000 miles per second), there is no perceptible time lag between the moment the player depressed a key and the moment the action takes place in the chest. This removed severe spatial limitations on placement of the console or the pipework.

The most common means of converting electrical energy to mechanical energy is by solenoids, also termed electromagnets. (For a discussion of electric circuits and solenoids see Chapter 4.) The simplest electric action, called Direct Electric Action (registered trademark, Wicks Organ Company, henceforth referred to as *direct action*), simply places a solenoid beneath each pipe. The solenoid has an *armature* which is attached to the pipe valve itself. When the solenoid is activated, the valve opens and the pipe plays.

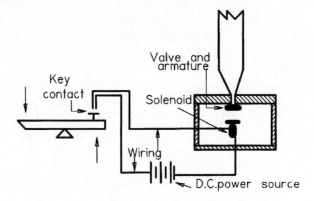

Figure 1.4 Direct Action

It would seem that the simplicity of this action would replace other more complex forms of electric action. This is not so for two reasons. The large number of solenoids necessary for organs of any size means that there is a large expenditure of current if many pipes are played simultaneously. Secondly, it is practically impossible to get a number of solenoids to fire precisely together when a number of pipes are played at the same moment. The result can be an annoying buzz before the sound is produced. The advantage of direct action is that it is extremely simple to build, so simple that an amateur can build these chests in his home basement with ease.

In an electro-mechanical action, electric circuits from console to chest actuate solenoids which, in turn, actuate the mechanical action in the chest, which opens the valves beneath the pipes. The electro-mechanical action can be viewed as a modified mechanical action in which the system of physical linkages has been replaced by electrical circuits activating solenoids. Instead of the energy of the player's fingers opening the valves, solenoids do this work. There are many examples of organs which were originally mechanical and have been "electrified" upon rebuilding.

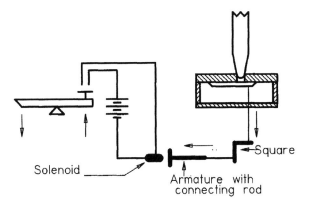

Figure 1.5 Electro-Mechanical Action

In electro-pneumatic action, a small bellows, circular in shape and called a *pouch*, is located beneath each pipe. This tiny bellows has a circular pad of felt attached to its top surface. This pad is held tight against the pipe hole by a small, internal spring. Exiting from the bottom of the bellows is a small pipe which leads to a solenoid outside the chest. When that solenoid is activated by the key action, it opens the pouch to outside atmosphere. The air pressure in the chest then causes the pouch to collapse. In so doing the valve is opened and wind flows into the pipe. It takes only a tiny solenoid using minimal current to open the pouch to atmosphere. This action, while it may appear complicated, is in fact highly reliable and very fast. Most organs which use electrical connections from console to chest use some form of electro-pneumatic action.

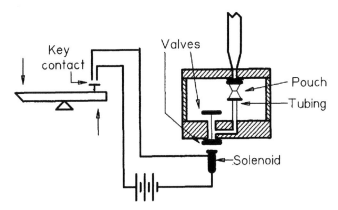

Figure 1.6 Electro-Pneumatic Action

The chests upon which the pipes stand are large wooden boxes, generally one per division, sub-divided within by wooden partitions. The pipes are arranged in a matrix in which the pipes for a given stop are most often arranged in a row from left to right and all the pipes for a given note (i.e., on all stops) are arranged in a line from front to back. As one looks from above, one can think of it essentially as a graph in which along the X axis one finds all the pipes for a given stop and along the Y axis all the pipes for a given note. If one wishes to locate the pipe for middle C on the flute stop, one counts from the bottom of the keyboard and discovers that the note is the 25th one. Since various sets of pipes are visually different from one another (see Chapter 8), one locates on the chest the flute stop and counts upward to the 25th pipe. A single set of pipes moving from left to right is called a *rank*. Many ranks of pipes move down from the longest pipe of the bass at one end of the chest to the shortest pipe in the treble at the other. Another pattern is to alternate sides of the chest in the following manner:

C D E F# G# A# c..............................etc. c# A F D# C#

This pattern of pipe placement gives a V pattern. There are also other arrangements less frequently encountered.

There are two types of wind chests, distinguished from one another by the way they are internally partitioned. In the *key channel chest*, the partitions run from front to back within the chest so that all pipes for a given note lie directly over a single channel. For a sixty-one note windchest there will be sixty-one channels, one for each note. In a *stop channel chest* the partitions run from left to right, and there will be one channel for each stop. As you can imagine, the mechanisms which actually open the valves in the two types of chests are essentially different.

The main chests of a division are usually mounted on a frame several feet above the floor. This facilitates placing the parts of the action which enter the chest from below and allows room for making repairs. It is often necessary to place some pipes, particularly those which are very large, on smaller chests away from the main one of a division. These small chests are called *offset chests* and are generally placed directly on the floor.

While there is a huge variety of organ pipes, and builders from time to time come up with new ones, they are essentially of two types: flue pipes and reed pipes. The flue pipes are essentially whistles, even though they may be thirty-two feet long. A flue pipe produces its sound by the phenomenon known as *edge tones*. An edge tone is the sound that occurs when wind passes over a sharp edge with adequate force. The phenomenon is often heard during a wind storm when wind passes around the corner of a building. When one couples an edge tone device with a pipe of specific length, the edge tone will cause the molecules of air within the pipe to vibrate at a specific pitch, determined largely by the length and structure of the pipe.

A *reed pipe* has a small metal reed in its foot so configured that the reed, when caused to vibrate by wind, will rapidly open and close the orifice from which the wind is coming. An organ reed has nothing in common with the reeds of orchestral wind instruments, which are made of particular members of the grass family. The organ reed is a thin sliver of brass carefully cut and bent. The initial vibration of this reed, which produces a decided pitch, is then coupled to the pipe itself, which by its length has a certain resonance. The pipe and the reed come to a compromise which constitutes the actual pitch of the pipe.

The organ is really a complex synthesizer, not an electronic synthesizer, but an acoustic one. Each organ stop has its own particular color, intensity, and pitch. The art of registration is the art of blending the many sound capabilities of the organ into beautiful and meaningful combinations. Many organ pipes are at the same pitch level as that of the piano. We say these stops are at 8' pitch since the lowest pipe on a principal stop must be about eight feet in length to produce that pitch. Other stops can be at 4' pitch, an octave higher; 2' pitch, two octaves higher; or at 16' pitch an octave lower. There are also pipes which sound other pitches in the *overtone series*. The result. in even an organ of modest size, is a vast pallet of sounds.

Finally, we need to mention pipe placement, since this causes some confusion to the layman. The time honored procedure is to place organ pipework in an ornate wooden case with the console directly at its center. These cases were often works of art in and of themselves, and stood completely within the room in which they were to sound. Often the casework reflected the order of the divisions of the organ, but sometimes not. Mechanical action and encased organs are inseparable brothers. When electric action became common late in the nineteenth century, this classic pairing could easily be broken. Pipes could be placed almost anywhere, even at considerable distances from the console which was to control them. Often the decision of where the pipework should be placed was made by architects with little input from organists. Pipework was often relegated to what were no more than large closets opening into the main room. Pipework was no longer visible in these organs in *chambers*. In reaction to this most un-musical procedure, some builders began to bring their pipework into the open and expose it in geometric patterns that reflected the "form as function" concept of modern architecture. Thus there are three ways pipework has generally been disposed: in cases, in chambers, and exposed within the room itself. As one can imagine, the placement of pipework has a profound effect on the success of any organ.

CHAPTER 2

The Wind Supply

We are normally unaware of the combination of gasses we know as the atmosphere. Yet these gasses exert a constant and omni-directional pressure which amount to no less than 14.7 pounds per square inch at sea level. What we colloquially term air, then, has considerable weight. In fact it presses upon us in such a fashion that if its force were suddenly removed, as in decompression in a high altitude aircraft accident, we would not long survive. However, since air is a combination of gasses and in gasses molecules are loosely in contact with one another, it can be compressed, and, in doing so, its pressure can be increased. We use compressed air for many purposes. The tires of our automobiles are made absorbent by being filled with compressed air. Paint sprayers and many other tools operate by compressed air, and the static molecules of air within an organ pipe are activated by a stream of lightly compressed air. Blow into a short organ pipe, if you can obtain one. If not, a recorder will do. To make the best sound on either you must blow gently but provide a fairly large volume of air. If one increases the pressure too much the sound will become harsh, and, if the pressure is further increased, the pipe will *overblow*. Organ pipes, then, need large amounts of wind at relatively low pressures.

The Measurement of Wind Pressure

The compression of air is normally measured in pounds per square inch, but this type of measurement is far too unwieldy for the light pressures used in organ design. Instead we

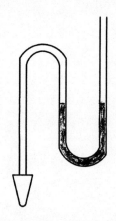

Figure 2.1 Manometer

measure pressure in inches of displaced water, and the instrument of measurement is the *manometer*. This instrument consists of a piece of glass tubing of approximately a half inch in diameter. The actual diameter of the tubing is not crucial. This tubing is bent into an S shape and fitted into a foot suitable to insert into a toe hole from which a pipe has been removed. The lower crook is filled with water as shown in the drawing. The upper end of the tube is open to the atmosphere. When the instrument is fitted into a toe hole, the valve beneath that hole is opened by depressing the appropriate key. Wind enters the tube and forces the water upwards. By reading the difference in heights of the extremes of the column of water, we read the wind pressure. Measurements are given in inches or millimeters.

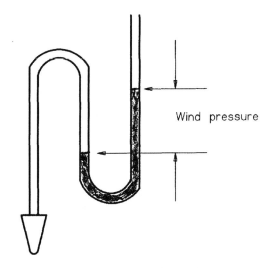

Wind pressure

Figure 2.2 Measurement of Wind Pressure

Wind pressures used in organ building rarely fall below two inches (c. 50 mm) and now, save in the case of high pressure reed stops, rarely exceed five inches (c. 130 mm). In organ building from the first half of the twentieth century, one sometimes encounters pressures of thirty or more inches. It should be noted that the pressures used in organ building are low. One inch of water pressure is equivalent to .036 pounds per square inch. Commonly used wind pressures in use today, then, range from .072 to .18 pounds per square inch. The structure of the Austin *Universal Wind Chest*, which we will discuss in the chapter on chests, actually allows a person to enter the pressurized chamber beneath the pipework. For a person inside the universal chest, the physical sensation caused by turning on the wind is simply a popping of the ears similar to that encountered in ascending a mountain in an automobile.

The Raising of the Wind

We have already said that organ pipes require a large volume of wind at relatively low pressure. The supply must be continuous; it must be adaptable to large demands at one moment and no demand at the next; and, no matter what, the pressure must remain constant within narrow limits. Not only must wind be provided for the pipes, it must also be available in some organs to operate much of the action.

Prior to the advent of the electric centrifugal blower, wind was raised manually by activating two or more bellows of the *cuneiform* type. A cuneiform bellows, sometimes called either a *diagonal* or *wedge bellows*, is made of two rectangular boards hinged together at one of their shorter ends. The space between is filled by some pliable material or more often by carefully cut, thin, wooden ribs. These are hinged together with fine leather and thereby made air tight. The drawing below from the eighteenth century treatise of Dom Bédos (see the bibliography) shows a large cuneiform bellows with five sets of internal ribs. They act not only to make the bellows more secure, but also to serve as rigid surfaces against which the air may press.

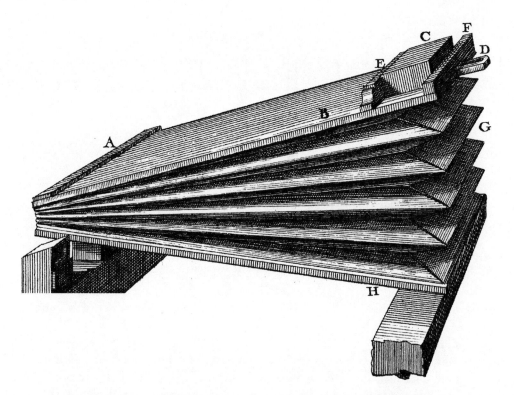

Figure 2.3 Large Cuneiform Bellows (Dom Bédos, Plate 48)

The manual raising of wind is still found in historical restorations. Some modern organs, particularly those with a strong historical roots, are provided with manual wind supplies as alternates to the centrifugal blower. The diagonal bellows used in such systems are often six or more feet in length and used in pairs. The bottom board of a *feeder bellows* (see the figure on page 17) is securely fastened to the floor of the organ. At one end of the bottom board a hole is cut which leads into the main wind trunk. At the other end of the bottom board a hole for the intake valve is cut. The top board is connected to a lever mechanism which allows the bellows to be raised. The top board is weighted, generally with blocks of lead. The placement of these weights, as well as their weight, is critical, since these are the principal factors in determining wind pressure. The heavier the weights and the fur-

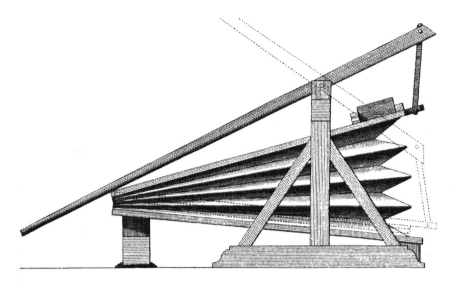

Figure 2.4 Manually Operated Cuneiform Bellows (Dom Bédos, Plate 72)

ther the weights are placed from the hinge of the top board, the greater the wind pressure. As one bellows of a pair descends and, in so doing, feeds air into the wind trunk, the other bellows is raised. Hence the wind pressure can remain essentially constant.

It is necessary to fit both the intake and exhaust ports of the bellows with *check valves*, also called one-way valves. If this is not done, wind will be expelled via the intake port on descent of the bellows and sucked from the organ as the bellows is raised. These valves are usually simple but effective *flap valves*. A flap valve allows wind to move in a single direction. In the figure below, wind moving from left to right forces the valve open. When the force is in the opposite direction, the flap closes and prevents wind flow.

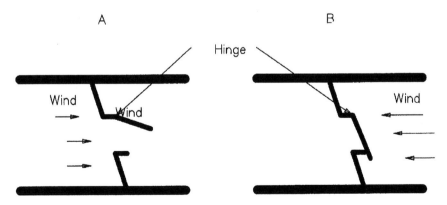

Figure 2.5A, *left:* **Flap Valve Open. Figure 2.5B,** *right:* **Flap Valve Closed**

The principal difficulty attached to manual raising of wind is obvious: the necessity of a person to work the bellows. There is also a limitation of the amount of wind which can be raised effectively. Even in the eighteenth century there were frequent complaints that winding was inadequate. The late nineteenth century change in taste which favored organs of more than about forty stops and wind pressures substantially above four inches spelled the doom of manual production of wind. Various systems involving steam, gasoline, and water powered engines were attempted before all were superceded by the *centrifugal blower* activated by an electric motor. These blowers are known by other names: squirrel cage, rotary and turbine blowers.

Air moving through any type of fan is mildly compressed. If a fan is contained in an air-tight casing which conforms to the spiral configuration of the fan blades it houses, wind of considerable velocity and ample pressure for use in organs can be obtained. Figure 2.6 is a schematic of such a blower.

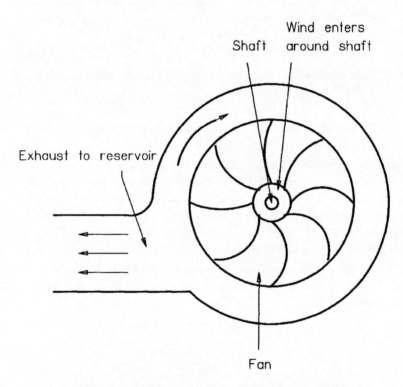

Figure 2.6 Schematic of a Centrifugal Blower

Air enters via an intake port surrounding the shaft. It is compressed by the fan and exits via the exhaust port. Blowers are made in many sizes to accommodate various organs. Modern blowers are essentially silent and can be mounted within an organ case or chamber. Blowers are designed to operate against the pressure of a wind system and should never be operated without that pressure. They will overheat and possibly fail.

The Regulation of Wind

In manually winded organs there is no further need to regulate wind than what we have already described. Raising greater wind or higher pressure than the organ requires is essentially impossible. As the instrument uses wind, the bellows deflates proportionately.

The weights atop the feeder bellows regulates the wind. As long as the bellows operator does his job properly, wind regulation is assured.

The electric blower, however, is quite different. It is intentionally designed to provide more wind and at higher pressure than is needed at any one moment. It is necessary, therefore to regulate the wind. The pressure at the outlet of the blower, known as its *static pressure*, is always higher than that used by the organ. Regulation therefore always involves lowering static pressure.

Wind from the blower is ducted into one or more *reservoirs*. These, in some ways, are similar to bellows in that they contain wind under pressure. The most common form is a rectangular box. Its top board is connected to the remainder of the box by airtight and hinged ribs similar to those we encountered in the diagonal bellows. They, however, surround the box on four sides. The top board, as it rises, remains in a plane parallel to the base of the bellows. Wind pressure is regulated by weights attached to the top board as in the cuneiform bellows, or by springs, either coiled or leaf. Sometimes both weights and springs are used together. Figure 2.7, A and B shows cross sections of rectangular bellows, *A* with coil springs and *B* with leaf springs.

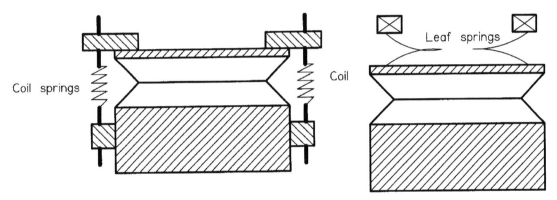

Figure 2.7A, *left:* **Reservoir with Coiled Springs. Figure 2.7B,** *right:* **Reservoir with Leaf Springs**

In flexible wind supplies, where variation of any element can easily become critical, weights are preferred over springs. Weights exert a constant downward force which depends solely upon unchanging gravity. Springs, however, exert somewhat different pressures at various points of their extension, which can result in momentary variations in the wind pressure.

To prevent the main bellows from receiving too great a capacity of air at high pressure from the blower, a valve mechanism is interposed between blower and reservoir. The most common types of valves used here are the *cone valve* and the *curtain valve*. Both work on much the same principal. When the top board of the bellows is at its maximum height, the valve is completely closed (i.e. the reservoir needs no more wind). As wind is exhausted from the reservoir, the valve opens in direct proportion to the wind which has been exhausted. With only a small flow of wind is being used, the valve will open only partially. As greater demands are made for wind, the valve opens wider.

Figure 2.8 shows a cross section of a rectangular reservoir fitted with a cone valve. The box is partitioned horizontally into two sections. Wind from the blower at static pressure is introduced via the duct at the left. While the lower section is at static pressure, the upper section is at regulated pressure. There is a circular port between the two sections. A large wooden cone is shaped so that it can completely close that port when the top board of the reservoir reaches its highest point. As wind is exhausted from the reservoir, the top board descends and, in the process, partially opens the port, admitting the appropriate amount of air. Wind pressure is determined by weights, springs, or both. Wind moves into the organ via the duct at the right. Larger feeder bellows may have more than one cone valve.

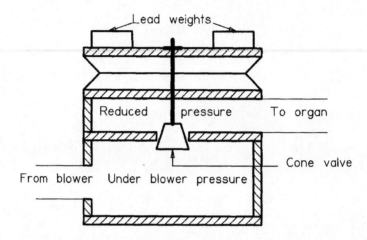

Figure 2.8 Reservoir Regulated by a Cone Valve

Figure 2.9 represents a cross section of a reservoir controlled by a curtain valve. In most elements of its construction it is obviously similar to the cone controlled variety. A small box is built across one end of the bottom board of the reservoir. This box is charged with static pressure. On the vertical wall of this box is a rectangular port through which wind passes to the regulated area of the bellows. A curtain, similar to an ordinary window shade, mounted upside down, is fixed on a spring loaded roller. The center top of the curtain is fastened to a cord that in turn is attached to the top of the bellows. As the reservoir top board rises, the port is closed by the curtain. The rising and falling of the curtain acts to admit or exclude wind exactly as the cone in the reservoir just described.

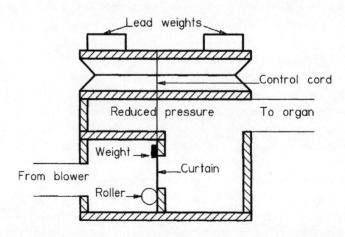

Figure 2.9 Reservoir Regulated by a Curtain Valve

The Distribution of Wind

Systems for the distribution of wind vary according to the size of the instrument and the functions wind is to assume. In a one manual organ the distribution system will more than likely be no more than a wind trunk from bellows to chest. In small organs wind lines will be short, and thereby one of the most common problems of wind conductivity is eliminated. Wind is an elastic medium (it tends to recover its original density as soon after compression as possible). The shorter the wind lines, the less chance for the wind to begin this restorative process. In large instruments the wind systems can be extensive. As a wind system becomes larger, keeping the wind stable becomes more of a problem. Major trunk lines must be carried to all major chests and branch lines to offset chests. If the motive power for parts of the action is pneumatic, as is often the case, lines must carry wind to the console, combination action, stop action, and the like.

Wind systems are made more complex by the fact that many organs use different wind pressures for various purposes. Parts of the action and offset chests for reeds may use significantly higher pressures than is used in the remainder of the organ. Major divisions of the organ may be on different pressures (i.e., the positive on 2½ inches, the great on 3 inches, the swell and pedal on 3½ inches). The feeder reservoir must have a pressure higher than that used anywhere in the organ. From it branch lines go to secondary reservoirs, which in turn step down the pressure to that needed locally. These secondary reservoirs have essentially the same design as the primary one. They are merely smaller.

Wind lines are made of many materials. The classical material is wood and the cross sections of wooden lines is normally rectangular. Galvanized pipe, similar to that used in home heating systems, is often used, particularly in situations in which wind must be carried a considerable distance. Flexible hose of various diameters is used. Builders sometimes use rigid polyvinyl chloride (PVC) pipe of various diameters. Cardboard tubing, of the type used to roll carpeting, has even been employed. When covered with shellac and kept away from moisture, it works remarkably well.

We have already said that wind is elastic. If it is ducted over a long distance, an unacceptable drop in pressure is inevitable. Builders sometimes place secondary bellows at the end of long lines to stabilize pressure before it enters the organ itself. Each supplementary bellows has the effect of smoothing out fluctuations of the wind. Nevertheless, the demands of playing can put an excessive strain on a medium as pliable as air. Rapid, loud, and thick chords can strain the capacity of the wind system beyond its capabilities. To rectify such a condition, builders who seek stable wind often use *concussion bellows* (also known as Schwimmer or winker bellows) to absorb sudden shocks against the wind supply. These bellows are rather small in size and are loaded by springs. They are often affixed directly to the bottom boards of the windchests themselves. Figure 2.10 on page 22 is a cross section of a concussion bellows attached to the bottom of a chest. Wind is ducted from the main reservoir to the interior of the chest. The port to the concussion bellows opens directly from the bottom of the chest. In the event that there is a sudden demand for wind that the reservoir does not have time to supply, this bellows absorbs the thrust.

The advent of the electric blower provided organ builders with a source of wind which is inexhaustible. Any serious fluctuations in winding can be avoided if the builder is conscientious and willing to size the components of his system adequately. This capacity for achieving stable winding, which no musical demand can threaten, was, for some years, con-

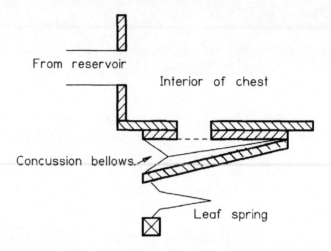

From reservoir

Interior of chest

Concussion bellows

Leaf spring

Figure 2.10 Concussion Bellows

sidered a positive accomplishment. Some builders, particularly those with a strong histor-ical orientation, now feel that such stable wind robs the musical performance of a live dimension. These builders have sought to design wind systems which intentionally fluctu-ate when large demands are made upon them. The player is expected to "play the wind." A flexible system has the following elements: large diagonal bellows, wind trunks of con-siderable size constructed of wood, care in leading these trunks in as direct a manner as possible, the use of weights instead of springs to load bellows, and the avoidance of sec-ondary or concussion bellows. The use of relatively low wind pressure (below about 3½ inches) is mandatory for *flexible winding.* Some builders even regard the centrifugal blower with suspicion. There are a few organs in which the lever arms of manual wind supplies are lifted and released electrically or pneumatically. Some builders offer both flexible and sta-ble wind supplies within a single instrument. This is accomplished by having all concus-sion bellows activated when stable wind is desired and deactivated when flexible supply is desired. Ports between the concussion bellows and the chests are open when stable wind is called for and closed when flexible wind is called for.

The Tremulant

The tremulant intentionally disturbs the stability of the wind in order to produce a desirable musical oscillation. Dom Bédos outlines the structure of two distinctly different types of tremulants. The first of these, the *tremblant doux* or soft tremulant, can operate effectively only in flexible wind systems. It operates by placing a pliable impediment to the flow of wind directly in the path of the main wind trunk. Figure 2.11 is a cross section of the device (see page 23). When it is not functioning, the device pivots on hinge A and is housed in the rectangular recess above the wind line. When its stop is pulled the mecha-nism falls down as a partial barrier in the wind line. The stop action holds it in the "on" position. Wind now moves through the small port and forces open the hinged flap (hinge B). That flap is delicately balanced against the light spring. It now wavers up and down. In so doing it imparts a light and subtle fluctuation to the wind. The soft tremulant is use-

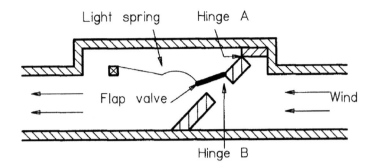

Figure 2.11 *Tremblant Doux*

ful only in soft registrations. Since the device impedes the main wind line, it would have only a negative effect in larger registrations.

The other type of tremulant Dom Bédos describes is the *tremblant à vent perdu,* or the tremulant that loses wind. Its function is to allow a moderate portion of the wind in the main wind line to be exhausted into the atmosphere in oscillating puffs. The alternation between full and reduced pressures produces the trembling effect. A simple version of the device is shown in figure 2.12.

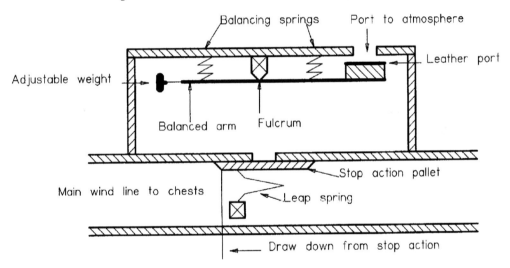

Figure 2.12 *Tremblant à vent perdu*

A box containing the device is mounted on the main wind line. There is a port from the wind line into the device which is closed by a pallet mechanism when the device is not functioning. A stop action opens that pallet to activate the tremulant. The device consists of a balanced arm that can be carefully adjusted by a weighted screw at one end. On the other end of the arm is mounted a leather padded port cover. The port opens to the outside. A cycle consist of upward motion of the port end of the arm due to wind pressure. The weight is strong enough to pull the arm back down, and the cycle repeats. Small puffs of air are released with each cycle. Most tremulants on modern organs work on a similar principal.

Some organs with historical roots have a single tremulant affecting the entire organ. Other instruments have tremulants which affect only a single division. It is obvious that the more rigid the wind system is, the more difficult it is to design an effective tremulant. The rigidity of the winding in the Austin Universal Windchest, for instance, requires a large revolving fan mechanism mounted above the pipework to simulate the effect of the tremulant.

CHAPTER 3

Mechanical Action

In a mechanical action, the connections between key and pipe valve and between stop control and stop action is via mechanical linkages. The physical action the player takes is appropriately transferred by means of rods, thin slats called trackers, levers, lever arms, and wire *pulldowns* to the chestwork itself. This type of action is often termed *tracker action*, although the trackers play no greater part in the mechanisms of such organs as do other parts of the action.

Mechanical action was the only organ action available for hundreds of years, and it continues to be used exclusively by some builders. The organ, which in Europe can certainly be traced to the tenth century, was entirely activated mechanically until the 1840s, when pneumatic assistance was provided on large organs to overcome excessive key resistance. Considering the physical size of even a modest organ, the distances between manuals and chests, and the minuscule pressure available in a player's fingers, it is obvious that the mechanisms of this type of action must indeed be designs of engineering artistry. Yet a well designed mechanical action can be made remarkably responsive in three and even four manual organs when designed and built by conscientious builders. The student is urged to find an opportunity to study the interior of a mechanical action instrument and marvel at its beauty, simplicity, and efficiency.

Advantages and Disadvantages of Mechanical Action

Despite the fact that many persons predicted the demise of mechanical action during the first two-thirds of the twentieth century, it remains alive and well into the twenty-first century. Indeed, it is the action of choice with some of the finest organ builders working today. Despite our reliance on electrical power to do everything from brushing our teeth to grinding our coffee, it seems strange that so ancient a system has persisted with few changes for centuries. Why is this so? The answer may be found in consideration of other musical instruments. Can one imagine a violinist or a pianist willing to disassociate himself from his or her instrument by the imposition of electrical circuits? The tactile sensations so important in sensitive musical performance would be lost. These tactile sensations are as important to many organists as they are to violinists or pianists. They remain the principal reason for the tenacity with which mechanical action has survived.

There are, however, other reasons for this persistence. Mechanical organ actions are a wonderful example of the KISS principal of engineering: "Keep it simple, stupid." The more complex an engineered system is, the less reliable it becomes, and good designers in any field attempt to solve problems with the least complexity possible. The simplicity of mechanical organ action results in high reliability with many organs serving congregations for literally centuries. Such organs, when initially well designed and reasonably cared for, have a longevity which is practically unequalled in the history of technology. Mechanical action depends merely on two power sources: a means to raise wind and the action of the player's hands and fingers. These power sources are as reliable as one can imagine. If a mechanical action organ with an electric blower is simultaneously fitted with an alternate manual means of raising the wind, then the instrument can operate on human power alone, and that, for power sources, is as reliable as one can obtain.

The majority of mechanical action organs are enclosed in free standing cases. These cases reflect the organization of their contents. In other words the action itself suggests, or even demands, the general outlines of the case. This symbiotic relationship between action and case imposes upon the builder constraints which other actions very often do not demand. As a result, mechanical instruments have a visual and tonal integrity frequently lacking in organs with other types of actions. It is, for instance, extremely difficult to exceed about forty feet in the horizontal dimension of an organ case. The action simply becomes too unwieldy and cumbersome. Vertical distances are less of a problem, but then these are often proscribed by the ceiling heights of the buildings in which organs are placed. As a result, the various divisions of a mechanical organ cannot be dispersed at will but must work as a cohesive whole. No better example of the dictum that form should follow function can be found than in a well designed mechanical action organ.

Organ cases are often works of art in and of themselves, and many reflect a visual beauty equaling their tonal beauty. Were this not true, there would have been little reason to preserve many ancient organ cases when their contents had long since been, unfortunately, destroyed. When the visual and tonal beauty of an instrument are both excellent, a real work of art results. This combination is rarely achieved in organs with other types of action.

Finally, as suggested above, a major advantage of mechanical instruments is that they are almost indestructible. Given reasonable and sensitive care and kept from vandalism, animal damage, fire, water, and injudicious organ repairmen, they will last for generations. Mechanical instruments are far less vulnerable to environmental damage than are electropneumatic organs. The longevity of mechanical organs is truly astounding. Some organs in Europe built in the sixteenth century still serve their churches, although they may have undergone major repair, rebuilding, and restoration from time to time.

The disadvantages of mechanical action are largely converses of its advantages. In the first place, there is a decided limit to the force available in the player's fingers unaided. This limited force requires a parallel limitation in the complexity and resistance in the action itself. Too much resistance, too much weight, or both can cause a mechanical action to become unplayable. If manuals are coupled, there is a corresponding increase in resistance and weight. If wind pressures become too high, the resistance in opening the valves (i.e., the *pallets*) becomes substantial. The larger the number of pipes mounted on a chest and the higher the wind pressure, the greater that pallet resistance will be. All in all, the player's fingers limit the size, the complexity of action, and the wind pressure of a sensitive mechanical action.

The first departure from pure mechanical action took place in the 1840s when increased size and wind pressure in organ design of the day outran the power the player himself could reasonably exert. The *Barker lever*, discussed at the conclusion of this chapter, assisted in pulling open the pallets. In so doing it made playable larger organs with higher wind pressures. The Barker lever functions much the same way that power brakes or power steering do in modern automobiles. Both devices assist the person actuating them in the mechanical tasks they must perform. Barker levers merely assist mechanical action; they do not replace it.

A second disadvantage of mechanical action is that it is simply difficult to build. The components which constitute an electric action instrument are, for the most part, produced in a factory environment where they can be produced en masse. These manufactured parts are then assembled into larger components, which in turn are assembled into entire instruments. While there are certainly some skills, such as pipe-making and voicing, requiring high levels of competence, much of the work involved is far less demanding. While some parts of a mechanical action can be produced in factory fashion, most require hand crafting, which is time-consuming, expensive, and requires from everyone involved a high level of skill. As a result, shops which build this action tend to be small and to produce only a few instruments per year. Sometimes larger shops building mostly electric action instruments will have small divisions that build mechanical action for their clients who demand it.

The majority of mechanical action organs are freestanding. Freestanding organs require floor space sufficient for the instrument's foot print and free space above for the instrument itself. This action does not adapt well to situations involving less than this open space. Particularly, mechanical action is ill-suited to organ *chambers* and to smaller, divided chancel churches. Any extensive distance from keyboard to pipework is difficult to span, and such elements as echo organs placed well away from the main instrument are impossible. Very simply put, mechanical action does not allow the freedom that electric action allows to display the organ in any way a builder or client might wish.

Closely related to this is the need which some organists demand to have complete visual access to a choir situated between console and pipework. Traditionally, the keyboards of mechanical organs are situated at the base of the organ case, a position which allows the shortest and most direct route between keyboard and chests. While it is possible to have detached mechanical consoles, the complexity in the action is unavoidably increased both by the distance and the necessary turns involved. Sensitivity of touch, the hallmark of good mechanical action, is thereby threatened. Some situations, particularly those in public auditoriums and some very large churches, demand that consoles be moveable. In these situations mechanical action is simply impossible.

The Lever

A lever is one of the simple machines. (Others are the inclined plane, the wheel and axle, the wedge, the pulley, and the screw.) A lever consists of a stiff rod revolving about a pivot called the fulcrum. The two other elements applied to the rod are a force and a weight. There are three classes of levers determined by the order on the rod these elements occur:

First class: The fulcrum *(FU)* is placed between the force *(F)* and the weight *(W)*.

Second class: The force and the fulcrum are at opposite ends of the lever with the weight in between.

Third class: The fulcrum and the weight are at opposite ends of the lever with the force in between.

In Figure 3.1, a common example of each type is given to the right of each pair: first class: a child balances a man on a seesaw; second class: a wheelbarrow; and third class: a pair of tongs.

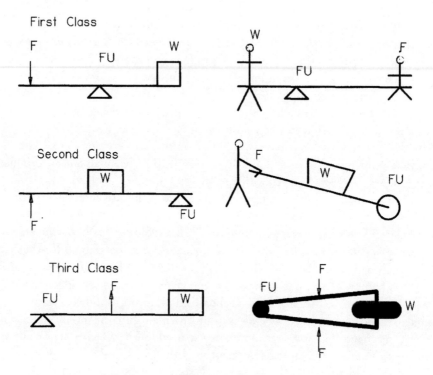

Figure 3.1 Three Classes of Levers

By far the most common type of lever used in organ building is the first class lever. The typical keyboard represents an example. Keys rotate around a fulcrum. Downward pressure of the fingers provides the force and whatever the key actuates constitutes the weight. (As we will see shortly, some organ keys are second class levers.)

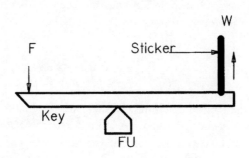

Figure 3.2 The Key as a First Class Lever

As long as the force and weight are equal and the lengths between force and fulcrum and fulcrum and weight are also equal, the first class lever is in balance. This can be expressed by the equation where L1 represents the length between force and fulcrum and L2 the length between fulcrum and weight:

$$(F)\ (L1) = (W)\ (L2)$$

The formula may be used to determine the lengths and weights necessary to balance any similar lever. Assume that F = 4 grams, L1 = 8 inches, and W = 10 grams. To solve for L2, the appropriate equation reads:

$$(4\ grams)\ (8\ inches) = (10\ grams)\ (L2)$$

The lever balances if L2 is 3.2 inches in length. In order to achieve a light and responsive action, the organ builder must balance levers with care.

Often one first class lever actuates another. In theory, one could have a chain of levers, and, as long as each is in balance, the sole force necessary to actuate the chain would be that to move the first lever and to overcome the frictional resistance in the chain itself. A first class lever changes the direction of the force and a second such lever restores it to the initial direction.

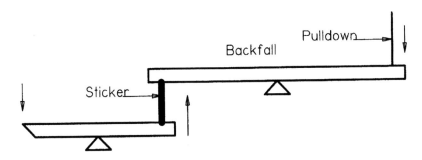

Figure 3.3 Key and Backfall Levers in Combination

If the product of the force and length to the fulcrum is greater than the product of the weight and the length from the fulcrum [(F) (L1) > (W) (L2)] , the lever has a mechanical advantage (i.e., it will require less force to move the weight than would be required in a balanced situation). If the reverse is true [(F) (L1) < (W) (L2)], the lever has a mechanical disadvantage. It will require more force than the weight itself to actuate the lever.

A first class lever can appear in several forms. The force may come from above or below, the fulcrum can be mounted above or below, and the weight can appear above or below. It is obvious that first class levers change downward motion to upward motion as well as upward to downward. If the arms of the lever are angled at the fulcrum, other directional changes can be made. If the arms are attached to the ends of a rotating rod which acts as a fulcrum, motion can be transferred over considerable distances in a lateral manner. It is even possible for a single lever arm to actuate two other arms in the form of a *T*. The weighted arms would, then, move in opposite directions.

Second class levers are far less common and third class are rare. One important use of the second class lever is in the key design of *suspended action*. In this action the connections between key and pallet are reduced to an absolute minimum by designing the action so that

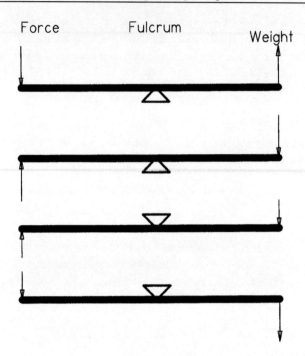

Figure 3.4 Four Types of First Class Levers

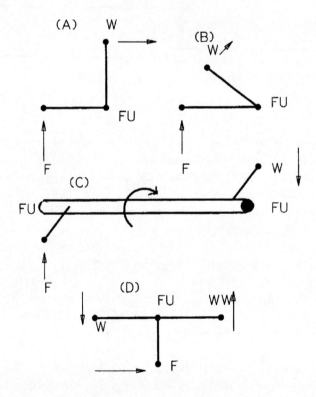

Figure 3.5 Various Forms of First Class Levers

it literally hangs on the pallet. The result is very sensitive control of touch. The key levers themselves constitute second class levers.

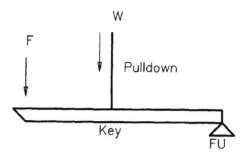

Figure 3.6 Key in Suspended Action

Hardware of Mechanical Action

Keyboards. There has never been a universally accepted norm for the range of manual keyboards. Perhaps the closest thing to a norm is the tradition that the lowest note (at 8' pitch) is *C*. For many years the American Guild of Organists specified a five octave range beginning with *C*, or sixty-one notes with the top note *c4*. This specification is often ignored in present day mechanical instruments. *G3* is often the highest note (a fifty-six note range), but there are other possibilities.

In historical organs even the convention of the lowest note is not universal. There was an English tradition, also found in some antique American organs, of the lowest note being GG, a fourth lower than the more common C. Another idiosyncrasy one finds in antique organs is the absence of some of the lowest notes, particularly C# and D#. These notes were rarely used in the seventeenth century, and since it was expensive to make large pipes of the lowest register, their absence was a matter of economy. Sometimes the appropriate sharp keys were simply omitted on the keyboards. At other times the keyboards were compressed in what is known as the *short octave*. In the short octave, a sharp key would be divided into front and back sections, one section playing one note and the other section another. Although there were many forms of the short octave, one such system used in Italian harpsichords of the period has the following lowest octave.

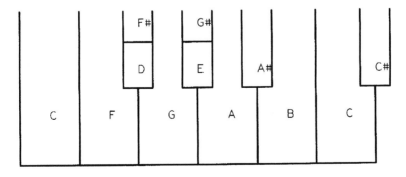

Figure 3.7 Example of a Short Octave

Key bodies are made of clear, soft wood. The key slips (coverings) are made of various materials. Ivory was, during the nineteenth and the first half of the twentieth century, the material of choice, but today ivory is unavailable. Instead many builders use animal bone. The traditional white for naturals and black for sharps is, of course, a meaningless convention. Many organ keys are covered with key slips of various types of hardwood, and darker naturals and lighter sharps are common. Plastic is a ubiquitous and cheap substitute. Many players object to the slick feel of plastic keys.

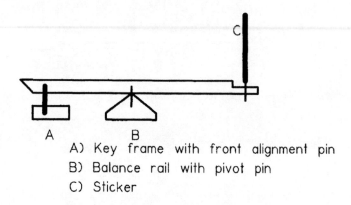

A) Key frame with front alignment pin
B) Balance rail with pivot pin
C) Sticker

Figure 3.8 Cross Section of a Typical Key

Figure 3.8 represents a cross section of a key. The *balance rail* runs under the keys, which it supports, and is attached to a wooden frame. A single steel pin provides the pivot (fulcrum). The front alignment pin keeps the key in proper alignment. These pins fit into slots cut in the bottom of the key, slots which are generally bushed with hard felt. The pins themselves are oval in cross section. By turning these, some adjustment can be made, particularly when a key tends to stick. The rear end of the key is trimmed as shown to allow whatever connection is to be made to it. In this drawing a sticker is shown.

The history of the pedalboard is one of variety, a variety that persists to this day. In fact, many historic organs had no pedalboard at all, and even where these existed they were often so rudimentary that they could do little more than sustain single notes. Spanish and English organs were almost entirely without pedalboards until well into the nineteenth century. Early Italian organs had little more than an octave of pedals, and these often were attached to the lowest notes of the manual by means of strings or light wires. It was to the northern Europeans, the Dutch and the Germans to whom we owe the development of serviceable keyboards to be played with the feet.

From time to time there have been efforts to standardize the pedal, both in overall design and in compass. The English attempted this in the late nineteenth century and the Americans, under the aegis of the American Guild of Organists, tried again in the early half of the twentieth century. These attempts were only moderately successful. The situation is now such that an organist who moves about the United States, much less Europe, will encounter a diversity of pedalboards upon which he must be fluent.

Dom Bédos, writing in the middle of the eighteenth century, describes the pedalboard that was common on French organs of the day. As Figure 3.9 shows, the pedals are so short that any use of the heel is simply precluded. They protrude through a covering board which served to keep out dirt. Occasionally this type of keyboard will be made by contemporary builders whose goal it is to reproduce antique French organs to the letter.

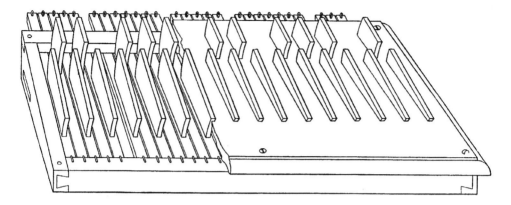

Figure 3.9 Early French Pedal Board (Audsley II, 123)

There are four types of pedalboards one may now encounter: flat and non-radiating, flat but radiating, concave and non-radiating, and concave and radiating. The first type is perhaps more characteristic of mechanical action organs than are the other types. Although it is the type of keyboard that one finds on many antique organs with full pedalboards. it is also found on many modern mechanical instruments. Its most common range is either a twenty-seven note (C to d") or thirty note (C to f'). Sometimes the sharp keys are lengthened in the bass and treble to make reaching them a bit easier. Audsley shows this in his drawing below.

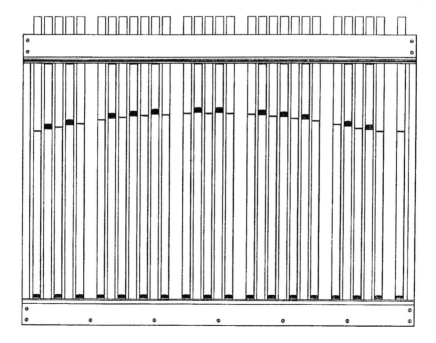

Figure 3.10 Flat Pedalboard with Varying Sharp Keys (Audsley II, 131)

Of the four types, flat and radiating is the rarest. It is still encountered on earlier Hammond electronic organs, but its use in pipe organ construction is hardly ever found. Concave-non-radiating pedalboards are common in Europe. These pedalboards favor those whose legs are shorter.

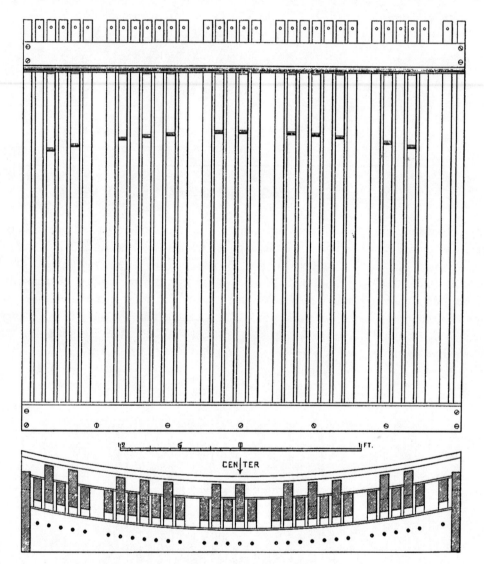

Figure 3.11 Concave Non-radiating Pedalboard (Audsley II, 133)

In the United States the most common pedalboard is of the concave radiating type. This is the form sanctioned by the American Guild of Organists. Their specifications indicate a range from C to g', or thirty-two notes. Audsley (II, 135) shows this form with a thirty-note range (C to f') (see Figure 3.12).

    Connections from the keys to the remainder of the mechanical action are much the same in the pedal as in the manuals. There is one significant difference: manual keys are normally returned by the action of the pallet springs. Such a small force, however, is inad-

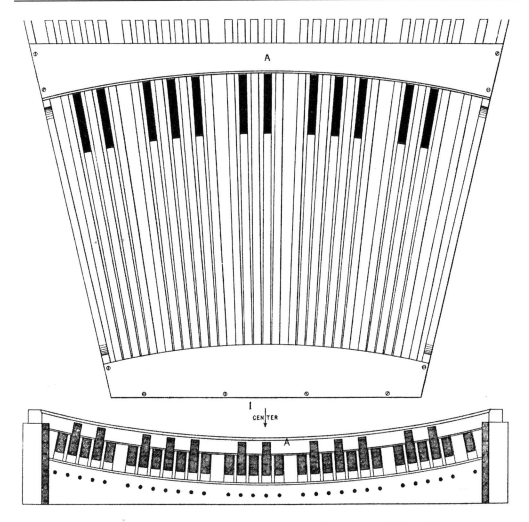

Figure 3.12 Thirty Note Concave Radiating Pedalboard

equate to return a pedal key. Therefore these keys work against springs. Figure 3.13 represents a side view of a pedal key. A heavy wire spring (approximately ⅛ inch in diameter) directly under the key returns it when it is released. The pivot is shown at the left end of the drawing. A pedal key is one of the rare uses of a third class lever in organ building. The force is the player's foot applied between the pivot (fulcrum) and the spring (the weight).

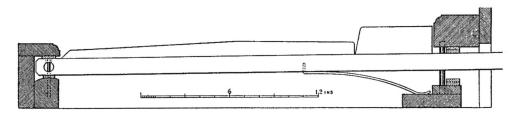

Figure 3.13 Cross Section of a Pedal Key (Audsley II, 131)

Trackers. Trackers are thin strips of wood approximately ⅜ inch wide and ⅛ inch thick. Other materials, such as plastic or aluminum, have been used with only minimal success. Since trackers are the most ubiquitous and visually the most obvious element in mechanical hardware, they have responsible for the none-too-accurate designation *tracker action* when mechanical action is the more accurate term. Trackers transfer motion in tension; that is, they pull, they never push. In order to attach these to other parts of the action, threaded brass or bronze rods, perhaps ³⁄₃₂" in diameter, are bound to the ends with silk or cotton thread, which is then shellacked or glued. Small leather nuts can then be threaded onto the rods. Figure 3.14 shows three possibilities.

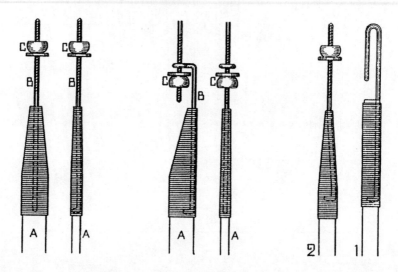

Figure 3.14 Methods of Finishing the Ends of Trackers (Audsley II, 163)

When vertical trackers exceed about five or so feet in length, they need some type of lateral support or guide to keep one from touching another. Audsley shows two methods; the first is a wooden comb, and the second has two functions: first to keep adjacent trackers apart and the second to attach the two parts of a long vertical tracker together.

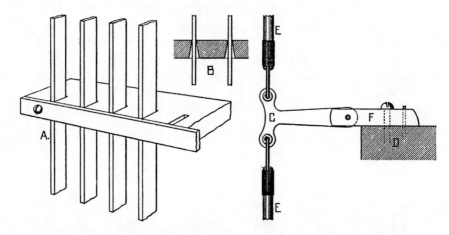

Figure 3.15 Supports for Longer Trackers (Audsley II, 185)

Stickers. Stickers, unlike trackers, operate in compression. They push; they do not pull. They are rarely longer that about a foot in length since they are prone to bending if longer. They are made of wooden dowels about ⁵⁄₁₆ inch in diameter, and generally require guides when they are used vertically. At one end they have threaded rods and leather nuts to connect to whatever element they actuate. In Figure 3.16, key lever *C* raises sticker *AB*. The end of the key lever is covered with felt or leather to reduce noise. *D* is a guide and *E* a small pin to prevent the sticker falling if the key below it is removed.

Squares. A square is a right angled component originally made of wood but sometimes of metal. It is pivoted at its corner. The purpose of a square is to change motion by 90 degrees, horizontal to vertical or vertical to horizontal. The tips of the arms of a square have bushed drillings to received connections from other parts of the action. Below is a typical square shown with its mounting bracket.

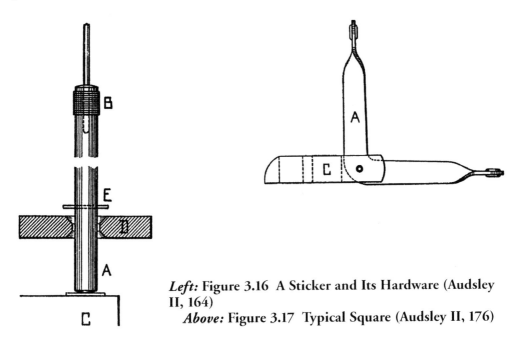

Left: **Figure 3.16 A Sticker and Its Hardware (Audsley II, 164)**
Above: **Figure 3.17 Typical Square (Audsley II, 176)**

The drawing on page 38 (top) shows the various changes of direction which squares can effect. Number 1 is by far the most common. Numbers 5 through 8 show that "squares" can also be made with acute and obtuse angles. Number 9 shows a compound square which changes horizontal motion to upward and downward vertical motion in a single unit.

Backfalls. Backfalls are levers of the first class, the purpose of which is most often to change downward motion to upward motion or upward motion to downward. They are by their nature more massive than trackers or stickers and are mounted in a secure beam which contains the pivot about which they rotate. That beam can support the backfall either from above or below.

In the upper drawing of the Figure 3.19 on page 38, *A* is the backfall mounted on the beam which contains the pivot *F*. Sticker *C* raises the left end of the lever. The right end goes downward, pulling with it the tracker *D*. In the lower drawing, the left end of backfall *B* is pulled downward by tracker *C*. As a result, the right end goes upward and, in the process raises tracker *D*.

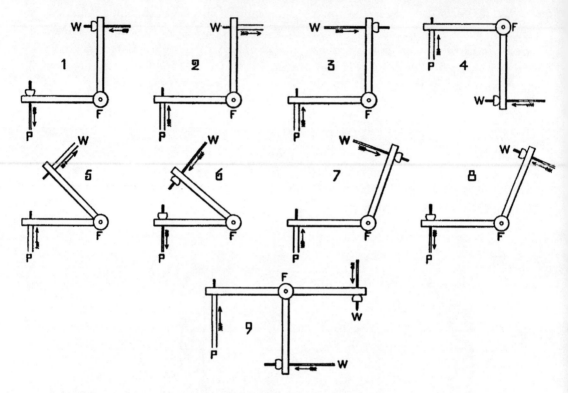

Figure 3.18 Directional Changes Effected by Squares (Audsley II, 167)

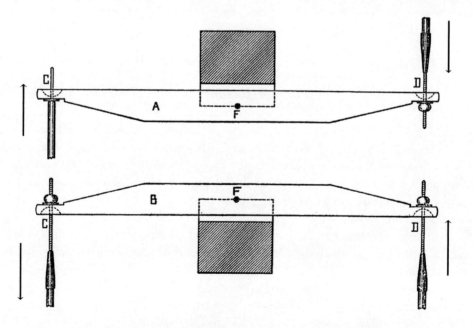

Figure 3.19 Two Types of Backfalls (Audsley II, 168)

Certainly the most common use of the backfall is in connecting the motion of a key to the pulldown connected to the *pallet* in the windchest. A frame bearing one backfall per note is mounted above and behind the keyboard. The action is simple. The front end of key is depressed and its rear end lifts. It pushes the sticker upward to activate the backfall. In turn, the other end of the backfall drops and, in the process, activates the pulldown.

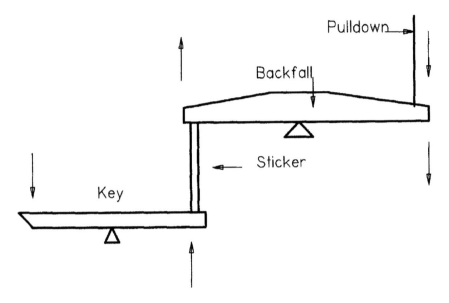

Figure 3.20 Key, Sticker, Backfall, and Pulldown

The beam on which these multiple backfalls are mounted has deep routings into which the levers are placed. With the backfalls in place, a single wire (*A* in Figure 3.21) is fed through each of them to serve as pivots. The wire is then fixed solidly in place.

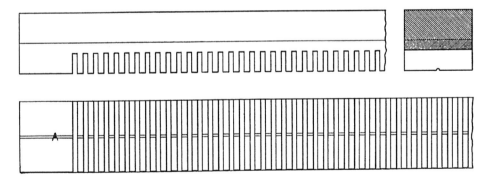

Figure 3.21 Frame for Multiple Backfalls (Audsley II, 169)

Fan Frame. The distance across a keyboard is much less than the space necessary to place a set of pipes across a chest. Therefore, it is necessary to spread the action as it moves from keyboard to chest. There are two ways this can be accomplished: the *fan frame* and the *roller board*, which we will discuss presently. The fan frame is merely a series of longer backfalls spread so that at one end each lines up with a sticker from a key and at the other with a pulldown entering the pallet box of the chest. Unlike the backfalls we just described, which could be pivoted on a common wire, each backfall in a fan frame must be individually pivoted since each follows a slightly different angle.

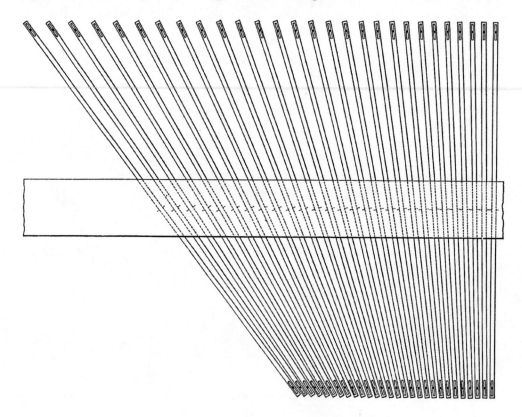

Figure 3.22 Fanframe (Audsley II, 171)

Fan frames were very common in small American organs of the latter part of the nineteenth century. Roller boards are now far more common.

The Roller Board. A roller board is a large, monolithic board as long as the chest it serves and as wide as necessary to support its components. On this board are mounted horizontal rotating rods, one for each note of the keyboard to which they are attached. Each rod is provided with two short arms, one on each end. One receives the key tracker and the other the pulldown tracker. The arms receiving the key trackers are spaced evenly as they come up from the keys. The arms for the pulldown trackers are spaced according to the spacing of the pallets they serve. In this way the appropriate spreading of the pipes as they stand on the chest can be attached to the smaller spread of the keys themselves. The principle is shown in Figure 3.23 on page 41. The board is shown as *A* with their rollers and their pivots mounted on it. Trackers leading down to the key action are shown at *B* and those leading up to the pulldowns are shown at *C*. When a key is depressed its roller rotates in the direction shown. When the first tracker of the lower right group is pulled downward, its motion is laterally transferred to the corresponding tracker of the group on the left. That tracker, in turn, pulls downward. Other pairs work similarly.

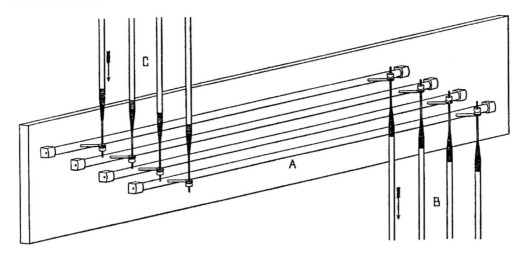

Figure 3.23 A Portion of a Roller Board (Audsley II, 187)

One might assume that it would be necessary for the pipes mounted above a roller board to be placed chromatically on the chest. Such is not the case, for by varying the length and each roller, almost any pattern of pipe placement can be achieved.

From Key to Pallet Box. A schematic of a typical mechanical key action from the key to the pallet is shown in Figure 3.24.

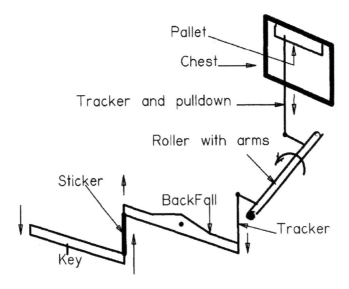

Figure 3.24 Schematic from Key to Pallet Box

As the key is depressed on the left the lever rises on the right. It forces sticker attached to it upwards; that in turn lifts the left end of the backfall. The right end of that backfall moves downward, and, as it does, it pulls downward the tracker attached to it. That tracker is attached to one of the arms on the roller, which now rotates. In turn that motion pulls down the tracker, which is attached to the other end of the roller arm. This tracker is attached to the pulldown wire entering the pallet box. The wire pulls open the pallet and wind is admitted into the groove upon which the pipe is mounted. It would be desirable, at this point, for the student to move ahead to Chapter 5 for a brief description of the slider chest.

Many antique organs and some of modern designs feature a division called the *Rückpositiv* in German or the *chair organ* in English. This division is placed behind the performer and often hangs over a balcony. In order to design such a division, it is necessary for its action to go down, under, and then back up to the pallet box. One solution to this is to place the roller board against the floor in a flat orientation. In Figure 3.25 the action moves

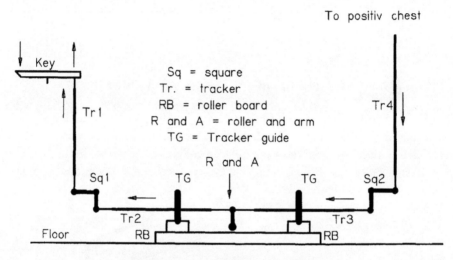

Figure 3.25 *Rückpositiv* **Action**

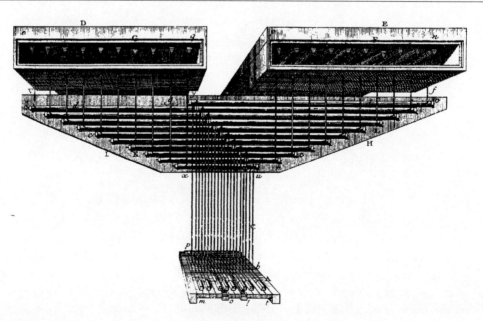

Figure 3.26 All Elements of a Mechanical Key Action (Dom Bédos, Plate 56)

- from the rear of the key, via tracker 1, to square 1 (upward motion)
- motion via tracker 2 to roller arm (leftward motion)
- motion from roller arm, via tracker 3 to square 2 (leftward motion)
- from the chest (not shown) via tracker 4 to square 2 (downward motion)

The drawing cannot show the two arms of the roller.

Figure 3.26 from Dom Bédos shows all the elements of mechanical action clearly. The engraving shows a short keyboard (20 note) and the action from key to pallet box. The keyboard, the trackers connected to it, the roller board, the pulldowns, and the pallets are clearly visible. Earlier, in the discussion of levers, we mentioned the use of second class levers (i.e., with the weight between the force and the fulcrum) in key design of suspended action. This is the action Dom Bédos shows, an action which approaches the sensitivity of harpsichord action. Its sensitively is the result of the few components between key and pallet, two trackers and a roller board.

CHAPTER 4

Electric Action

In an electric action organ the connections between the keys and chest valves and the stop controls and the stop action are controlled by electric circuitry. The key levers and the stop controls are reduced to nothing more than switches. The connections from keyboard to chest valves and from stop tab or knob to stop action are made via small gauge wires bundled together into cables. As we said in the opening chapter, the player is merely a maker and breaker of switches. The signals the player sends are instantaneously transmitted to the pipe and stop action in a system that is relatively simple and reliable.

In the introduction, we mentioned that the history of the organ reflects the history of technology. In the last thirty years there has been no greater technological change in organ building than that of the introduction of *solid-state switching* to replace the older electro-mechanical switching. However, the bulk of this chapter will deal with this older, pre-transistor system for two reasons. First, there are simply thousands of electric action organs which still rely on it. The system is reliable, and to replace it for the sake of modernity alone is wasteful. While many organs have been retro-fitted with solid state switching, the majority of organs built before about 1985 have not. The second reason is pedagogical in nature. We can see, touch, visualize, and conceptualize electro-mechanical switching in a manner that is impossible with the fixed, self-contained modules of micro-electronics. The important thing to remember is that these modules are doing precisely the same thing that is done by the hardware of the older system. To understand what the older system is doing is to understand what the newer system is also doing. We will return to solid state switching at the end of this chapter.

The Advantages and Disadvantages of Electric Action

The advent of electric action in the last half of the nineteenth century was perhaps the most radical technological development in organ building since the invention of the slider chest in the sixteenth century. One might assert that the pneumatic (i.e. Barker) lever might rival it as a radical innovation. Certainly it made possible much larger organs operating on higher and higher wind pressures. But electric action potentially changed everything, from the detachment of the player from the pipes to the nature of playing the instrument. The player could now control a hundred stops, possibly scattered throughout the hall, with identically the same effort he could control a single flute. He could rapidly change from fortissimo sounds to pianissimo ones with the press of a button. Not only did the instrument itself undergo a radical change there was, then, an equally radical change in the nature of the music written for it and played on it. Electric action seemed to provide the organist with the ultimate adaptation of technological modernity to music making. The theater organist, rising magically from the orchestra pit on his pneumatic lift and in control of his banks of switches, had a mystique about him not unlike the stars of the movies he accompanied.

The advantages of electric action to the organ builder were legion. Electric circuits are easy to lay out and simple to construct. The limitations which mechanical action placed on the builder, particularly the close connections between the keys, stop action, and chests, were no longer an issue. One can switch on a light bulb at the back of one's yard as easily as one can switch on the light in one's bedroom. One could open a chest magnet in an electric action chest one hundred feet distant as easily as one could open a chest magnet in a chest ten feet away. The builder, but progressively more the architect, could place pipework wherever he chose with few, if any, mechanical, electrical or architectural hindrances.

The hardware for the electric action was much easier to fabricate by the process of the modern assembly line. Much electric action hardware used today had its inception in the mind of one who was not primarily an organ builder but an engineer, Robert Hope-Jones. The hardware he imagined, particularly chest magnets and switches, could be fabricated quickly and as easily as could parts for an automotive carburetor. Two organs, radically different from one another, could use identical electrical hardware. The assembly line method of construction was rapidly applied to larger and larger organ components such as chests, and eventually entire instruments were essentially the products of it. The organ builder became more and more the organ assembler. The high level of quality control demanded of a mechanical organ builder could now be forgotten. In many cases the skill of his employees could be essentially the same as those of an automotive assembly line worker. In the same way that Henry Ford's assembly line reduced the difficulties inherent in automotive production, the electric action and its assembly line reduced the difficulties inherent in the building of organs.

The disadvantages of electric action are really corollaries of its advantages. The ease with which the builder could locate pipework remote from the console led most builders, particularly those in the United States, to destroy the architectural integrity of the instrument, an integrity that was over five hundred years old. In many cases, pipework was relegated to chambers, hardly more than huge closets, opening poorly into the space in which the organ was intended to sound. Organ pipework was often regarded as hardly more worthy than the plumbing or heating systems to be kept out of sight and out of mind.

The ease of the assembly line process hindered the close connection between the organ builder and his instrument. The small builder, working at one time on one or two instruments and exercising high quality control, was at the financial mercy of the factory builder. Most small builders did not survive. The ease with which changes of registration were possible and the large palette of available organ voices often led to regarding the organ as a one man orchestra. The organ was seen not as a musical instrument in its own right, but a substitute for the orchestra. A glance at organ programs from the early part of the twentieth century reveals the ubiquity of orchestral transcriptions. Composers often shied away from an instrument that now was largely detached from its historical roots and literature and one acting as a substitute for the more expensive orchestra.

The most serious disadvantage in electric action, however, lay in the player's loss of musical intimacy with the speech of his pipes. Even in large mechanical organs the player has a tactile sense as he plays, a sense lost in electric action. To reduce the motions in playing to merely switch controlling is unmusical and would hardly be tolerated in other fine musical instruments. The speed with which the player's finger depresses a key in a mechanical action has considerable effect on the manner in which wind enters the pipe, and the manner the wind enters the pipe has an important effect on the speech of that pipe. In electric action, a valve under a pipe is either closed or it is open. In an electric action, the speed with which the player depresses a key makes no difference whatsoever in the speech of a pipe.

The Simple Electric Circuit

An understanding of simple electrical circuits is a pre-requisite to understanding electric action. These circuits use low *voltage* (from about 12 to 18 volts) *direct current (DC)*. Voltage is a measure of the force with which electrons move through a circuit. Typical home voltages in North America are either 120 for most uses and 220 for such appliances as clothes dryers and water heaters. So, in comparison, the voltages used in organ circuitry is low indeed. Since such low voltages cannot override the resistance one's body has to current flow, no one need ever worry about shock from such circuits. Many persons cannot feel direct contact with 12 to 18 volts at all. Direct current implies that the electron flow in a circuit is in one direction only. Alternating current (AC) rapidly oscillates from current flowing in one direction to current flowing in the other direction. Typical home current in North America is alternating at 60 cycles per second, approximately the pitch of CC.

Since electrical power for an organ is derived from common line sources, it is necessary to convert 120 AC to 12–18 DC. High voltage current would wreck the delicate circuits used in organ building and, therefore, must be reduced. The 60 cycle oscillation of AC current would produce a permanent and audible buzz were it used for organ circuits. So, then, the common AC current must be smoothed out into DC. The device which reduces voltages from high to low and smoothes AC into DC is called a *rectifier*. Before rectifiers were available, organs' blowers sometimes had attached to them generators similar to those used in automobiles of the period. These generators produced DC current at the appropriate voltages. These were often plagued by worn brushes and fouled commutators, and most have now been replaced with rectifiers.

While voltage is the force behind electrons, *amperage* is the amount of current being forced through the circuit. Since there are many circuits in even a medium size organ, considerable amperage must be provided. Hence, it is necessary to have large rectifiers, and sometimes a particularly large organ might have more than one. Rectifiers are easy to identify. They are contained in steel boxes and are generally close to the power supply which drives the blower. (Blowers operate on 110 or 220AC current.) The advent of solid-state circuits has greatly reduced the amount of amperage necessary and, hence, reduced the size and number of rectifiers.

Now that we have defined the type and source of current used in organ actions, our next task is to conceptualize a circuit. A simple analogy based on Figure 4.1 will help. The drawing represents a piston pump which forces water around a closed loop. The piston is shown in its exhaust position, forcing water out of the open exhaust valve 2. The intake

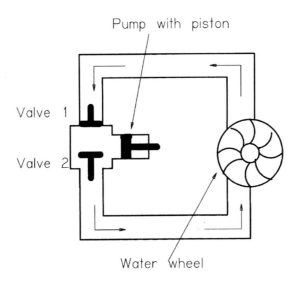

Pump with piston

Valve 1

Valve 2

Water wheel

Figure 4.1 Piston Pump, Water Loop, and Water Wheel

valve 1 is closed. In the course of its travel the force of the water actuates the impeller of the water wheel, causing it to rotate. When water wheels are completely encased they become far more efficient. In this case they are known as turbines. Some useful device, even an organ blower, might be attached to the shaft of that impeller and useful work could be accomplished. As long as the pressure in the loop is maintained, the rotor will turn. Hydraulic pressure has been converted into mechanical force.

The electron flow in a simple electric circuit is analogous to the flow of water in this drawing. A source of DC current, such as a rectifier, is analogous to the pump. Copper wires carry electron flow as pipes carry water. As water power is converted into mechanical force by the turbine, electromotive force is converted into mechanical force by the *electromagnet*, also known as a *solenoid*. Figure 4.2 on page 48 is a schematic of a simple electrical circuit. In electrical drawings, single wires are represented by lines. The symbols for power sources and switches, open and closed, are given on the drawing. The power source is at the left. When the switch is closed (shown open here), power flows through the circuit as shown by the arrows. Any wire which carries an electric current generates around it lines of electromagnetic force. These lines of force are weak as long as the wire follows a single path. However, if wires are clustered by being doubled back upon themselves in a spiral or helix fashion, the weak force of a single strand is added to the force of adjacent strands. A coil produced in this way can exert a significant magnetic force. If a soft iron rod is placed in the middle of the coil, it will become temporarily magnetized whenever current is passed through the coil. It will lose its magnetism within a microsecond whenever the current is interrupted. The device made in this way is called a *solenoid*.

Magnetized metals, of course, attract to themselves other metals containing iron. Whenever a piece of ferrite metal is mounted so that it intentionally moves in the direction of the solenoid core, that piece of metal is called an *armature*. The solenoid in Figure 4.2 has an armature mounted on a pivot. Whenever the switch is closed the solenoid is charged and the armature, normally held upward by a spring which is not shown, moves downward. We have converted electro-magnetic force into mechanical force. Such simple circuits with their

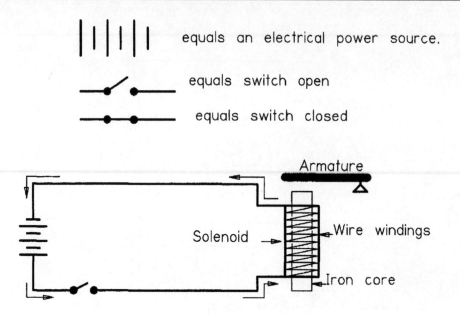

Figure 4.2 Simple Electrical Circuit

power source, switches, and solenoids are the basis for electric action organs. We can now return to our pump, water, and turbine analogy.

Figure 4.3 is a schematic of a single pump connected in parallel to a number of turbines (*ABCDE*). As long as the pressure in the pump is adequate, it can force each of the wheels into motion at the same speed and force. The hydraulic pressure at the pump is converted into mechanical energy at each turbine equally. Note that each turbine is part of a loop similar to the single turbine loop discussed earlier. As long as the pump pressure is adequate, an infinite number of pumps and valves may be added, each with its own circuit.

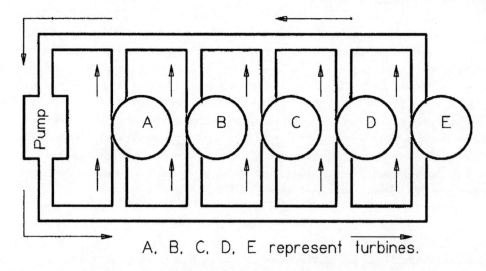

A, B, C, D, E represent turbines.

Figure 4.3 Multiple Turbines, Water Loops, and Pump

In a similar fashion, electrical circuits can be multiplied by the addition of more and more loops. As long as the voltage and amperage are adequate, an infinite number of such circuits can function. DC current has polarity. A convention in organ building is that the current leaving the power source is always positive and its return is always negative. All wires returning power normally go to a single heavy wire called the *bus bar*. Figure 4.4 represents several electrical circuits returning to the bus bar, represented by the heavy line at the top of the drawing. The symbol for a solenoid is given in the drawing.

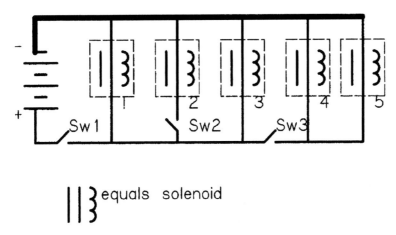

Figure 4.4 A Single Power Source, Multiple Circuits, Switches, and Solenoids

Study the switches in the diagram. If switch 1 is open, no circuits function. If switch 1 is closed and 2 and 3 are open, solenoids 1 and 3 operate. If switches 1 and 3 are closed and switch 2 is open, solenoids 1, 3, 4, and 5 operate. If all switches are closed, all circuits operate. By adding more switches, it would be possible to activate any circuit or circuits one might choose. In an electric action organ of any size, there are hundreds of such simple circuits leading from a single power source to a single solenoid and returning via the bus bar to the negative terminal of the power supply. Some circuits activate key action, others stop action, others various registrational aids such as the combination action, some the swell shutters, and such devices as the *tremulant* and *cymbelstern*. These circuits are always organized in a reasonable fashion by the organ builder, and it takes surprisingly little time to locate a single circuit among its many cousins. Each circuit is a simple loop, and complex circuits, such as those typical of electronic devices, are never used.

The type of wiring used in these circuits is known as *parallel wiring*. Each circuit is directly connected to the positive side of the power supply and returns directly to the negative side. The voltage at any point in such circuits is the same as that delivered by the power supply itself. *Series wiring*, in which all elements consuming electrical power fall along a single continuous circuit, is never used in organ building, save by accident. The voltage at any solenoid in the series-wired circuit drawn below is one-fourth of the voltage at the power supply itself.

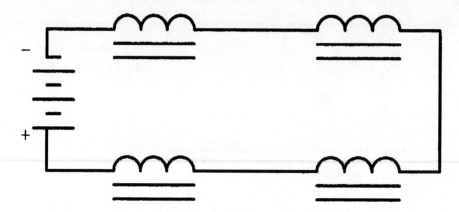

Figure 4.5 Series Wiring

The Hardware of Electric Key Action

The hardware of electric key action consists of the wires which carry current, various types of electro-mechanical *switches*, and *junction blocks* that connect wires and cables, The wire used in organ cables is relatively fine copper wire of 24, 26, or 28 gauge. The size of these wires range from approximately .020 to .013 inches. Older wire was covered with fine cotton insulation and impregnated with paraffin. Newer wire has plastic insulation and is similar to the wire typically used in telephone installations. Cables can be purchased already made up which contain 36, 48, 72, or 84 wires. Some have groups of wires color coded for quicker identification. Cables can also be made up in the shop and covered with plastic electrician's tape.

Three types of switches are employed in electric action: *key contacts*, *relays*, and multiple or *gang switches*. The key levers of electric action organs are normally of the first class (i.e., the fulcrum is in the middle of the lever). Since a key has no pallet with its spring to actuate, it is necessary to provide some type of spring mechanism against which the key can work. Either coil or leaf springs are used. There are two types of key contacts, although the principle behind each is the same. A bar of copper or phospher bronze, actuated in one system by the key and in the other directly connected to the key, intersects a set of *feelers* made of silver or gold wire. These metals resist *arcing*. Either the bar itself or one of the feelers is positively charged by a direct line from the rectifier. Since the bar contacts each of the feelers when a key is depressed, all the feelers become electrically charged.

At a microsecond before a switch is fully closed and a microsecond before it is fully opened, a current may leap across the gap between the two elements of the switch. This arcing can produce a spark which easily corrodes some metals. Silver and gold resist this corrosion, and hence these are the metals of choice in electrical switches throughout the organ. The higher the amperage involved, the greater the chance for serious arcing. Switches activating large solenoids, such as those used in direct electric action, will corrode faster than those opening the tiny chest magnets used in electro-pneumatic action. Corroded key and other switch contacts caused by arcing are perhaps the most prevalent cause of failures in electric action organs. Figure 4.6 on page 51 represents two types of key contacts. The four feelers of the drawing on the left lead to the rectifier, to the great chest magnet for that key, to the swell to great gang switch, and to the positive to great gang switch. The bar is

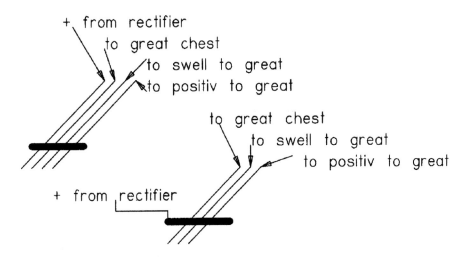

Figure 4.6 Two Types of Key Contacts

attached to the key, and when it is depressed the current from the rectifier is transmitted to the other feelers. The drawing on the right is similar. The only difference is that the bar itself is connected to the positive pole of the rectifier.

These feelers are set in small blocks of wood sawed to fit them. Each key of both manuals and pedalboard normally has a single block. The number of feelers in each block relates to the number of functions that key will be called upon to perform. For instance, a key on the great manual might require three contacts — for the great main line, swell to great, and positive to great. If the builder chooses to actuate the contacts with one of its own feelers, there would be a fourth. If the organ were complete with unison off, sixteen, and four foot couplers, there might be a great many more feelers, one for each function. There is obviously a limit to the number of contacts that can be placed in a small block under a single key. Sometimes there is a second contact block for each key or it may be necessary for one feeler to lead to a *relay* away from the keyboard, from which the lines may branch out to their respective functions.

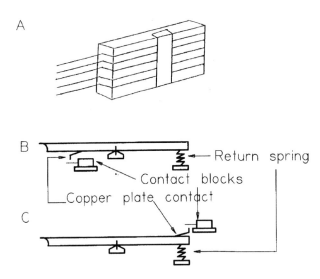

Figure 4.7 A: Contact Block; B and C: Methods of Mounting These Blocks

In the figure above, A is a typical key contact with five feelers. Part B of the figure is a cross section of a key lever mounted on a board which runs the length of the keyboard. The contact block is a piece of copper generally tipped with silver, screwed to the key, and bent as shown. The copper serves as the contactor. Notice that there is a spring which loads the key. Part C of the figure shows the contact rail mounted at the rear of the keys.

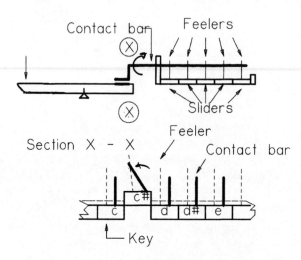

Figure 4.8 Slider Type of Contact Action

Figure 4.8 represents another type of electric key action which combines key contacts with the function of the gang switch. Mounted in a tray-like frame, the sides of which are not shown in the upper drawing, is a series of sliders. Each of these sliders has mounted on it a set of vertical feelers. There are as many feelers on each slider as there are notes of the keyboard. There will be as many sliders as there are functions controlled by that key. One of the sliders has feelers which are positively charged. It remains permanently in the right position. The moveable sliders are controlled by solenoids activated by the stop action.

A copper contact bar of heavy wire is bent and mounted as shown on the upper drawing. It is mounted so that when its key is depressed, the far end of the key rotates the bar in the direction shown. If a slider is in a position to the left, the rotation of the contact bar cannot touch its feelers. Those sliders which are in the right position will be charged when the bar rotates to the left. The lower drawing shows a section X-X of the upper drawing. The C# key has been depressed raising its other end. Its bar has rotated to the left and contacted the feelers for that note.

The purpose of a relay is to allow a single electrical circuit to activate several other circuits simultaneously. Figure 4.9 represents a relay seen from the side and from the top. The primary circuit energizes the solenoid through its leads. In so doing it draws the steel armature, which is pivoted at one end, upwards at the other. A contact bar attached to the armature intersects the feelers. One of these feelers is positively charged by a line to the rectifier. When the contact bar meets the other feelers, it charges all of them simultaneously. Relays may have as few as five to as many as twenty feelers activating that many circuits. We have already suggested the use of relays to reduce the number of feelers in key contacts. Pedal divisions, which often have their large pipes scattered at various places throughout the organ, are often wired by using relays. Figure 4.10 shows the wiring of such a pedal key relay.

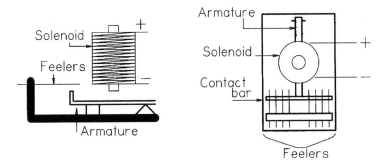

Figure 4.9 Side and Top Views of a Relay

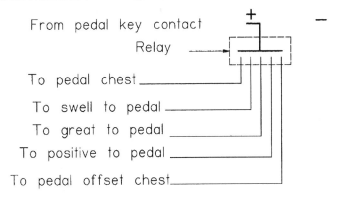

Figure 4.10 Pedal Key Relay

A multiple or ganged switch is a compound switch (i.e., a series of single switches grouped together) so mounted that all the switches open and close simultaneously. These switches relate to a single function such as opening a single coupler. Figure 4.11 shows the principle in schematic form.

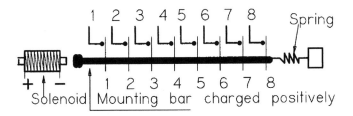

Figure 4.11 Schematic of a Gang Switch

The steel mounting bar holds as many feelers as there are circuits to be completed. The feelers are electrically isolated from one another. The bar normally remains in a position to the right with all switches open. When the solenoid is energized, the steel rod moves to the left, causing its feelers to engage a set of contact points. Each feeler mates with its appropriate contact. Ganged switches for organ use are made in sizes relating to the number of notes which they will be called upon to control: 32, 44, and 56 for pedal notes, pedal notes plus one octave, and pedal notes plus two octaves; and 61 and 73 for manual notes and manual notes plus one octave. These relays are small in size. One for 61 notes may be no longer than ten to twelve inches in length. Relays and gang switches fulfill the same function. The gang switch, however, can accept far more circuits.

The purpose of a junction block is to join cables together. A junction block is constructed of a slat of wood which serves as a base. Into this slat a row of brass or copper nails, which can accept solder, are driven. On each side of this row of nails are strips of wood which serve as spreaders and guides for the wires to be joined. Small holes are drilled into these strips at the same intervals as the nails had been driven. Individual wires, as they come from the cables in a logical order, are threaded through the holes in the strips, stripped of terminal insulation, wrapped around the nails, and soldered. Figure 4.12 represents a cross section as well as a view from above of a typical junction block.

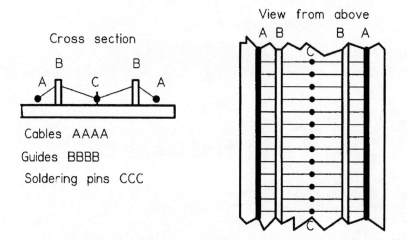

Figure 4.12 Two Views of a Typical Junction Block

Wiring of an Organ — Key Action and Coupler Action

Now that we are familiar with the basic concept of a DC electrical circuit, the ways such circuits can be endlessly compounded, and the hardware used in these circuits, we are in a position to describe the wiring of a modest size instrument with swell, great, and pedal divisions and with unison couplers for swell to great, great to pedal, and swell to pedal. The following cables are necessary:

Swell main line: From the swell key contacts to the swell junction block and hence to the swell chest magnets.

Great main line: From one set of great key contacts to the great junction block and hence to the great chest magnets.

Pedal main line: From one set of pedal key contacts directly to the pedal chest magnets.

Swell to great: From one set of great key contacts through the swell to great gang switch and hence to the swell junction block.

Swell to pedal: From one set of pedal contacts through the swell to pedal gang switch and hence to the swell junction block.

Great to pedal: From one set of pedal contacts through the great to pedal gang switch and hence to the great junction block.

Figure 4.13 on page 56 is a schematic diagram of the routing of the cables. Notice that for the swell only one key contact is necessary since no manual couples to the swell. For the great, two key contacts are required: one for the great itself and one for the swell to great. Three are necessary in the pedal: one for the pedal itself, one for the swell to pedal and one for the great to pedal.

Gang switches are the devices by which electro-mechanical coupling is effected. For example, a swell to great coupler requires that one set of the great key contacts lead to one side of a ganged switch. The other side of the gang switch leads to the swell junction block. The switch is wired so that note 1 of the input is switched to note 1 of the output, note 2 to note 2, and so forth. When the switch is open, the coupler does not work. When closed it allows the great key contacts to act in lieu of the swell key contacts.

The wiring of octave couplers is similar. The key contact for a great to great four foot will lead first to a gang switch. The lowest feeler on that switch will represent note 13 (an octave higher than unison pitch), the second feeler, note 14, and so forth. Assuming a 61 note manual, a four foot coupler will have a gang switch leading to notes 13 to 49 of the great junction block. A great to great 16' coupler does not affect the lowest octave of manual notes. Key contact number 13 is wired to a gang switch at number 1 of the output, note 14 to number 2, and so forth. The gang switch is then appropriately connected to the great junction block. Again assuming a 61 note manual, a 16' coupler will have a gang switch leading to notes 1 and 49 on its output side. Inter-manual couplers are wired in the same fashion. Figure 4.14 is a schematic of the wiring of four and sixteen foot couplers. Part A represents the four foot; part B the sixteen foot.

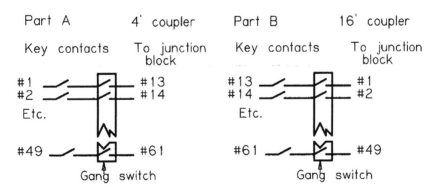

Figure 4.14 Wiring of Four and Sixteen Foot Couplers

Unison off requires a special wiring. Each key contact for the unison off is wired to a gang switch in a conventional manner: input number 1 to output number 1, input number 2 to output number 2, and so forth. This gang switch must be interposed on the main line between the key contacts of a particular manual and its junction block. In all other couplers the gang switches are open unless the coupler is desired. In a unison off the gang switch is normally closed, allowing current to pass from the key contacts to the junction block and hence to the chest magnets. When the unison off is pulled, the switch opens and interrupts

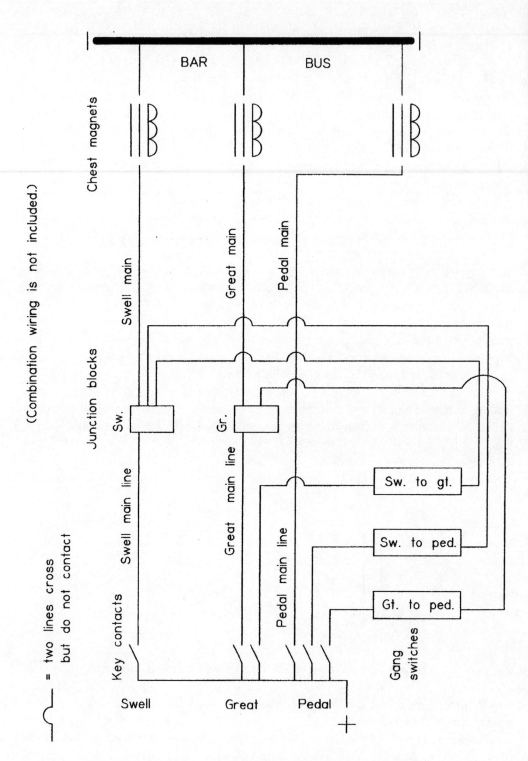

Figure 4.13 Wiring Schematic for a Two Manual Organ

the current for unison pitches. When it is open, the unison off gang switch negates the great main line from its unison key contacts to the junction block.

Stop Action Wiring

The wiring of electric stop action is remarkably simple. The stop tab or stop knob merely activate simple switches. These activate the stop action magnets in the chest. Although we will deal extensively with the function of the stop action chest magnets later, for now we need only to understand that they either activate the sliders of a note channel chest or admit wind to the stop channels of that type of chest. In either case a single circuit is all that is required. In coupler action the knobs or tabs merely activate appropriate gang switches for the functions called for.

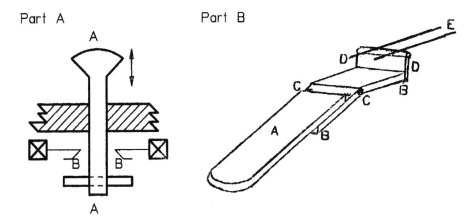

Figure 4.15 Stop Knob and Stop Tab

The figure above shows two types of stop controls one generally encounters, part *A*, the knob form and part *B*, the tab form. When the knob is drawn, the metal contact rod extending through the shank of *AA* intersects the two contacts *BB* and completes the electric circuit. In the tab type, the tab itself *(A)* is affixed to a metal bracket *BB* which is bent at its pivot point *CC*. A contact plate *DD* is welded to the bracket. When the tab is depressed, the plate contacts feelers *E* and completes the circuit.

Figure 4.16 represents the stop action wiring of a great division of a relatively large organ. Part A shows the stop action and part B a fairly full complement of coupler controls. Part A also indicates that two stops, the Quintaton 16' and the Trumpet 8', are to be borrowed in the pedal. Notice that the portion of these stops to be borrowed must be placed on offset chests in order to affect their doubled function. Since the pedal will use only notes 1 to 32 of these stops, their remaining pipes will be mounted on the great chest. The solenoids represented in the drawing are the stop action magnets at the chest.

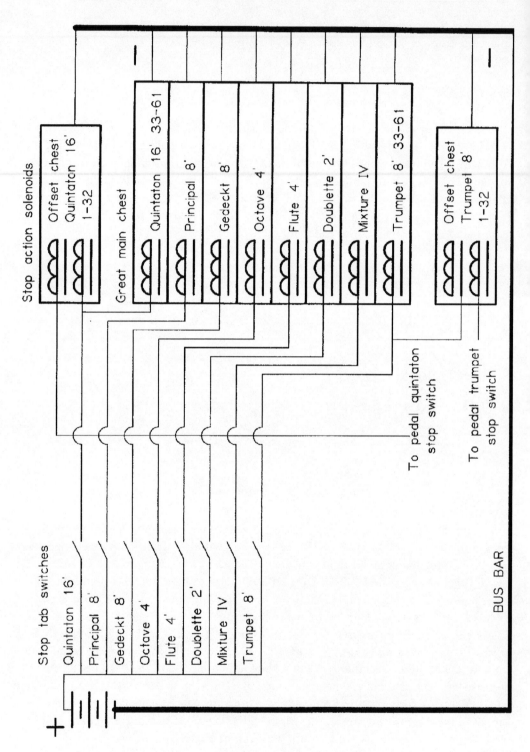

Figure 4.16 Stop and Coupler Wiring for a Great Manual.
Part A — Stops

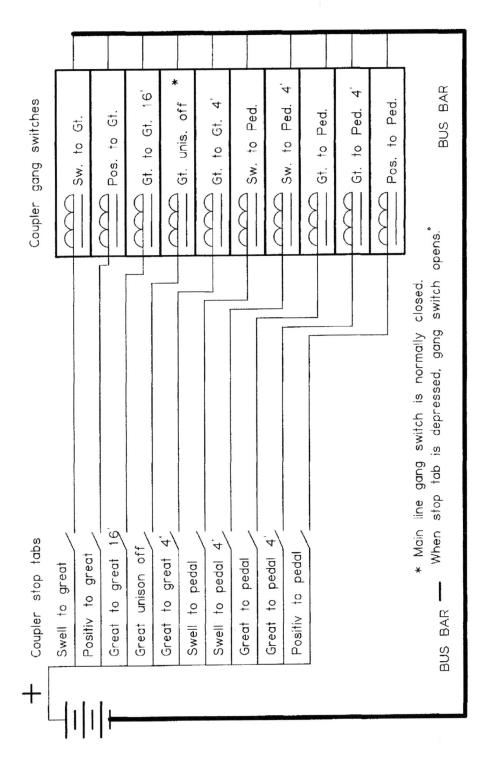

(Figure 4.16) Part B — Couplers

Solid State Switching

As we said earlier in this chapter, most electric action organs now being built, and many which have been retrofitted, use electronic switching (also known as solid-state switching). While the complexity of integrated circuits lies beyond the confines of this book, the principle of the electronic switch is not difficult to understand. Many materials, such as metals, conduct electrons well (conductors) and many, such as glass, resist electron flow equally well (insulators). There are some substances which conduct well in certain circumstances and resist conductance in other circumstances. The most common of these semiconductors is silicon. The device by which this quality of silicon is used to affect switching is the *transistor*.

The typical transistor used in switching sandwiches one type of silicon (the base in Figure 4.17) between two sections of another type of silicon (the emitter and collector). The base opposes the flow of electrons (i.e., it acts as an insulator), and no current can flow in the circuit *ACB*. The transistor is acting as a switch in the off position (Figure 4.17, upper drawing). In the lower of the two drawings, a minute charge from power source at *D* is introduced into the base. This changes the character of the base from an insulator to a conductor. Now current flows in the circuit from emitter to collector. The transistor acting as a switch is in the *on* position.

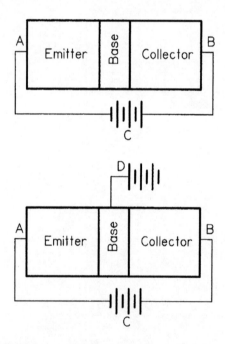

Figure 4.17 Schematic of a Transistor Used as a Switch

It takes an incredibly small amount of silicon to act as a transistor, and perhaps the most significant engineering achievement of our day is the development of micro-processing. The first computer micro-chip, produced in 1971 by the Intel Corporation, contained 2300 transistors. By 1999 a chip could contain twenty million. One can easily understand that the relatively few circuits used in the electric action organ can be reduced to small components using integrated circuitry. The complex array of switches, relays, and junction blocks we have described can be incorporated in small, easy to install electronic *modules* requiring minimal space.

Each key of an organ with electronic switching needs a single mechanical key contact for each note and a single mechanical stop contact for each stop. These few key and stop contacts are the only mechanical switching necessary. The amperage required in these few circuits is very low, so that even in these the chance of corrosive action is slight. All other switching is done within the modules themselves without any mechanical movement whatsoever. As a result, the failures characteristic of electro-mechanical switching, such as corroded contacts or crossed or shorted circuits, are essentially non-existent. Since each switching module is factory tested, the chances of errors is slight. Those of us who use computers are aware that eventually electronic devices fail, and this is also true of switching modules. Their design, however, is such that a repairman can easily locate the problem, remove the card that is involved, and simply plug in a replacement.

The output from the switching module is a single cable, similar to those used in computers, which leads to an interface with the standard cables leading to the chest magnets. This single cable can replace the multiple cables necessary in the older system. Some builders have replaced it with a *fiber optic cable*. In a fiber optic cable the *digital* information from the switching module is transferred to the interface by means of electronic pulses carried by tiny strands of pure glass. The purpose of the interface is to convert the signals from the module to the conventional electrical signals the organ magnets normally use.

Each switching module is a generic board designed by its manufacturer to fit a builder's specifications. The ease with which circuits can be fabricated within a module allows complete flexibility. If a builder desires a complete complement of couplers (16', 4' and unison offs on all manuals) these are readily available, or he may choose only those which he thinks are appropriate to his instrument. These modules make retrofitting a console easy indeed. The little space they consume is far less than the complex of relays necessary even in a small organ with a few couplers. Console shells can be retained, new keyboards added if necessary, old switching discarded, and the new system easily installed. If it is impractical to lead new cables from console to chests, the interface may be mounted in the console itself and the old cables retained. It is very easy for a builder to design for expansion of the organ by specifying extra circuits for future use. The speed with which electronic switching takes place (i.e., at the speed of light), means that there is absolutely no delay from the moment the player makes an action and the action is transmitted to the chests. As we will see the Chapter 7, combination actions are available which are equally responsive and far more flexible than any other present system. These allow as many potential combinations as the builder and client think would be useful.

All in all, solid-state switching answers the problems associated with electro-mechanical switching. It does so with no specific drawbacks. For the person learning about electric action, however, we must stress again that understanding the older method of switching is the key to understanding the newer. They do precisely the same thing. The newer system is simply more reliable, more compact, easier to install and maintain, and more flexible than the old.

CHAPTER 5

Organ Chests

Organ chests serve three functions:

- they provide support for the pipework,
- they provide space directly beneath the pipes which may be charged with pressurized air, and
- they contain the elements of the action which allow specific pipes to speak at the will of the player.

Chest design is determined by the type of action the builder employs, the aesthetic design of the organ, and the disposition of the *stops*. Some chests support entire divisions of an organ and support up to 1000 pipes. Others, generally termed *unit* or *offset chests*, may support merely the pipes of a single stop or even a portion of a stop.

Although there are important exceptions to this pattern, pipes controlled by a single key are aligned from front to back on a chest. Pipes for a given stop are aligned from left to right on a chest. Again, there are exceptions, but many times pipes are staggered in the manner shown in Figure 5.1. This reduces the overall length of a chest considerably. The following drawing is a schematic of the disposition of the lower octave of pipes on many chests.

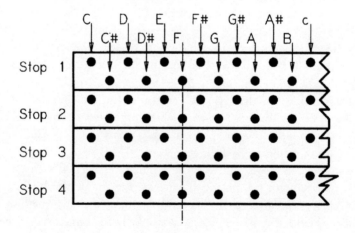

Figure 5.1 Possible Placement of Pipes on the Lower Octave of a Four Stop Chest

There are several common patterns for lining up the pipes of a chest. The simplest, although not necessarily the most common, is to place the pipes in descending chromatic order. The largest pipes appear at one end of the chest and gradually diminish in size as the rank moves to the opposite end.

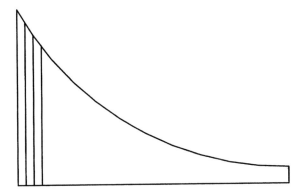

Figure 5.2 Chromatic Order of Pipes

A chest with chromatic order is easy to build and, in mechanical action, requires no *roller board*. A *fan frame* can be used instead. This form of pipe disposition is not necessarily the most common, probably because it produces a situation in which the weight on the chest is out of balance. In order to correct this unbalance, some chests place a few bass pipes at the treble end of the chest. The aesthetic appeal of this type of chest is obviously limited.

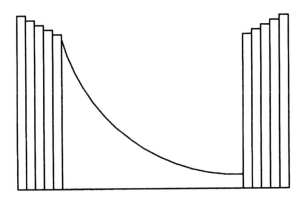

Figure 5.3 Modification of Chromatic Order

The most common type of chest is the V. Here pipes corresponding to consecutive notes alternate from left to right on the chest. The basses are at the ends of the chest and the trebles are in the middle. The two sides of the chest are termed *C-side* and *C-sharp side*, terms which reflect the two whole tone scales resulting from this figuration. When viewed from the front of the chest, the C-side is on the left, the C-sharp side on the right. The visual appearance of this type of chest is balanced and pleasing.

Less common is the A order. Here the largest pipes are in the center of the chest, and the progression from the ends of the C and C-sharp sides is in the direction small to large.

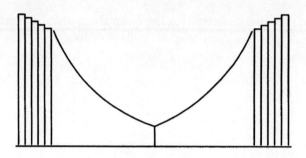

Figure 5.4 The V Order

This figuration provides a visual contrast to the V form, and is frequently found in the design of organs with exposed pipework.

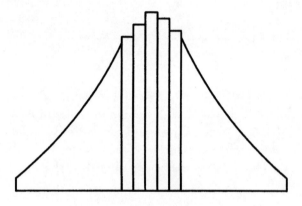

Figure 5.5 The A Order

Offset or unit chests are most frequently used for pipes which are too large to be conveniently mounted on main chests. For instance, the lowest notes of an open eight foot stop would simply not fit on the main chest of a swell division whose chamber has only an eight foot ceiling. The bass notes of such a stop would usually be placed on an offset chest close by. Many small organs have only a few pedal stops. In such cases there may be no main pedal chest, and these stops are mounted on offset chests.

Although many pipes in organ façades may be no more than dummies (i.e., they do not speak), others are true speaking pipes. Such speaking pipes are placed on offset chests crafted to fit the case design. Unless offset pipes are part of a façade design, they are usually arranged in chromatic order.

Stop Channel and Note Channel Chests Contrasted

There are basically three kinds of organ chests: *note channel chests*, *stop channel chests*, and chests for direct action, which, for now, we will put aside. In the first two types of chests, pipes must be placed in specific order that is a result of the action which controls them. Imagine for a moment that you are standing on a ladder looking down at a large organ chest without pipework. Think of the top boards of the chest as a graph with the X axis running from left to right and the Y axis running from back to front. Along the X axis run the pipes of a given stop. Along the Y axis run the pipes for a given note. If one plays a single note on a single stop, let us say cl on the 8' principal, wind must be admitted to the *toe hole* for that pipe via both the X and Y axes. From the player's point of view, he or she selects two things: what stops to pull (the stop action on the X axis) and what note to play (the key action on the Y axis). The action of these chests is thus divided into two parts, the stop action controlling the X function and the key action controlling the Y function.

Both types of chests are divided into sections called channels. Chests in which the channels run along the X axis are called stop channel chests; those with channels running along the Y are termed note channel chests. In a stop channel chest, there will be as many channels as there are stops on the chest. In a note channel chest, there will be as many channels as there are notes on that chest. A five stop chest of sixty-one notes would have five left to right channels if a stop channel chest were employed. It would have sixty-one channels if a note channel chest were employed.

In many stop channel chests, wind is first admitted into a channel by pulling a stop knob or depressing a stop tab. As long as that stop is on, that channel is charged with wind. When a note is played, a valve under the pipe in question is opened and wind flows from the channel into the pipe. In a note channel chest, wind is first admitted into a channel (called a *groove*) by depressing a key. If no stop is pulled, no note will sound since a barrier prevents wind from moving into the pipe. When a stop is activated, that barrier is removed and wind is allowed to move freely into the pipe. In both types of chests, both a key action and a stop action must take place simultaneously for a pipe to speak.

The Slider Chest

The most common type of key channel chest is the *slider chest*. It is this type of chest employed in all modern mechanical action organs, and it is often the chest of choice by builders of electro-pneumatic organs. Its reliability and straightforward construction has hardly changed since its invention in the sixteenth century. It, however, requires excessively precise woodworking skills, and, as a result, it has never adapted well to factory production. The slider chest has advantages in the voicing of pipes, advantages which derive from the fact that wind pressure must first build up in the channel before it moves into the pipe foot. This micro-second delay is important in establishing the proper transient sounds upon which proper pipe articulation depends. This advantage is most evident when this type of chest is activated by traditional mechanical action, but to some degree it is evident even when used with electro-pneumatic action.

Figure 5.6 on page 66 represents a cross sectional view of a slider chest. The pallet box (EFGH) runs from one end of the chest to the other. It is directly connected to the wind supply and is continuously charged with air. *ABCD* represents a key channel called a *groove*. There will be as many of these grooves as there are notes on the chest. They will vary in width to accommodate the diameters of the pipes placed above them. Obviously bass grooves will be the widest and treble the narrowest. Each groove or channel is carefully sealed from those running parallel to it. Any cross bleeding of air from one channel to the next is a potential disaster since two notes would play when only one was intended. *Pallets*, which are the valves of the slider chest, are made of light wood, are rectangular in shape, covered

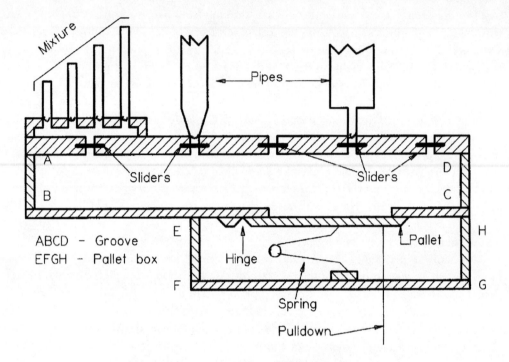

Figure 5.6 Cross Section of a Slider Chest

with leather to seal them from the groove they supply, and hinged in the back. They lie directly below and completely cover an inlet into the groove above. The wire pull down is attached to the front of the pallet on one end and to the key action at the other. It passes from the pallet box to the outside via a hole bushed so that its exit is essentially airtight. A heavy wire spring keeps the pallet tight against the bottom of the groove when the pipes above the channel are silent. When a key is depressed the pulldown wire is actuated; the pallet moves into its open position, and air is admitted from the pallet box into the groove. When the key is released, the pallet spring returns the mechanism to its static position.

Figure 5.7 on page 67 represents a section of the chest viewed from the front. The pallet box is continuously charged with air. Grooves, pallets, pulldowns, and the *sliders*, which are the essential elements in the stop action, are shown. Sliders are thin slats of wood, which move from left to right in cavities between the *table* and the *toe boards* and are actuated by the stop action. These sliders are carefully drilled so that they match precisely the drillings in the table below and the drillings in the toe boards above. Running parallel to the sliders and completing the slots in which the sliders travel are spacers called *bearers*. The sliders are slightly thinner than the bearers and are free to travel in the slots formed by the table below, the bearers on the side, and the toe board above. Figure 5.8 shows the table, the slider, bearers, toe board and pipe foot.

Before we describe the sliders themselves, we must say a few words about the table and the toe boards. The table is a monolithic wooden member covering the entirety of the chest directly above the grooves and under the sliders. Indeed, the upper surfaces of the groove partitions are glued to it and the sliders work directly atop it. In older instruments the table was made of several wide boards selected for their stability and carefully glued together. In modern slider chests, the table is almost always constructed of some type of wooden lam-

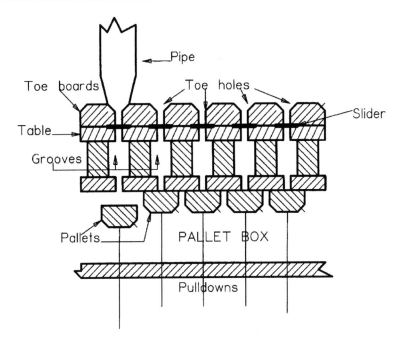

Figure 5.7 Sectional View of a Slider Chest from the Front

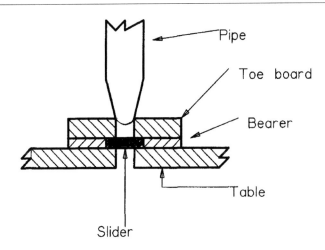

Figure 5.8 Cross Section of a Slider and Its Surrounding Elements

inate which can resist expansion, contraction, and warping. Toe boards run from left to right across the chest. The borings through the toe boards, the sliders, and the toe boards align precisely. Each stop has its own toe board screwed tightly to the spacers below. A *mixture* stop, one that contains more than a single rank of pipes, requires a specialized type of toe board, shown in Figure 5.6.

Figure 5.9 on page 68 represents a portion of a slider. Sliders are drilled so that they may be moved from side to side alternately opening the wind passage between the table and the pipe foot, or, in the other position, closes that passage. When a stop knob is pulled, the stop action at one end of the chest, shifts the slider so that the wind passage is open.

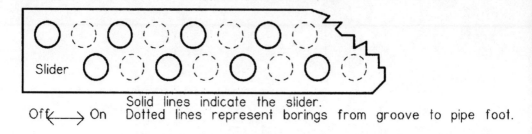

Solid lines indicate the slider.
Dotted lines represent borings from groove to pipe foot.

Off ⟵⟶ On

Figure 5.9 Schematic of a Portion of a Slider

Then a pipe will speak when the pallet below it has been opened by the key action. When a stop is retired, the slider is shifted into its off position. In Figure 5.9 the slider is shown in the off position. As has been pointed out before, pipes will speak only when both the key and stop action permit. Stop action can be either mechanical, where the motion occurs via a series of linkages from stop knob to slider; electrical, where a solenoid effects the action; pneumatic, where a small bellows makes the motion; or electro-mechanical, where a solenoid admits air into the bellows which, in turn, works the slider. At present a very popular format is the use of mechanical key action and electric (or electro-pneumatic) stop action. This blend allows the sensitivity afforded by mechanical touch and the freedom of modern stop selection and combination action.

In order for sliders to work properly and not jam or freeze, they must have freedom of movement. To that end, sliders and their bearing surfaces are lubricated with powdered graphite. Some free play must exist between slider and table and between slider and toe board, which, no matter how carefully controlled, cannot allow the slider to be air tight. This might lead to the ultimate horror of the slider chest, the unwanted transfer of air from one groove to another or from one toe hole to another. To avert such *runs*, the table and the toe boards have shallow grooves called *spiderings* routed between the drillings in a diamond pattern similar to that below. These grooves (not to be confused with the grooves of the key action) intercept any unwanted air and lead it outward to atmosphere.

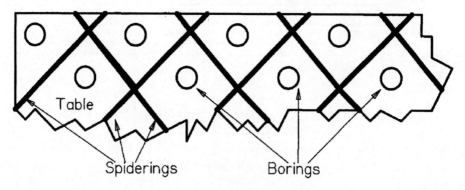

Table

Spiderings   Borings

Figure 5.10 Spidering

The construction of the slider chest has been remarkably the same for centuries. One could follow very exactly the construction details for this type of chest given by Dom Bédos in the eighteenth century and hardly depart from the procedures used in the best modern shops today.

Divided Stops and Divided Chests

A *divided stop* is one which is split into two parts, bass and treble. A *divided chest* is one in which all its stops are split in this fashion. One encounters these most often in small, one manual, mechanical action organs where they are used to provide flexibility of registration. The advantage here is that the lower portion of a manual can serve as accompaniment using single or multiple soft stops while the upper part of the manual can be used for solo registers. The reverse is also possible: the solo in the bass and the accompaniment in the treble.

From the mechanical standpoint, all that is required is that the bass and the treble each have a half slider, the left hand half actuating the bass notes, and the right hand half, the treble. Each half must have its own stop action and stop controls. Good design mandates that both treble and bass stop controls be adjacent, preferably close enough so that a single hand motion can pull both when an entire stop is desired.

The bass-treble break traditionally occurs at two places. The break which derives from Spanish tradition occurs between c' and c#'. The English and French tradition places the break a semi-tone lower, between b and c'.

Pneumatic Assistance to the Slider Chest — The Barker Lever

The force necessary to open a well designed pallet is a function of three elements: (1) the size of the pallet, which depends upon the type and number of stops it supplies; (2) the register (bass or treble) of the pallet (bass pipes require far more wind than do treble pipes), and (3) the overall wind pressure of the pallet box. If the number of stops is large, if the stops selected draw considerable wind, and if the wind pressure is high, the pallets become unacceptably difficult to operate, the action becomes sluggish, and ultimately the instrument becomes unplayable. Organ design changed rapidly in the first half of the nineteenth century. This was the result of larger instruments and stops of grander scale which required both higher wind pressure and a greater volume of wind. Pallets became too difficult for the limited action of the fingers alone. This problem was alleviated by the introduction of the Barker lever invented by Charles Barker in 1839. Figure 5.11 is a simplified drawing illustrating the mechanism.

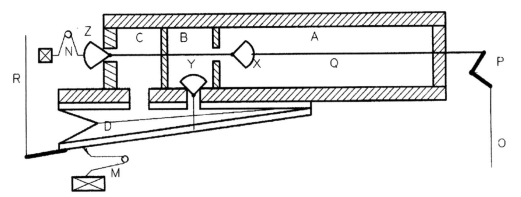

Figure 5.11 The Barker Lever

A small secondary chest is mounted under the bass portions of the main chest. Treble registers, since they offer less resistance, hardly need assistance. The Barker chest is divided into three sections: *A*, *B*, and *C* in the drawing. Section *A* runs throughout the length of the chest and is charged with high wind pressure. Sections *B* and *C* represent channels separated, as are grooves in a slider chest. Each serves a single pallet, and each note is provided with its own mechanism. The action for each key is provided by three cone valves: *X*, *Y*, and *Z*. Mechanical assistance is provided at a pneumatic bellows, *D*, ample to pull down the chest pallet it assists. The device is shown in the drawing in its functioning position, i.e., a note is being held.

The action of the device is simple. The pull down wire *O* is attached to a typical mechanical key action. The square *P* transfers the downward motion of the pull down wire to lateral motion of the action wire *Q* on which cone valves *X* and *Z* are mounted. When a note is played, valve *X* admits air through valve *Y* and hence bellows *D* is inflated. At the same time valve *Z* closes, preventing the escape of air. As the bellows inflates it pulls down wire *R*, which, in turn, opens the pallet in the main chest. Over inflation of the bellows is prevented by closing of check valve *Y*. When the key is released, valve *X* closes preventing further air from moving into *A* and *B*. Valves *Y* and *Z* open, exhausting both *A* and *B*. The spring *M* forces the bellows to collapse and return the pull down wire to neutral position.

Much as a power steering unit on a modern automobile operates, allowing a minimal force to do a maximum of work, the Barker lever reduces the force necessary at the keyboard to the amount needed to activate the assisting device. Pneumatic energy actually does the harder task of opening the chest pallets. The application of the Barker lever made it possible for builders to maintain something of the desired features of mechanical key action while allowing them to increase the number of stops and the wind pressure they desired.

Tubular Pneumatic Action and the Slider Chest

There are strong similarities between the Barker lever and full tubular pneumatic action. In this action, now essentially obsolete, small tubes, originally made of lead, connect the key action to small auxiliary bellows attached to the chest. There is a single tube and bellows for each note of the chest. These small bellows or pneumatics open the chest pallets exactly as do the bellows in the Barker device. Figure 5.12 on page 71 is a schematic of the simplest type of pneumatic action. The key valve box is charged with high pressure air. When a key is depressed, disc valve A opens and disc valve B closes. These actions allow a strong jet of air to move down the lead tubing. The small pneumatic now inflates. The channel containing the small pneumatics is open to atmosphere. This provides an opening to outside air for the bellows. This now collapses due to the wind pressure on its upper surface. In so doing, the pallet is now opened. When the key is released, there is no longer pressure in the tubing. The process reverses; the bellows rises due to the pull of the pallet spring, and the pallet closes.

Tubular pneumatic action, invented in the late nineteenth century, was an effort to replace the complicated connections of mechanical action with a more flexible system. While there were numerous improvements to the simple system diagrammed in Figure 5.12, tubular pneumatic action was ultimately doomed by the advent of electric action. Pneumatic action's numerous fragile tubes, which were difficult to position and very easy to damage,

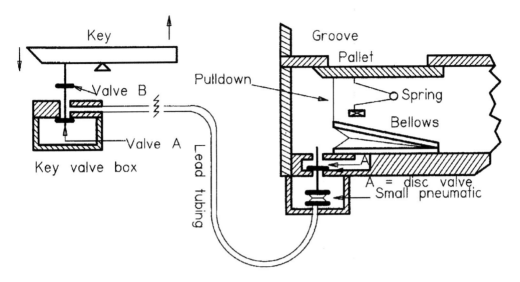

Figure 5.12 Tubular Pneumatic Action

were no match for the flexibility and durability of electric wiring. Since air is an elastic medium, pneumatic action could never be as responsive as electric action. Tubular pneumatic action, however, still remains in many organs built as late as the First World War.

The Slider Chest in Electric Action

There are now two ways to electrify a slider chest, the old way and the much simpler new way. The basic problem is clear. When a key is depressed, how can it actuate a pull down electrically? Until recently solenoids alone could not effect this motion without using undue amounts of current. It was necessary to accomplish this action via electro-pneumatic force.

Before we describe the mechanism by which this is accomplished, we need to examine the most common type of chest magnet used in electro-pneumatic action.

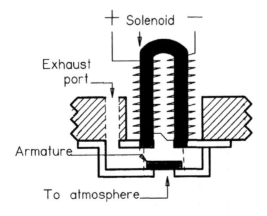

Figure 5.13 Schematic of a Chest Magnet

Chest magnets are small, self-contained units no more than two inches high and designed to fit into a one inch boring normally in the bottom of a chest. The purpose of the magnet is simple: to allow air under pressure to exhaust through the port to atmosphere. The type of magnet used is a horseshoe magnet which places both poles of the magnet in a position to decisively draw the tiny armature upward. The armature itself is a thin disc smaller in diameter than a dime. The top surface is steel to allow the magnet to attract it. Its lower surface has a cloth-like face to cover its port completely. When the magnet is energized, the armature moves upward. In the process it opens the port to atmosphere.

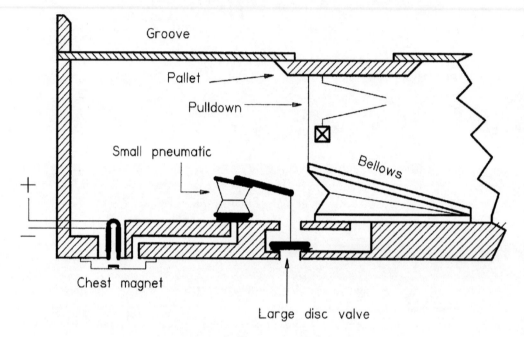

Figure 5.14 Method for Electrifying a Slider Chest

The drawing shows the chest magnet unit in place. Its exhaust port opens into a channel leading to the small pneumatic. When the magnet is energized, that pneumatic exhausts. Wind pressure in the chest forces it to collapse. As it collapses, it lifts the arm attached to it. That lifts the large disc valve, the bellows collapses, and, in the process, pulls down the wire to the pallet. Wind enters the groove. If the slider(s) are in the right position, the pipe(s) will sound.

The modern method for doing this is very simple. Efficient solenoids using relatively little amperage are designed to drawn the pulldown wires directly and thus open the pallets. The KISS principle wins again.

Stop Action on the Slider Chest

The function of the stop action on the slider chest is merely to move the sliders the appropriate distance from right to left and left to right as a stop is pulled on or retired. In an organ with mechanical stop action, this is accomplished by use of the same components used in the key action: trackers, stickers, rotating rods, and squares. These, however, are much more massive in scale than those used in key action. The task they must perform is far less intimate and requires much more energy. A schematic of a typical stop action is shown in Figure 5.15. *B-B* are called *traces*. Their motion is horizontal. *C* is a vertical member that acts as a first class lever and is called a *trundle*. By controlling the length of its arms, greater or lesser leverage can be obtained. The slider *E* is actually moved by the rocker arm *D*. A is the stop knob. The arrows indicate the motion when drawing on a stop.

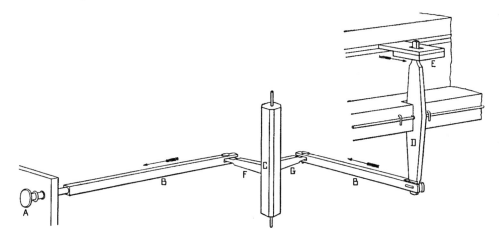

Figure 5.15 Typical Mechanical Stop Action (Audsley II, 362)

The sliders of tubular pneumatic organs and older electric action organs operate by inflating and deflating large pneumatics similar to that discussed above. These pneumatics are attached directly to the sliders at one end of the chest or the other. They are adjusted to move the sliders only the appropriate amount. In tubular pneumatic action, the slider action pneumatics are connected via independent tubing to the stop controls. If electrically operated, they are connected by circuitry to the stop controls at the console and the combination action. In modern electric action instruments, pneumatics are replaced by small electric motors designed specifically for this purpose. Many builders of mechanical action organs favor electric stop action. For all intents and purposes, flexible combination action is impossible using mechanical linkages alone. Blending both systems allows the sensitivity of mechanical key action and the flexibility of modern electric stop action.

The Spring Chest

The spring chest is encountered only on organs built before 1700, by which time it had been superceded by the slider chest. Nonetheless, spring chests still exist on some important antique organs. Both types of chests developed and were used simultaneously. The slider type ultimately was preferred because of its greater simplicity and reliability. The spring chest and the slider chest have similar pallet boxes and pallets. The spring chest is also divided into note channels (grooves) similar to those in the slider chest. Within the grooves, however, lies a relatively complex stop action. Figure 5.16 is a cross section through a single groove.

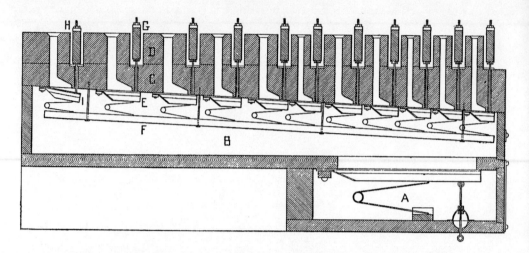

Figure 5.16 A Groove within a Spring Chest (Audsley II, 227)

In Figure 5.16, *A* represents a pallet box, pull down, and key pallet identical with those of the slider chest. *B* represents a note channel (groove). Below each toe hole on the chest there is a small pallet held closed by a spring mounted against a solid bar *F*. It is from these springs that the chest gets its name. Short stickers, *G* and *H*, bear down on the note pallets through the toe boards. The stickers for all notes of a given stop are bound together by a common slat (not shown), which is depressed when the stop is drawn. When a slat is in the down position, all the small note pallets for that pitch are depressed and air is free to move into any pipe of that stop where the key pallet *(A)* is open. The note pallets, the note springs, the stickers, and the depression slats together fulfill the function of the slider on a slider chest. The complexity and fragility of the spring action makes it easy to damage. Stops must be drawn and retired with care to prevent significant damage to the mechanism.

Two Types of Stop Channel Chests

A stop channel chest is one in which the channels run from left to right on the chest with a single channel servicing a single stop. There are two types of stop channel chests: those which allow air into a stop channel only when the stop is drawn, and those which admit air into all the stop channels whenever the organ is being played. In the former type, stop channels are winded only when a stop has be selected; in the latter type the channels are winded at all times that the organ is in use. In the first type of chest, the *ventil* chest, stop action is effected merely by admitting air into a stop channel and reducing its internal pressure to atmosphere whenever the stop is retired. In the fully winded type, the *pitman chest*, the action must, of necessity, be more complex, since it must act both as a stop and as a key action. The justification for the complexity of this type of chest is that it provides an ease and rapidity of stop action equaling that normally expected of key action.

The Ventil Windchest

In a ventil windchest, air is admitted into a stop channel only when its stop is drawn. Each airtight channel supports a single stop, and at the end of each channel is a large valve, activated by pneumatic or electro-pneumatic means, which can quickly charge or discharge the channel as determined by the stop action. When a stop is on, the valve is open and the stop channel is winded. When the stop is retired, the valve opens and the channel discharges. Unless these two actions are relatively fast, the stop action will be sluggish. Particularly, if the discharge is slow, it will cause a stop partially to speak when the stop has just been retired. Sometimes these two valves are on opposite ends of a lever arm. When one end is down it winds the channel; when the other is down, it discharges the channel.

In the ventil windchest, as in all other stop channel chests, each toe hole (and hence each pipe) is provided with its own small pneumatic valve.

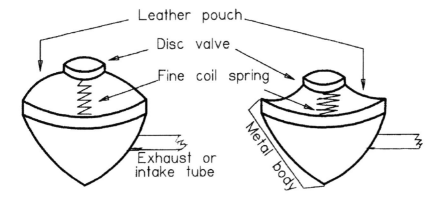

Figure 5.17 Pneumatic Chest Valve

Figure 5.17 represents one of the small pneumatic valves that is affixed directly to the toe boards of channel chests. On the left the valve is shown expanded and on the right it is shown discharged. A small fiber disc covered with felt is sized to fit tightly over the toe hole. The pouch is a circular piece of extremely fine and pliable leather onto which the disc is glued. The perimeter of this leather is glued tightly to the body of the pneumatic. Inside the leather pouch is a fine coil spring, whose purpose is primarily to align the disc. The tube exhausts or fills the pneumatic as the situation demands.

The action of these pneumatics is simple. As long as the high pressure air from the intake line is available, the disc is tight against the toe board and wind is prevented from entering the toe hole above. When that wind is cut off and the pressure inside the pneumatic is now that of atmosphere, the wind in the chest works against the leather pouch and forces it down. Wind is now permitted to flow into the toe hole above.

Two wind pressures are used in many stop channel chests. One is the pressure required by the pipework and the other (and higher one) is used to operate the action. Pneumatic pouches take forms other than the one shown above. However, the principle behind each is essentially the same: high wind pressure holds the unit closed, and discharging that wind pressure opens the unit. Pneumatics are made in different sizes to accommodate the various types and diameters of pipes and other appliances they serve.

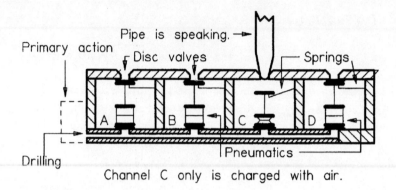

Channel C only is charged with air.

Figure 5.18 Cross Section of a Ventil Chest (No Primary Action Is Shown)

Figure 5.18 represents a cross section of a four stop ventil chest without its primary action. When no stop has been pulled and no key depressed, the drilling through the bottom board of the chest is charged with high pressure wind via the primary action. All the pneumatics are held tightly against the top board. The drawing shows a speaking pipe above channel C. The ventil activated by the stop action has admitted air at lower pressure only into that channel. When the key is depressed, the high pressure in the drilling is exhausted to atmosphere. The pneumatic in channel C exhausts and collapses due to downward pressure of the wind in the channel. The pipe, then, speaks. The springs hold the inactive disc valves in the upward position.

The Primary Action of the Ventil Chest

Stop channel chests, whether they are of the ventil or pitman type, employ a primary action whose purpose it is to exhaust the passageways leading to the pneumatics that control the opening or closing of the toe holes. The primary action and the passageways (generally drilled) constitute the key action of the ventil chest and both the key and stop functions of the pitman chest. In a ventil chest with tubular pneumatic action, depressing a key forces a small impulse of air from the key box to be sent through the appropriate connecting tube to the primary action of the chest. This impulse provides the force necessary to inflate a small bellows, which in turn opens a valve which allows the drilling to exhaust.

Much more common is the electro-pneumatic primary. Here the key action at the console opens a circuit leading through the main cable to a solenoid in the primary action. When this circuit is activated, it opens a small pneumatic that in turn allows the key action to function. The drawing below shows the same chest as that of Figure 5.18 with the primary action in place.

Just as in Figure 5.18, the drawing is shown with the pipe speaking. The primary action consists of two channels running the entire length of the front of the chest. The first, channel A in the drawing, has no partitions and is charged with high pressure air. Channel B is divided into sections, one for each note of the chest. Each has its own solenoid and passages. When the solenoid is *not* activated, the portion of channel B allotted to that note as well as the channels in the bottom board of the chest are charged with high pressure air. When current is applied to the solenoid, its armature rises. In the process it causes the

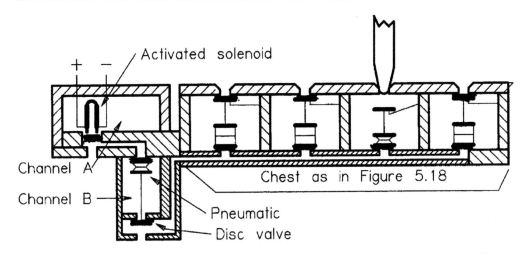

Figure 5.19 Cross Section of a Ventil Chest with Primary Action

pneumatic in channel B to collapse and the disc valve to rise. This opens the long channel under the pipe valves to atmosphere. The remainder of the action has already been described.

The Pitman Chest

The liability of the ventil chest lies in the time lag required to charge or discharge the air from an entire stop channel. Instantaneous changes of registration, demanded by many players, are precluded. The invention of the pitman chest, which maintains air in the stop channels at all times, answers this problem. Within the larger stop channels, which remain

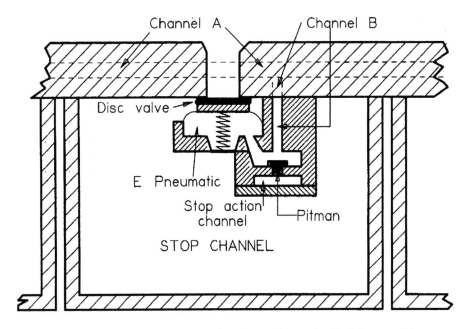

Figure 5.20 Cross Section of a Stop Channel of a Pitman Chest

winded when the organ is being played, there are much smaller channels controlling stop action that can be quickly winded or exhausted. The essential element of this type of chest is a short, moveable rod, called a *pitman*, that acts for each note channel as a fast and effective valve. The pitman action provides the performer with split second effectiveness when adding or subtracting stops.

Figure 5.20 represents a cross section of a single stop channel of a pitman chest as constructed by several builders. The channel is charged with wind at all times when the organ is being played. There is a lengthy drilling (channel *A*) through the top board leading from the primary action. *B* is an offshoot of channel *A* leading into the pitman mechanism. There is a narrow stop action channel that is charged with high pressure wind when the stop is off, exhausted when it is on. The channel runs the length of the chest. The pitman itself is cast in lead, and its circular upper surface is softly leathered in order to act as a valve against the end of channel *B*. A passageway leads from the pitman compartment into a pipe pneumatic similar to those that have already been described. The pitman action, which is admittedly complex, is best understood if it is analyzed in four situations:

1. *The stop is off. The key is not depressed.* The key channels *A* and *B* are under compression by means of the primary action, and the narrow stop action channel is under compression by means of the stop action. The pneumatic is winded, and the pitman remains in its downward position, since the pressure both above and below it is equal. Since the pneumatic is inflated the toe hole is not winded.

2. *The stop on. The key is not depressed.* The position of the pitman does not change. The narrow stop action channel is now exhausted by means of the stop control. The pitman is held downward by the higher pressure above it than below it. The toe hole pneumatic remains charged, as it was in position 1.

3. *The stop off. The key is depressed.* The key channels *A* and *B* exhaust by the key action. The pressure in the stop action channel forces the pitman up closing channel *B*. The wind in the pneumatic *E* cannot escape and it remains inflated. This is the only one of the four situations in which the pitman actually moves. Its purpose is to detach the pipe pneumatic of a stop that has not been drawn from the key channel serving it. In so doing, it keeps the pneumatic it serves from deflating.

4. *The stop on. The key depressed.* The stop action channel exhausts by virtue of the stop control. Channels *A* and *B* as well as the pneumatic are also exhausted by means of the key action. The pitman remains in the lower position since atmospheric pressure exists both below and above. The pipe wind in the large stop channel now acts on the pneumatic, which is now forced down. Wind enters the toe hole, and hence the pipe speaks.

Despite its seeming complexity, the mechanism is extremely fast and reliable. Stop changes can even be made while a key is being depressed.

Wind Chests Without Channels:
The Austin Universal Wind Chest

We now move to two specialized wind chests which do not divide their interiors into sections. The first of these is the highly individualized chest made only by one builder, the Austin Organ Company. The tenacity with which this company has adhered to this idiosyncratic chest certainly indicates that, for them, it has certain virtues which they cannot ignore. The first of these lies in the fact that one can enter the interior of what the company calls the universal chest through an airtight door and quite literally make repairs to it with the blower in operation. The second virtue is certainly the great reliability of the design. Even in the event chest components malfunction, which in practice they rarely do, each component is easily accessible and can be replaced with the least of effort.

The principle of the Austin chest blends electro-, pneumatic-, and mechanical key action with electro-mechanical stop action. The universal chest itself is a large airtight chamber which must be made at least two feet in height. In practice it is sometimes much higher, and often it spans the height from the floor to the toe board. This provides considerable headroom for the person working inside. The key action consists of a large pneumatic motor activated electro-mechanically via a conventional primary action, not shown in Figure 5.21. Here the similarity to other chest construction ends.

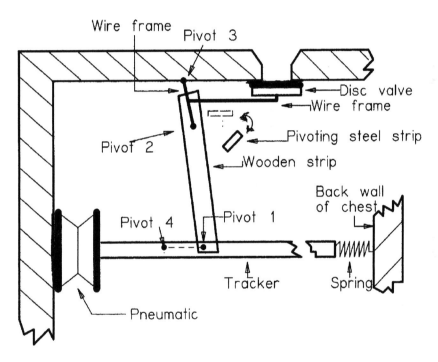

Figure 5.21 Single Note Action for the Austin Universal Chest

The action of a single note of this type of chest is given in Figure 5.21. It is shown with neither the key depressed nor the stop drawn. The large pneumatic is actuated by a primary action similar to that described above. Attached to it is a long tracker running from the front to the back of the chest and bearing the key mechanisms for all pipes of that pitch. In a sense, this tracker fulfills the same function that the groove serves on a mechanical action chest. Unless a key is depressed, the pneumatic is inflated when the organ is on. When the key connected to the solenoid which activates the pneumatic is depressed, the pneumatic discharges and draws the tracker to the left. A spring attached to the end of the tracker and the rear of the chest returns the tracker when the pneumatic is again charged. Deflating the pneumatic is analogous to opening the pallet of a mechanical chest. No note will play unless the stop action is actuated.

Short wooden strips, one per valve, are attached to the tracker so that that they are free to slide from pivot 1 to pivot 4. These arms are mounted so that they are free to pivot about pivots 1 and 2. A wire frame holds the disc valve *C*. This frame can pivot at pivot 3. As long as a stop is not pulled, movement of the tracker does not affect the wooden strip. It is free to pivot harmlessly around pivot 2. Its lower end slides equally harmlessly from pivot 1 to pivot 4. The disc valve, held by the chest wind, remains tightly in place. Continuing with our analogy to the slider chest, the tracker and all its attachments are similar to a groove filled with wind but with no slider engaged.

Stop action is effected by a steel strip running laterally across the chest. The stop action moves this strip from a neutral position shown in the drawing to an engaged position, shown in dotted lines. This motion effectively locks the wooden strip so that it can no longer pivot on pivot 2. In essence the components from pivot 1 to the disc valve are now a single stable unit pivoting at pivot 3. The tracker is now able to rotate the arm mechanism, and, in the process, pull open the pipe valve. The movement of the steel bar is analogous to engaging a slider on a mechanical chest. I urge the student to enter an Austin Universal Chest and observe at first hand its remarkable action.

Wind Chests Without Channels: Direct Electric Action

The simplest type of wind chest merely places a disc valve mechanism beneath each toe hole and pipe foot and connects that mechanism to the arm of an electromagnet. This type of action is termed *direct action* or Direct Electric Action. The latter is a registered trademark of the Wicks Organ Company, which has used this type of action extensively.

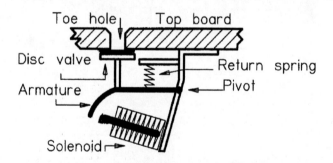

Figure 5.22 Direct Action Chest Magnet

The drawing above represents a mechanism for a single pipe in such a chest. The chest magnets are screwed directly under the toe board, which may be a large monolithic board covering the entire top of the chest. When a solenoid is energized, the soft iron armature is drawn downward. This in turn opens the disc valve which admits air into the pipe. When the circuit is closed, the armature is returned to its original position by the spring. These chest magnet units are made in various sizes to accommodate the various pipes that they serve.

The selection of both stop and key action is merely a function of switching and wiring outside the chest. No channels, complicated woodwork, complex action, or any pneumatic devices are necessary. Pipes may be placed on the chest at the whim of the builder, a capability which is attractive in the design of organs with exposed pipework.

Were these virtues of direct chest action the builders' only concerns, this type of electric chest would have supplanted others long ago. This type of chest, however, has considerable liabilities. In the first place, the amperage required to energize a number of large solenoids simultaneously is high, and therefore there is a limitation on the number which can be used. Even small organs with this type of action can suffer voltage drop and become sluggish as a result. The second liability is that it is a practical impossibility to get numerous solenoids to act simultaneously. The result can be ragged attack and poor pipe speech. Some of this may be alleviated by drilling small expansion chambers beneath each pipe foot in thickened toe boards. This allows the air to have some cushion before it enters the pipe.

A more sophisticated direct chest action interposes a pneumatic device between the magnet and the valve itself. These require only small chest magnets drawing limited amperage. Thereby the problem of high current is solved. They also are much easier to adjust for simultaneous action than the direct magnet valves.

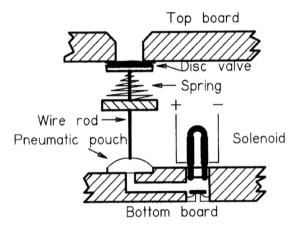

Figure 5.23 Direct Action Pneumatic Chest Magnet

The device is similar to other pneumatic devices we have studied. The chest magnet is activated by its circuit. The armature is pulled upward allowing the pneumatic *pouch* to discharge. The pouch collapses under the force of the chest wind and pulls down the disc valve. Wind is, then, admitted into the pipe. The spring holds the disc valve tightly against the toe board when the circuit is neutral. Some units combine the magnet, pneumatic, valve, and spring in a single body which may be screwed directly to the toe board. The exhaust must, then, take place via tubes to the outside.

Offset Chests

Up until now we have discussed only multi-stop chests. Frequently in the design of an organ, it is necessary to place larger pipes of a stop or even an entire stop on a small, detached chest termed an *offset chest.* In organs with mechanical action and frequently with pneumatic action instruments this can be accomplished only by running tubes from the appropriate hole on the top board of the main chest to the appropriate toe hole of the offset chest. The pipes of the facade of a classically designed mechanical action organ are almost always tubed from the main chest. Tubing is naturally cumbersome and has only restrictive use. Electric action offset chests, however, are easy to build, easy to wire, and can be placed wherever the builder desires. These normally employ direct chest action. We will return to these chests in the next chapter, which deals with duplication and unification of stops.

CHAPTER 6

Unification and Duplexing

Unification and *duplexing* (also called borrowing) are closely related and often depend upon the same technology. Duplexing is the use of a single rank of pipes to produce two or more stops often on two different manuals. For instance, a reed stop might play on the great, pedal, and swell even if the stop was inherently a part of the swell division. A very large organ may have a large ceremonial trumpet that does not fit within the ensemble of any division, yet may be played on all manuals. Such a stop is called a *floating stop*.

Unification is the derivation of multiple pitches from the same rank of pipes. Thus an 8' principal might also appear as a 4' octave, even on the same manual. An 8' swell reed might appear as a 4' solo reed in the pedal. A single extended 16' flute might appear on various manuals and pedal at 16', 8', 4', and 2' pitches. Assuming that one has a 61 note manual, this would require 97 pipes with the lowest pipe CCC and the highest c7. The derivation would be as follows:

16 foot:	CCC to c4	pipes 1 to 61
8 foot:	CC to c5	pipes 13 to 73
4 foot	c to c6	pipes 25 to 85
2 foot	c1 to c7	pipes 37 to 97

On the face of it duplexing and unification would seem to make considerable sense. They would seemingly contribute to a greater variety of sounds with a smaller number of pipes. Admittedly, duplexing does accomplish this, and many of the finest organs use the device in limited ways. When used perniciously it destroys the integrity of an organ. A purist would argue that a single stop can adequately fulfill only a single function, and to force it to serve in other than its principal function is to force it to do what it is inherently incapable of doing. On the other hand, one might argue that drawing down a four foot reed to the pedal is infinitely better than having no four foot reed in the pedal at all.

The concept of unification, however, is more insidious. Assume that one pulls a unified principal at eight and four foot pitch and then plays a chord. An analysis of that chord will reveal that some notes contained in it are played at both eight and four foot pitch. Others, however, are played at only one of the pitches (i.e., only one pipe sounds at that pitch). If one plays the following C major chord on an 8' principal stop, the pitches in the lowest row sound. If one adds to that a 4' derived from the same stop by unification, there are no new pipes sounding for the blackened notes in the upper row. They are already sounding. The chord is unbalanced and weak. Moreover, the *pipe scale* (the scale of a pipe is the ratio between its diameter and its length) of a good 8' principal is very often different than the

83

Figure 6.1 A Chord Played on a Unified 8' and 4' Rank

scale of a good 4' octave. In an ensemble they function in different ways, and to expect one pipe scale to serve both is a musical compromise.

There is one situation in which unification is more justified, and that is in a single pedal stop. Since the pedal normally plays a single line of notes, the derivation of two, or even three, stops from a single rank of pipes is acceptable. Thus a pedal bourdon 16' might be extended to provide 8' and even 4' flutes from a single set of pipes. Reed stops, since they are particularly expensive, are often unified in the pedal.

Duplexing and Unification in Electric Action

Duplexing is difficult to achieve in pneumatic and mechanical action, and it is used in these actions only for special purposes. Unification in these actions is even more difficult. Due to its flexibility, electric action is ready made for both. It is a rare electric action instrument that does not use either one or both in its design. The reason is simple: wiring can be led almost anywhere. Pneumatic lines and mechanical connections cannot.

Duplexing takes place in larger electric action organs largely for reeds and 16' stops. Borrowing of reed stops is due mostly to the need to make their use as solo stops more flexible. Sixteen foot stops require considerable space and are expensive to build. They are often borrowed from manual to pedal as a cost and space saving measure.

It is the offset chest which makes this duplexing possible. If the pipes to be borrowed are set on one of these, it is a simple matter to feed each of its magnets with two electrical circuits, one from the manual to which the stop normally belongs, and one from the keyboard which is borrowing it. Either circuit will play the note. Assume that, on a larger organ, there is a 16' manual bourdon that the builder wishes to duplicate in the pedal. He places the necessary pipes on an offset chest. Each pipe on the offset chest has its own action and solenoid valve. The solenoid is fed by two circuits: one manual the other pedal. Either will play the note.

The figure on page 85 is a schematic of the wiring of pipe number 1 in an offset chest similar to that just described. We will assume the pedalboard has 32 notes. The first 32 pipes will, then, be on the offset chest. The remainder of the stop lies on the manual chest from which the borrowing takes place. Console stop switches, whether tabs or knobs, open and close gang switches, one for the manual and one for the pedal. When either of these switches is closed, it completes a circuit and activates the appropriate gang switch solenoid. As a result, the lower portion of the gang switch moves to the left. This prepares the circuit for pipes to play whenever the key contacts for the proper notes are depressed. If manual key number 1 is depressed, the pipe sounds. If pedal key number 1 is depressed, the same note plays. One might think that two gang switches are redundant. Such is not the case. Unless two switches are used, a note played in either the manual or pedal will sound on both. The effect would be a manual to pedal coupler.

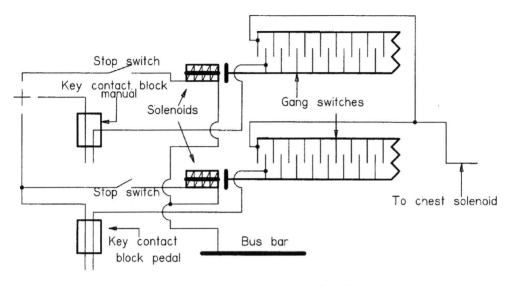

Figure 6.2 Schematic for a Duplexed Stop

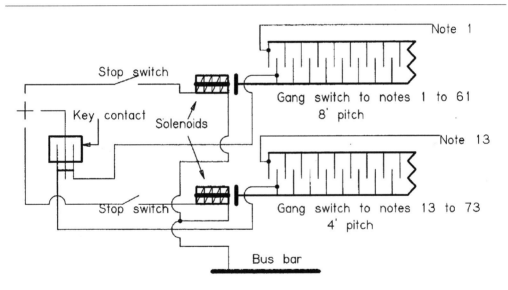

Figure 6.3 Schematic for a Unified 8' and 4' Stop

Unification is even simpler than duplexing. Figure 6.3 is a schematic of a unification of a single stop at eight and four foot pitch. Eight foot pitch requires notes 1 to 61 on a unit chest. The four foot requires notes 13 to 73. Each unified stop will require a 61 note gang switch and stop switches (either tab or knob). These switches work the solenoids which provide the stop action. The key action comes from the contact block feelers connected to the proper feelers on the gang switches. The drawing shows the wiring for chest note 1 on the 8' stop and chest note 13 on the 4' stop.

The Unit Organ

There are entire small organs, called *unit organs*, that depend entirely on the concept of unification. In essence, there are no divisions. All pipes are free to appear on any manual in any way the designer finds useful. Perhaps a half-dozen sets of pipes may appear as twenty stops on the console, which would, then, appear far more impressive that the organ deserves. Here is a hypothetical unit organ of six stops disposed on two manuals and pedal. The stop tabs suggest that there are 1017 pipes in the organ. There are actually only 499.

The Actual Stops

1) Gedeckt 16'	97 pipes
2) Dulciana 8'	61 pipes
3) Quintedena 8'	73 pipes
4) Principal 4'	73 pipes
5) Mixture II	122 pipes
6) Krummhorn 8'	73 pipes

The Stop List

Manual 1

Gedeckt 8'	number 1, pipes 13 to 73
Dulciana 8'	number 2
Principal 4'	number 4, pipes 1 to 61
Quintedena 4'	number 3, pipes 13 to 73
Flute 2'	number 1, pipes 37 to 97
Mixture	number 5
Krummhorn 8'	number 6, pipes 1 to 61

Manual II

Quintedena 8'	number 3, pipes 1 to 61
Dulciana 8'	number 2
Flute 4'	number 1, pipes 13 to 73
Principal 2'	number 4, pipes 13 to 73
Krummhorn 4'	number 6, pipes 13 to 73

Pedal

Bourdon 16'	number 1, pipes 1 to 32
Gedeckt 8'	number 1, pipes 13 to 44
Octave 4'	number 4, pipes 1 to 32
Mixture II	number 5, notes 1 to 32
Krummhorn 8'	number 6, pipes 1 to 32
Krummhorn 4'	number 6, pipes 13 to 44

All this is accomplished by an extension of the technology we just described in a single unification. The action of such instruments must, of necessity, be direct chest action in which each pipe is provided with its own solenoid activated valve. Key and stop actions are reduced merely to switches and circuits, and the chests to no more than simple boxes. No couplers are required.

Duplexing (Borrowing) and Unification in Mechanical Action

Both duplexing and unification are expensive in mechanical action. It is often simpler and less expensive to build a straight mechanical instrument than to resort to borrowing or unifying. Nevertheless, the procedures are possible and useful in some situations.

The basic problem in duplexing (borrowing), whether in electrical or mechanical action, concerns negating what we might call *backflow*. If one is borrowing a stop say from one manual to the pedal, a very common borrowing, a pipe will be winded via both pedal and manual actions. Backflow occurs when one source of wind intrudes in an unwanted fashion into the other. In electrical action it is a simple matter to prevent this backflow by the use of two gang switches, one activating the stop in its parent position and the other the stop in its borrowed position.

The solution to backflow is more difficult in mechanical action and the solution described below is merely one of several possibilities. Something analogous to an electronic *diode* is necessary. (A diode allows electrical energy to move in one direction but forbids it to move in the other.) It is first necessary to provide duplicate grooves on the parent (manual) chest for each note which is to be borrowed. One groove is for the borrowed trumpet itself. The other groove is for the manual stops. See figure 6.4A. This shows a small corner section of the chest with top boards removed and viewed from above.

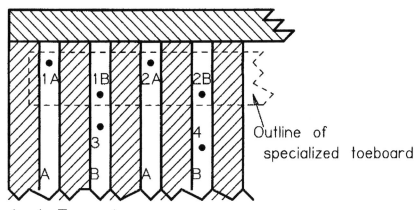

A, A   Trumpet grooves
B, B   Manual grooves
1A, 2A   Drillings for notes 1 and 2 on trumpet
1B, 2B   Drillings for notes 1 and 2 on manual
3, 4   Drillings for notes 1 and 2 on second manual stop

Figure 6.4A Double Grooves for Borrowing a Trumpet Stop

Both grooves are provided with independent pulldowns and pallets. The pedal pulldown is connected to the pedal action and the manual pulldown to the manual action in the conventional way. See the cross section of the chest in Figure 6.4B. Note that there are two sliders for the trumpet stop, one for its use in the pedal and one for its use in the manual.

It is necessary to mount a specialized toe board screwed tightly to the main toe board. The specialized board has drillings that mate precisely with the appropriate toe holes in the

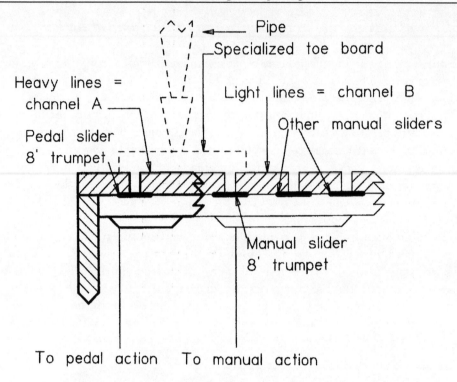

Figure 6.4B Cross Section of a Double Grooved Chest

original board. These drillings move diagonally and connect note 1 on the pedal groove to note 1 on the manual groove, note 2 to note 2, etc. See Figure 6.4A. They must move diagonally since we have two sliders to accommodate. Now observe the drillings (Figure 6.4C).

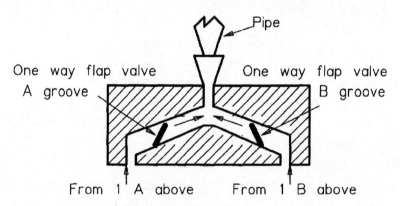

Figure 6.4C Cross Section of the Specialized Toe Board

These drillings take the form of an inverted Y with its base the toe hole for the pipe itself.

Each arm of the Y is provided with a simple check valve of the flap variety. Each prevents air entering one arm of the Y from flowing backwards into the other arm. It functions, then, as a diode. Observe the following situations.

1. Neither manual nor pedal stop is drawn. The sliders prevent any air from entering either arm of the Y.

2. Both manual and pedal stops are drawn. The pressure is equal within the Y and both check valves are open. The pipe sounds.

3. The manual stop alone is drawn. The check valve on the B groove opens and feeds the pipe. Wind, however, cannot pass the check valve on the A groove and hence cannot back flow to the pedal stop. The stop plays only on the manual.

4. The pedal stop alone is drawn. The reverse situation takes place. Wind may flow freely in the A drilling but cannot pass the B check valve. Hence wind cannot wind the remainder of the manual note channel. The pipe plays only in the pedal.

A similar procedure using the same dual grooves allows other stops to be borrowed from manual to pedal in precisely the same manner. One builder uses this principle in small organs in almost a universal fashion. Thereby he derives two manual divisions from the pipework placed on a single chest.

The most common situation in which unification in mechanical action takes place occurs when a builder desires to augment the single sixteen foot bourdon of a small organ by the addition of an 8' flute. The bourdon is, of course, already mounted on an offset chest, most likely of thirty or thirty-two pipes. The extension of the stop to eight foot pitch would require an additional twelve pipes in each case. Many builders who build mechanical actions will, in this situation, resort to some type of pneumatic or electro-pneumatic action and avoid the problem entirely. If, however, the builder wishes to remain within mechanical action, he must modify the backfalls leading to the pedal pulldowns.

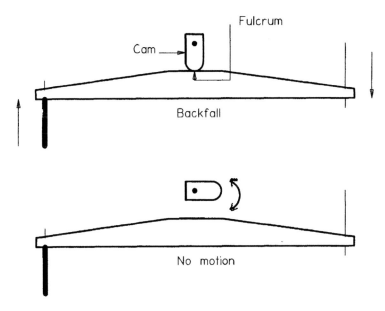

Figure 6.5 Backfall with Cam Mechanism

Figure 6.5 represents two views of the same backfall. In the upper view the *cam* is in the downward position and can act as the fulcrum of a first class lever. When the cam is rotated upward, as in the lower view, it is out of play. It can no longer serve as a fulcrum, and the backfall can no longer function. If a series of cams, one for each backfall of a stop, is attached to a rod so that the cams can move simultaneously, this can act as a stop action. When the cams are rotated into their downward position, the stop is on. When rotated into a neutral position, the stop is off.

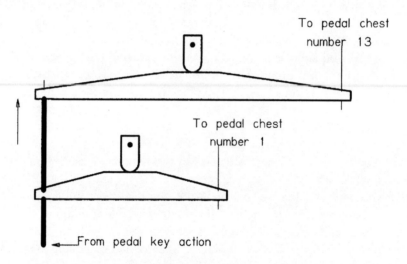

Figure 6.6 Pedal Stop Action Using Backfalls and Cams

Figure 6.6 represents a side view of the action for note 1 of a unified pedal stop. It is necessary to superimpose a second set of backfalls for the 8' pitch above those of 16' pitch. The 8' backfalls must be the longer since these must move in a diagonal fashion in order to pull down notes on the chest an octave higher. Both sets are fitted with the cam mechanism in order that each stop can function independently. The schematic below shows the path both sets of backfalls must take. The solid lines represent the backfalls for 16' pitch; the dotted lines represent those for 8' pitch. Only the first octave of the mechanism is diagrammed.

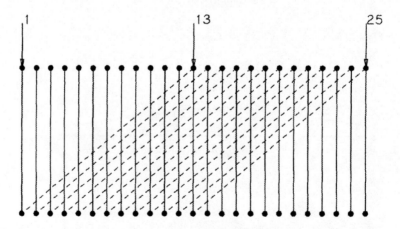

Figure 6.7 Backfall Paths for a Unified 16' and 8' Pedal Stop

A similar procedure can be used on a manual to produce a 4' *super coupler*.

CHAPTER 7

Aids to Registration

Couplers

The purpose of *couplers* at the organ is to allow the stops of one *division* to play on another keyboard, either one of the other manuals or the pedal. The order of manual keyboards is different in European practice than it is in American. In Europe the normal arrangement of a three manual organ is to place the great keyboard on the bottom with auxiliary manuals stacked above. Coupling, then, is always downward: the third and second manuals couple downward to the great and at least some of the manuals couple to the pedal. On a two manual American organ the first auxiliary keyboard (swell is the most common) is above the great, and the second auxiliary keyboard (positiv or choir) is below the great. Typical American practice, at least on electric action organs, is for the swell to couple downward to both the choir or positiv and to the great. The choir or positiv couples up to the great, and all manuals couple down to the pedal.

By far the most common coupling is at unison pitch (swell to great 8', choir to great 8', swell to choir 8', and great to pedal 8', swell to pedal 8', choir to pedal 8'). Some organs, but by no means all, have couplers which couple at the octave. Here a note coupled from the swell appears on the great either an octave lower (swell to great 16') or an octave higher (swell to great 4') than it would on the swell itself. Similarly there are also intra-manual couplers that, when pulled, play the key depressed an octave higher or lower (swell to swell 16' or swell to swell 4', for instance).

Perhaps the most extraordinary of "couplers" (although it does not actually couple anything) is what is know as the *unison off*. The unison off is an intra-manual device which literally cuts off unison pitch. It can be the bane of the unaware, since once it is pulled and no other intra-manual coupler pulled, the manual is essentially dead. What can be the rationale for what is seemingly a negative device?

Assume one has a 16' swell reed stop that one would like to use as an 8' solo stop. By pulling the swell to swell 4' coupler and the swell unison off, this is available. Assuming that the manual contains sixty-one notes and the chest has sixty-one reed pipes, the highest octave will now lack pipes. When this device was much in vogue, it was not unusual for builders to design seventy-three note chests to provide the "missing" pipes.

91

Coupling in Mechanical Action

Coupling in mechanical action must, of necessity, be restrained. Coupling of auxiliary manuals to the great and all manuals to the pedal at unison pitch is common, but all octave couplers are rare. The principle employed in mechanical coupling is to place some mechanism between two keyboards so that the manual to which the coupling is to be made actuates the keys of the manual being coupled. One such means is what is known as a *drumstick coupler*, a name it receives by virtue of its looks in cross section. Audsley (II, 105) gives a drawing. Here the upper manual is being coupled to the lower.

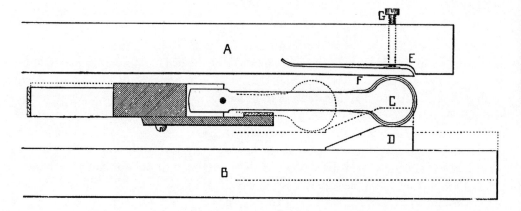

Figure 7.1 Drumstick Coupler (Audsley II, 104)

When not engaged, the device lies within the dotted line. The coupling action moves the drumstick to the right, forcing it up an inclined plane to rest solidly between the two manuals. As the lower key lever moves upward, it forces the upper key lever to do the same. The screw shown in the drawing is for adjustment. Notice that couplers in mechanical action almost always move the keys which are being coupled.

Another type of manual to manual coupler involves a sticker affixed to the lower manual. This sticker is hinged so that it can be moved to one side by the coupler action when the mechanism is off. When vertical, it forces the upper manual key to rise. When pulled to the side, it no longer has any effect. In Figure 7.2, A is the sticker shown in its on position. Its off position is shown in dotted lines. E is the coupling mechanism which moves the sticker one way or the other. Notice that the upper key is recessed so that it will not engage the sticker in its off position.

Figure 7.3 on page 94 is a drawing of the keyboards of a three manual organ with complete unison manual and pedal couplers. All are of the sticker variety. *A* is the choir manual; *B* the great manual; and *C* the swell manual. The manual couplers are as follows: *D* swell to great, *F* choir to great and, *H* swell to choir. The pedal couplers are: *R* great to pedal; *S* choir to pedal and, *T* swell to pedal. *O* and *Q* are two backfalls connected by sticker *P*. These are connected to a pedal roller board (not shown) via pulldown *W*. A pedal coupler roller board is necessary to reduce the larger lateral spacing of pedal keys to the narrower spacing of manual keys to which the couplers are directly connected.

The choir to great coupler is a special case. Here the manual being coupled lies below

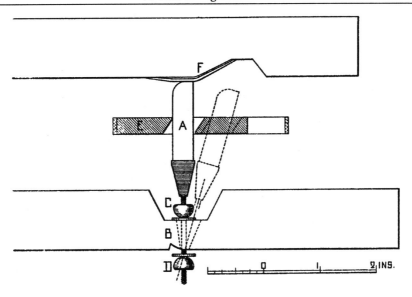

Figure 7.2 Mechanical Manual Coupler — Sticker Type (Audsley II, 108)

the coupling manual. The great key pulls the choir key up rather than pushing it up, as do the other couplers. The figure below shows how this sticker differs from the others.

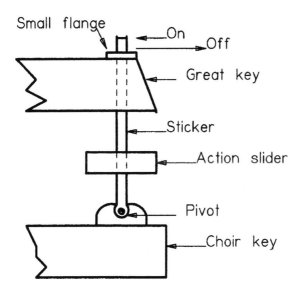

Fig. 7.3 is on page 94　　　**Figure 7.4 Choir to Great Coupler**

The sticker goes completely through the great key and has a small flange attached to it. This flange allows the key to lift the sticker when the coupler action is on. The sticker is, then, attached by a pivot to the choir key. When the end of the great key lifts, the choir key simultaneously lifts. When the coupler action is off, the sticker mechanism rotates on the pivot to the right. The flange can no longer be engaged by the great key.

A schematic of a pedal coupler action is given in Figure 7.5 on page 95. Depressing the pedal key pulls down the left arm of the backfall through the roller board. The roller

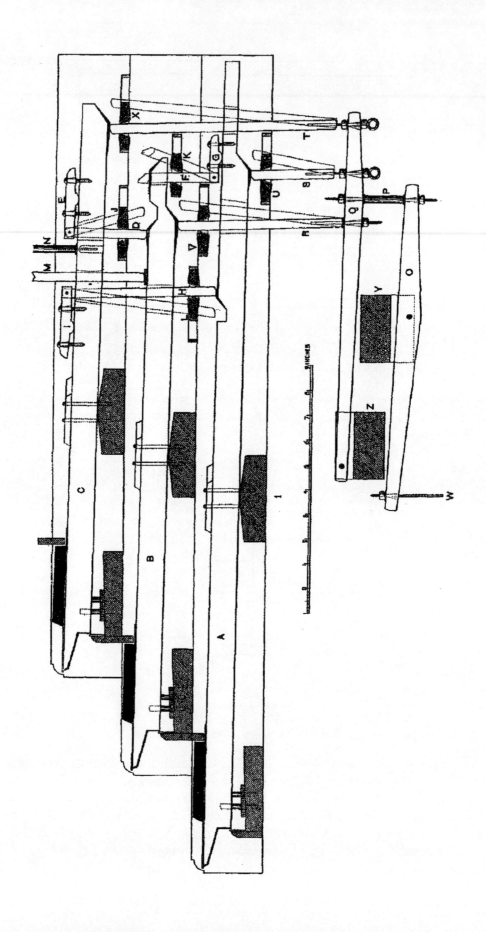

board is necessary to accommodate the difference in lateral dimensions of the pedal and manual keys. The right arm of the backfall rises and pushes the sticker upward, raising the manual key. The action cam is operated by the coupler control and is shown in its *on* position. When rotated to the *off* position, it no longer affects the backfall. Notice that the pivot of the backfall is mounted off center to the right. The downward motion of a pedal key is much greater than the upward motion of the tail of a manual key. The leverage must be computed accurately to take these motions into account.

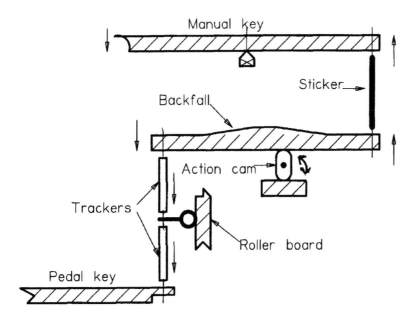

Figure 7.5 Mechanical Pedal to Manual Coupler

Coupling in Electric Action

While coupling in mechanical action can be complicated and expensive, coupling in electrical action amounts merely to cables and switches. In new instruments and in many retrofitted ones, solid state switching has replaced electric switching. Review the comments made on this in Chapter 4. One cannot "get inside" a computer chip, but one can see the operation of a gang switch. Remember that both technologies are doing the same thing.

The gang switch is the principal hardware element in electric coupling. If, for instance, we merely joined the main swell cable via a junction block with the main great cable, the result would be that the two manuals would be identical; what is played on the swell would be playable on the great. There would be no way to disconnect the two manuals. To prevent this unwanted feedback from the great to the swell, we interpose a gang switch which prevents its occurrence. Figure 7.6 is a schematic of a single note of a swell to great coupler:

Opposite: **Figure 7.3 Mechanical Couplers for a Three Manual Organ (Audsley II, 109)**

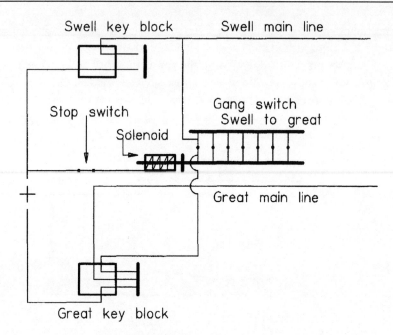

Figure 7.6 Electric Action Swell to Great Coupler

The drawing shows the stop switch closed and the coupler in operation. The great key block shows the note is depressed. The coupling circuit goes from the key feeler, through the gang switch, and hence to the swell main line. The note plays on both swell and great. If the swell key is depressed at the same moment that the same great key is depressed, the coupler has no effect. If, however, the swell key is depressed but the great key is not, there is still no circuit to the great main line. It is interrupted by the open great key contact. If the gang switch is open, there will be complete detachment of the swell from the great.

In inter-manual couplers there is no feedback problem. All that is necessary for a great to great 4' coupler is a gang switch operated by the stop tab connecting great note 1 to note 13, note 2 to note 14, note 3, to note 14, etc. A unison off "coupler" presents a unique situation. The main line from a manual to the chest is interrupted by a gang switch. This switch is wired so that it remains closed at all times except when the device is actuated. Then it opens and breaks all leads on the manual main line. Unless an intramanual coupler is simultaneously pulled, the manual is silent.

More Electric Hardware

Reversible Switch. A reversible switch is one that, when activated the first time, makes a desired contact. Normally it is immediately released and opened. When activated the second time, it reverses the action it took in the first place. Figure 7.7 on page 97 is a schematic of this type of switch.

The drawing shows the switch on line 7 having just been momentarily opened. This action has moved the armature and the contact plate attached to it to the right. Wire 6 is also momentarily charged. Its charge is carried through the contact plate to output wire 1, which activates the device the switch serves. The circuit remains open only for the instant

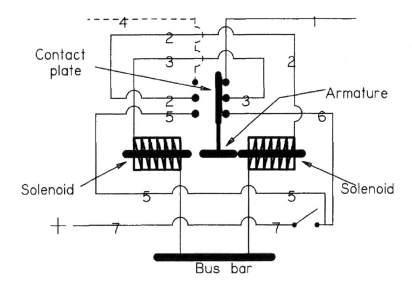

Figure 7.7 Reversible Switch

that this action circuit does its job. The next momentary closing of the switch will activate the left solenoid through line 3. The armature and contact plate move to the left and negate circuit 1. The device is in the off position. This action sets up the potential circuit: wire 5, contact plate, wire 2, which will next return the armature and the magnet to the right. By adding another contact point and wire, indicated by the dotted line, it is possible to use the switch to activate two devices, one when the armature has moved to the right and the other when it has moved to the left.

Two Specialized Switches. Reversible switches and many other contrivances on a console are activated by two types of simple switches, one mounted directly under the keyboards to be pressed with the player's thumb, and the other directly above the pedal board pressed by the player's toe. For reasons completely unknown, the first type is termed a *piston*. The second is a toe stud. Both are shown below, A, the piston, and B, the toe stud. Pressing either of the devices forces a metal contactor between feelers completing circuits. When released, both devices are returned by springs not shown in the drawing. Toe studs and pistons are used to activate combination actions, certain couplers, the forzando, and even the cymbelstern.

Reversible Stop Controls. If stops are to be used in conjunction with electric combination action, they must have a means of being turned off and on via electrical circuits. The first of the two drawings below shows the means by which this is accomplished using stop tabs. Two solenoids, marked *on* and *off*, actuate a curved armature. When the armature moves to the upper solenoid, the stop tab is moved down. When the lower solenoid is activated, the stop tab returns to the *off* position. A circuit is completed by a switch attached to the *on* end of the armature.

Figure 7.10 shows a draw knob action. When the knob is pulled manually or actuated by the combination action electrically, it closes contacts at the left, leading to the stop action. The two solenoids are designed to work in opposition. One pulls the knob out, the other returns it. The device is similar, but much smaller, than the electric motors that work mechanical sliders.

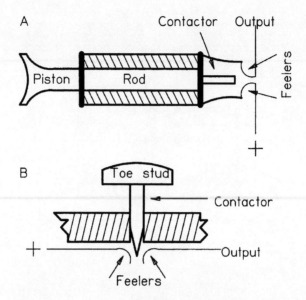

Figure 7.8A: Manual Piston; B: Pedal Toe Stud

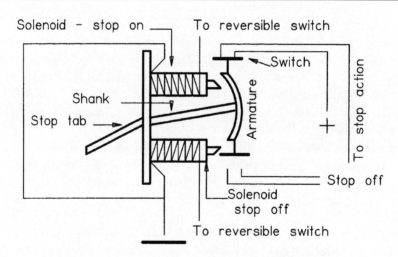

Figure 7.9 Reversible Stop Control — Stop Tab Type

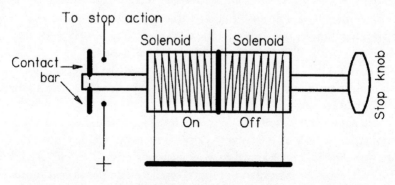

Figure 7.10 Reversible Stop Control — Draw Knob Type

Combination Action

The medieval organ had neither stop action or any kind of combination action. The desire to make the instrument flexible begins with no flexibility and gradually moves to modern combination action of infinite flexibility. The earliest device which might be called a *combination*, a preset group of stops which the player could activate when he or she willed, was probably the *machine stop* found almost entirely on manual organs in the eighteenth century. A machine stop was simply a means by which a group of sliders, generally those controlling the upper work of the instrument, could simultaneously be engaged by means of a pedal. By careful manipulation of the device, which was normally spring loaded so that it returned when released, one could effect a forte vs. piano effect.

A nineteenth century development, normally associated with the organs of the French builder Cavaillé-Coll, divided each of the main chests into two sections. One held the eight foot flue stops, of which there were many, and the other held the upper work and reed stops. Ventils allowed wind into each wind chest as the player desired. These ventils were controlled by pedal mechanisms placed directly above and in front of the pedal board. (The chests themselves, however, were of slider, not ventil, construction.) While this system provided considerable variety, it was nonetheless a system determined by the builder over which the player exercised only nominal control. More complex systems, activated mechanically alone or in combination with pneumatic assists, begin to appear on large organs in the late nineteenth century.

Combination action over which the player exercises complete control (i.e., he or she may preset stops and actuate them immediately) had to await electric action. Electric combinations begin to appear in the early years of the twentieth century and actually constitutes an early form of computer. The basic component of these systems is either the stop tab switch shown in Figure 7.9 or the stop knob switch shown in Figure 7.10. These components allow for either manual or electrical stop changes. We will describe two combination systems: the first is the setter board and the second the capture system.

Central to the action of the setter board is the *toggle switch*. A toggle switch is a simple on-off switch. When flipped in one direction it is on; when flipped in the other it is off. The toggle switch and the stop tab switch are the two components of this simple system. The setter board, which is often placed in a situation remote from the console, consists of rows of toggle switches, a single row for each combination. The following schematic represents a single combination on a great manual. The combination has been set to pull three stops: Principal 8', Octave 4' and Doublette 2'. Their toggle switches are set to the left. The other stops have not been selected, and their switches are set to the right. Two complete circuits are shown in the drawing: the Quintaton 16', shown in the off position at the stop tab switch, and the Octave 4', shown at the on position of its switch. When the combination button is pressed, it activates the stop tab solenoids according to the toggle switch settings. When the combination button is released, the stops stay in their set position until the player acts otherwise. The setter board, which no doubt is less convenient than the capture system, is nonetheless very simple, inexpensive, and highly reliable.

Much more convenient to the player is an all electric capture system by which one can set various registrations onto pistons without leaving the console. The basis of this system is to duplicate the stop tab settings made at the console with identical settings at a remote location. These can be saved at that location and retrieved by a thumb piston when required.

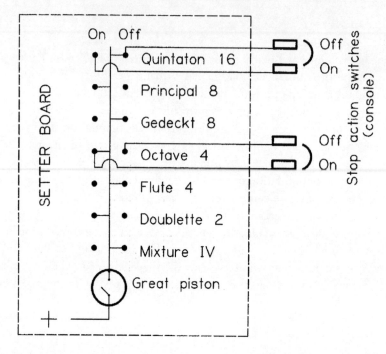

Figure 7.11 Setter Board Schematic

The remote location can be in the console itself. In other organs it is situated in an adjacent space.

In the drawing below represents a single stop on a single combination. A is the stop tab switch of the type shown in Figure 7.9. B is a similar switch in a remote location. It has no stop tab for obvious reasons. Four circuits, which are numbered in the drawing, connect the two switches. The setter button controls the switches on circuits 2 and 4. The piston controls the switches on circuits 1 and 3.

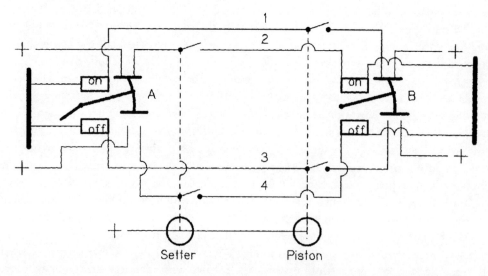

Figure 7.12 Schematic of a Single Stop in a Capture Combination System

The device operates in the following manner:

- Circuits 1, 2, 3, and 4, connecting the stop tab switches to the remote switches, are open except when setting and using combinations is involved.
- The player sets manually the combination desired.
- The setter button is now pushed, which closes the switches on circuits 2 and 4. This activates the remote solenoids *B* to duplicate what the player had set at *A*.
- While the setter button is still held, the piston (combination button) is now pushed. The switches on circuits 1 and 3 are now closed. Solenoids at *B* will be duplicated at *A*.
- Both buttons are now released, leaving circuits 1 and 3 open and 2 and 4 closed. Whenever the piston button is pushed, the position of switch *B*, which has now been "captured," will be duplicated by switch *A*.

While the drawing shows only the manner of saving a single stop on a single piston, the principle is extended to encompass an entire combination system. Although it may seem unnecessary to repeat this, the system just described is now obsolete. Solid state switching is now the norm both in new organs and retrofitted ones. However, what the microprocessor does in these systems is essentially what has been described above. Electro-mechanical switching, however, is generally limited to about a half dozen combinations for the manuals and pedal and no more than a dozen general combinations. Solid state switching, however, allows as many combinations as any dozen players might want. It does this in complete silence.

The Forzando or Full Organ

The forzando or full organ, generally operated from a reversible toe stud and also, at times, from a manual piston, actuates the majority of the stops of the organ instantaneously. When the switch is pushed a second time, the device is removed. Softer stops and celeste stops are generally left out of the circuits. The device functions in a blind fashion (i.e., the stop tabs or knobs do not move when it is actuated). There is often, however, a warning light which comes on when the device is active. The wiring of the device, illustrated in Figure 7.13 on page 102 is simple.

The forzando is activated by pressing either the manual piston or the pedal toe stud. This actuates a gang switch that is normally open (as shown in the drawing) when the device is inoperative. The piston and the toe stud are simple switches. These feed into a reversible switch which either can operate. When the reversible switch is in the on position, the gang switch closes and charges each circuit leading through cable. Each of the wires in this cable leads from the gang switch and intercepts a circuit leading from a manual stop key or draw knob to the stop action for that stop. Four circuits are show in the drawing. When the gang switch is closed, each lead from it activates a circuit leading to a stop switch on the chest. Pressing the piston or stud again deactivates the forzando. The warning light comes on when the forzando is functioning.

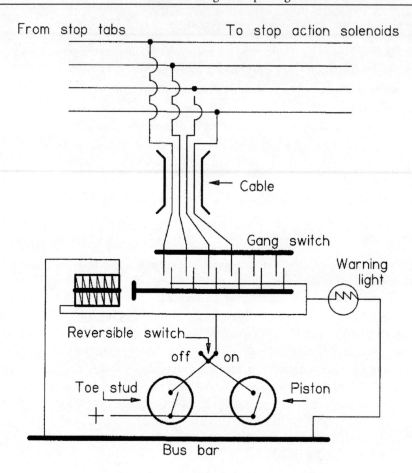

Figure 7.13 Wiring of a Forzando

The Crescendo Pedal

Closely related to the forzando is the crescendo pedal. It, too, brings on pre-set stops which cannot be selected by the player. It, too, operates in a blind fashion, so that the player does not know which stops are on or which or off. The device, which operates by means of a large pedal generally to the right of the swell pedal, brings on stops beginning with soft ones and progressively building until a forte is achieved. Figure 7.14 on page 103 shows one form of the device.

A large wooden drum is so fixed that it will partially rotate when the swell pedal is depressed. Mechanical linkages transmit the motion from pedal to drum. This pedal is normally directly above the pedal board in the center of the console. The drum has attached to it a triangular copper plate that is positively charged. When the drum with its plate is rotated, it cumulatively contacts a set of feelers, one for each stop in the crescendo progression. Each of these feelers is connected to a stop action wire in much the same fashion as in the forzando. In the drawing the softer stops are on the right side of the feeler plate and the louder stops on the left. The drawing shows that some of the soft feelers have already contacted the plate and actuated their stop actions.

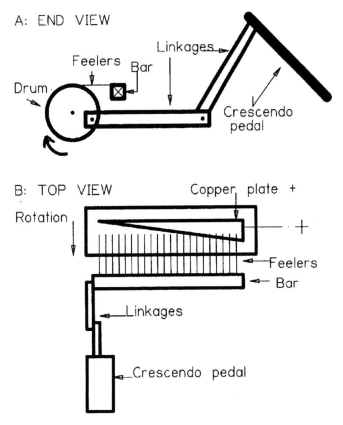

Figure 7.14 Crescendo Pedal Action

The Swell Box

On the many multi-manual organs, one (and sometimes more than one) division is *under expression*. This means that the pipes of that division are housed in an enclosed box fitted with Venetian type shades which may be opened or closed at the player's discretion. The act of opening the shades effects a crescendo and closing them effects a decrescendo. Note that the volume of the pipes themselves does not change. The shades merely place a partial barrier between the pipes and the outside of the box. Shades are normally controlled by a large pedal to the left of the crescendo pedal, and, if more than one division is under expression, other pedals are to the left of that. The primary division under expression is termed the *swell division*.

The idea of enclosing pipes in a box to dampen their sound is found in the seventeenth century in French organs with a miniature division mounted high up in the organ case and called the *echo*. It allowed no gradation of sound. The English experimented with the swell concept throughout the eighteenth century. Crude sliding doors opened enclosed divisions until 1789, when Samuel Green adapted the Venetian shades to the organ. These have been consistently used since.

Organ shades are, of course, much more massive than the window variety. Each shutter is perhaps ten inches to a foot wide and is constructed of wood generally about two inches thick. Swell shades are most commonly in the front of the swell box, but they may also be found on the sides and even on the top at the discretion of the builder. The shades themselves may be mounted either horizontally or vertically, with the latter the more common. In order to effect as tight a box as possible, one shade overlaps the other, and the overlap is thickly felted. Not only does the felt serve to seal the shades when closed, it reduces any undesirable sound when the swell box is closed.

Below is a schematic of four swell shades viewed from the top (assuming they are mounted vertically). Each is pivoted at its center. The pivots must be as free of friction as possible and strong enough to support the shades securely. On the upper edge of each shade is affixed a nub which is freely pinned to an action rod. When this rod is moved to the left, the shades attached to it all open. In the figure A shows the shades closed; B shows the shades partially opened.

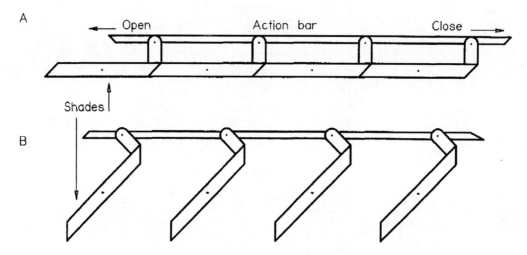

Figure 7.15 Swell Shades — A: Closed, B: Partially Open

If a swell box is free-standing, it is carefully constructed of wood of substantial thickness. It is important that the box is tight and free of any tendency to vibrate. In organs placed in chambers, a chamber itself often constitutes the swell box with the front wall only of wood and containing the shades.

To achieve smooth crescendos and decrescendos it is necessary to open and close the shades in a linear fashion; that is, they must open without any jerking or stalling. To achieve this builders have gone to excessive lengths. The controls of early swell boxes made this impossible, since the swell mechanism required the player to lock down the pedal at some point of his or her choosing. In other words, if the player released the pedal without using the lockdown mechanism, the box would close. Since early English organs had no pedal keyboard, the performer's right foot was free to work the box at all times. Save for their presence on antique organs, these hitch-down swell pedals have long since been replaced by the *balanced swell pedal*.

A balanced swell action is so designed that the swell shades will remain in the position they hold when the pedal controlling them is released. In mechanical action, the connection between pedal and shades is similar to that used to activate the slider mechanism. Both move components from left to right as the player demands. The swell control differs from the slider control by being more rugged and so fixed that at any point at which the player removes his or her foot, the action is balanced and holds in place. The builder controls this by balancing the weight of the mechanism's components and the springs which hold the shades closed. Since mechanical swell action is absolutely linear (i.e., the motion of the player's foot is precisely duplicated in the opening or closing of the shades), it is often preferable to other pneumatic or electro-pneumatic swell actions.

On a large swell the weight of the shades may be such that some assistance is needed. Audsley shows a pneumatic assist, which he attributes to E.M. Skinner. The device is placed between the mechanical arm from the swell pedal and the arm which actually opens the shades.

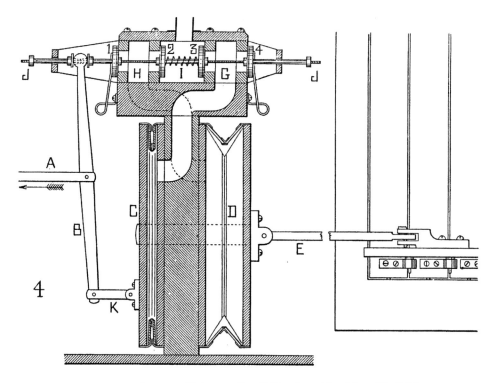

Figure 7.16 E.M. Skinner Swell Engine (Audsley II, 671)

In the drawing above, the swell shades are open and closed by rod *E*. The bellows *D*, which closes the shades, is shown inflated, and the bellows *C*, which opens the shades, is deflated. The bellows are tied to one another. When one is inflated, the other deflates. Chamber *I* is charged with air whenever the organ is being played. Four disc valves (*1, 2, 3, 4*) are threaded onto rod *JJ*. If the swell pedal is not operating, the disc valves are all closed. Rod *A* is connected to the swell pedal. When that rod is pulled to the left (opening the shades), lever arm *B* causes rod *JJ* to move the left also. Valve *3* now opens; bellows *C* is inflated through *G*; and the shades are opened. When rod *A* is moved to the right, valve *2* is opened, bellows *D* is inflated through *H*, and the shades are closed. Valves *1* and *4* are exhaust valves.

Electro-pneumatic swell actions pose a problem. In order to effect a smooth crescendo-decrescendo effect, some ten or twelve levels of opening and closing of the shades are desirable. The result with fewer is jerky and uneven action. The swell pedal can be connected to a device similar to that used to control the crescendo pedal (Figure 7.14). A feeler is provided for each degree the shades are caused to move. Another device, which works on the same principle, is shown in Figure 7.17.

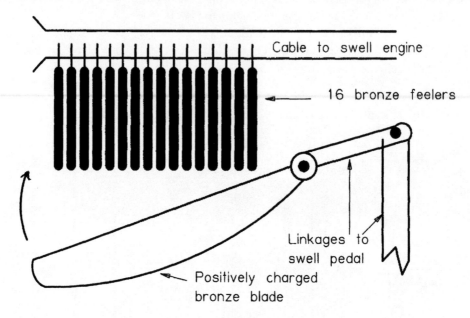

Cable to swell engine

16 bronze feelers

Linkages to
swell pedal

Positively charged
bronze blade

Figure 7.17 Swell Shade Control

The drawing shows sixteen bronze feelers each connected to a single stop action magnet. The bronze blade is positively charged. Its linkages are connected to the swell pedal. As the blade pivots due to the linkages being pulled downward, it contacts one feeler after another beginning on the right and ending on the left. Each feeler opens a single swell shutter when it is energized via the blade.

The problem now is how one converts multiple electrical charges from the swell pedal mechanism into progressive movements of the arm which opens the shades. Robert Hope-Jones went to the extravagant means of fitting each swell shade with its own electro-pneumatic motor. When a pneumatic inflated, the shade to which that pneumatic belonged opened. There was no common rod opening the shades. More often builders employ various types of *swell engines.* One of these is the *whipple-tree* type. The dictionary definition of a whipple-tree is "the pivoted and swinging bar to which the traces, or tugs, of a harness are fastened." Figure 7.18 on page 107 is a schematic of a whipple-tree swell engine.

The box is charged with air when the organ is being played. There are sixteen pneumatic motors actuated by the swell pedal switch similar to that described above. (The electric action is not shown.) Each pneumatic is attached to a pivoting arm called a trace. The other end of that trace is attached in similar fashion to that pneumatic's adjacent neighbor. Since there are sixteen pneumatics, there are eight such pairs. Each of these pairs is, then, attached to a higher level of traces. The pairs at that level are attached in similar fashion to the next level. These various levels finally attach to a single trace, outside the box. That lever, then, is attached to the rod actuating the shades.

As the swell pedal is depressed, it causes the motors to deflate in order from left to

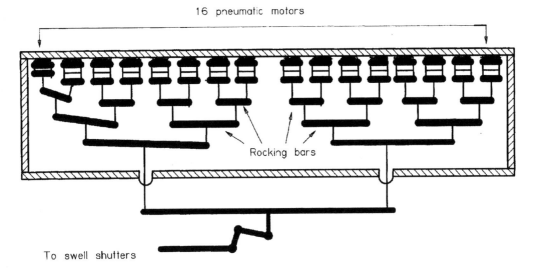

Figure 7.18 Schematic of a Whipple-tree Swell Engine

right. The drawing shows the first pneumatic deflated. That motion constitutes one-sixteenth of the potential motion of the engine, and that small motion is transmitted from one level of traces to the next, and finally, to the swell arm. The greater the number of motors that are deflated, the greater the motion imparted to the swell rod. For instance, if eight of the pneumatics are deflated, the swell arm moves half way. If all are deflated, the swell shades are fully opened. As individual motors are re-inflated as the swell is closed, the shades are closed by action of large springs.

Another form of electro-pneumatic swell engine is shown in Figure 7.19.

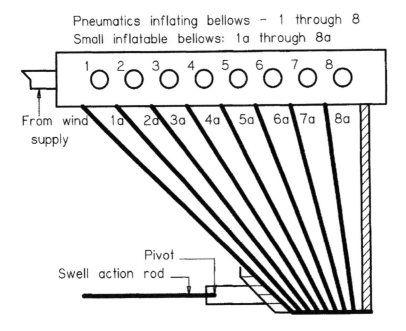

Figure 7.19 Another Form of Pneumatic Swell Engine

At the top of the drawing is a box charged with air. It contains eight electro-pneumatic valves (numbers 1 through 8) which pressurize eight small diagonal bellows (1a through 8a). These pneumatics are electrically fed through the feelers on the swell pedal switch. Each feeler feeds one of the bellows. The right wall of bellows 8 is secure and does not move. The same panel is used for the front of one bellows and the rear of its neighbor. As the bellows are progressively inflated by the action of the swell pedal and the valve mechanism, the swell action rod is forced to the left and the swell box is opened. As the bellows are progressively deflated, the arm is moved to the right and the swell box closes by the force of springs.

There are all-electric systems employing motors controlled by rheostatic devices and two-way motors to actuate the shades. A *rheostat* is a device controlling the amount of current entering an appliance. In these systems the rheostat is actuated by the swell pedal. By depressing it, more current goes to the swell motor. By varying the amount of current into the motor, the number of swell shades being opened or closed is similarly controlled.

Although mechanical swell mechanisms remain for smaller instruments the ultimate in finesse, for larger organs with larger swell openings these become impractical. Something of that finesse can be recaptured by systems dependent upon micro-processing. Such systems have a micro-processor activated by the swell pedal. The processor is then connected by a single cable to a motor module which activates the shades. Perhaps the best way to describe the capabilities of these systems is to quote from the catalogue of one of the principal manufacturers of these components.

> The RC-150's microprocessor based motion control system automatically compensates for various load conditions to smoothly accelerate and decelerate the shades. Beginning with standard factory settings, the organ builder may match the RC-150's shade position and shade parameters to the individual characteristics of a particular swell shade system by pushing buttons in response to clearly worded instructions on a LCD message screen. A number between 0 and 100 represents the amount that the shades will open at each shoe position. The speed of each increment of open and closed direction travel is represented by the words Slow, Medium, or Fast [Peterson Electro Musical Products, Inc. (www.Petersonemp.com) catalogue, page 19].

The Best Aid to Registration of All

We save the best aid to registration, and the most time honored, for last. It is simply the reliable and knowledgeable assistant. No matter how well equipped a console may be, an assistant is to be recommended. Assistants remove much of the stress of performance by making stop changes which are difficult or impossible, turning pages, by stepping in to correct the inevitable incorrect stop change, and even to remind the player which piece is due to come up next. For the student serving as an assistant, there is really no better instruction.

CHAPTER 8

Acoustics of Organ Pipes

Before we begin a discussion of the pipework, it is necessary to have some knowledge of basic acoustics, the science of sound. Since the production of specialized sounds is the basic function of organ pipes, acoustical matters become important.

Wave Motion

Many phenomena from tsunamis to microwaves depend on wave motion. Depending upon the *frequency* of a wave, the number of waves within a specified amount of time, we perceive waves as motion in water, various types of radiation, as light, or as sound. Sound is wave motion within a specified band of relatively slow frequencies. Figure 8.1 is a diagram of a single wave. It follows the form of a sine curve. From one vertical dotted line to the next is a single *cycle*. Two cycles are shown on the drawing. The span of time required for a single cycle is termed the frequency and is the determinant of pitch. Frequency is measured in cycles per second. A single cycle is called a *hertz* (Hz) after a famous nineteenth century physicist, Heinrich Hertz. The frequencies of organ pipes fall in the range of from 16 Hz for the lowest pipe of a 32' stop to about 4000 Hz for the highest note of a 2' stop. The expression A 440 is an indication that the pitch of A above middle C (a') is 440 Hz.

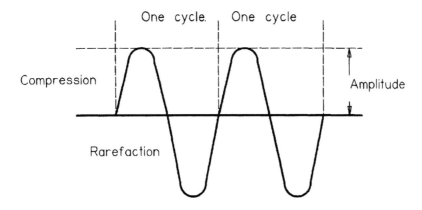

Figure 8.1 Single Cycle Wave Form

The solid horizontal line represents the neutral point. There is first a compression of air molecules. The limit of that compression, represented by the dotted horizontal line, is the limit of the wave's *amplitude*. The greater the amplitude of a wave, the louder the sound; the smaller the amplitude, the softer the sound. At the moment of the greatest amplitude a decompression or rarefaction begins. That rarefaction exactly balances the previous compression. At the maximum point of decompression, compression again begins. A single cycle concludes when this new compression reaches the neutral point. The type of motion represented here is termed *simple harmonic motion*. It is continuous, repetitive, predictable, and measurable. The limits of audibility are often given as 20 to 20,000 Hz, although the limits vary somewhat from person to person. Since the lowest note on a 32' stop, CCC, vibrates at only 16 Hz, the lowest notes of a thirty-two foot stop are often felt more than they are actually heard.

At this point it might be well to observe a pendulum (represented in Figure 8.2). A pendulum is an excellent example of simple harmonic motion. A single cycle is represented by movement of the weight from its neutral point *(E)* outward to the left *(A)*, a return to the neutral point, a movement outward to the right *(B)*, and then return to neutral. As long as the length of the cord *(CE)* remains the same, each cycle will take precisely the same amount of time. Hence the use of the device to control clockwork. Typically, friction will cause each cycle to become shorter, but the time for each cycle, no matter how far the weight travels, will be identical. Gradually the pendulum will come to rest. Amplitude is represented by the distance of displacement of the weight from its neutral point *(E to A)*. If the pendulum is displaced to *D* and then freed, then the motion *DEFED* will take exactly the same time as the motion *AEBEA*. The amplitude of the former, however, is greater.

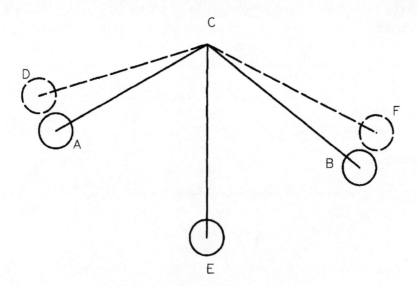

Figure 8.2 Movement of a Pendulum

Modification of the length of the cord will alter the length of the cycle. Shorter lengths will cause the cycle to speed up; longer lengths will cause the period of a cycle to slow down. The phenomenon is the same in musical instruments. Assuming that other factors such as tension of the vibrating body remain the same, the larger the mass of a vibrating body—

be it a string, a drum head, or a column of air — the lower the pitch. The smaller the mass, the higher the pitch.

Overtones

Pristine cycles of a single pitch do not exist in the live musical world. These can only be reproduced electronically. When an oboe gives the A = 440 Hz by which an orchestra is to tune, that frequency may predominate, but above it will be a complex of other pitches in a predictable pattern called the overtone series. Think for a moment about a violin string. Let us use the *A* string (440 Hz). It is excited by the hairs of the bow. We hear the nominal pitch of the string, but at the same time, higher tones are also present. The string vibrates along its entire length, but it also vibrates in smaller segments at the same time. Half the length of the string vibrates at 880 Hz or an octave higher than nominal pitch. Thirds of the string vibrate at 1320 Hz or *E* above the higher *A*. Quarters of the string vibrate at 1760 Hz or two octaves above the nominal pitch of the string. The process continues in specified order called the *overtone series*. That series is shown below with the fundamental being low *C* (the lowest note on an eight foot stop on a typical manual organ keyboard). The blackened notes are out of tune. Each member of the overtone series is called a partial. The fundamental is the first partial; the first overtone is the second partial; the second overtone is the third partial; etc.

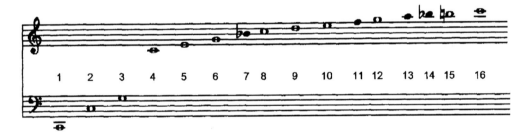

Figure 8.3 Overtone Series on *CC*

The pronounced difference in sound between two orchestral instruments, two organ stops, or even two human voices is dependent upon the various strengths of the overtones present in each source. The German term *Klang*, best translated as sonority, is the technical term for the complex of overtones characteristic of a particular musical tone. Some musical instruments have a simple overtone structure; others are highly complex. An oscilloscope is an electronic machine with a screen which can display the wave forms of various musical sources. A tone from a flute (either orchestral or organ), with its uncomplicated *Klang*, might show up on the screen with a single variation from the sine curve, a variation which indicates that the second partial is strongly present. A tone from a trumpet (again either orchestral or organ) with its extremely complex *Klang* might show up on the screen as a series of spikes and valleys.

The overtone series (sometimes called the harmonic series) has a precise mathematical basis. The relationship between any two partials is a ratio derived from their respective numbers in the series. Hence the octave is 2:1, the perfect fifth 3:2, the perfect fourth 4:3,

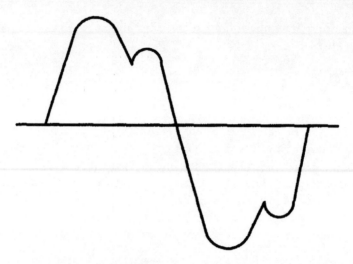

Figure 8.4 Possible Wave Form for a Flute Sound

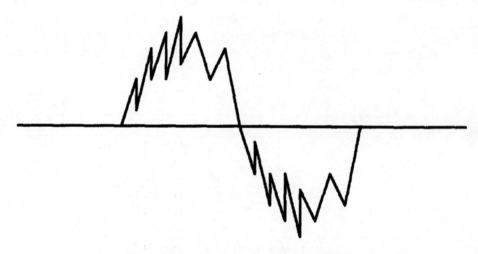

Figure 8.5 Possible Wave Form for a Trumpet Sound

etc., with the larger number representing the higher of the tones of the interval. If we define piano middle C (c1) as vibrating at 256 Hz, then the octave above will vibrate at 512 Hz, the perfect fifth at 384 Hz, the perfect fourth at 341+ Hz, and a major third 320 Hz. All perfect intervals and major and minor forms of seconds, thirds, sixths and sevenths have intervallic relationships present in the series. Here they are:

Unison	1:1	Perfect fifth	3:2
Minor second:	16:15	Minor sixth	8:5
Major second	9:8 or 10.9	Major sixth	5:3
Minor third	6:5	Minor seventh	16:9
Major third	5:4	Major seventh	15:8
Perfect fourth	4:3		

Augmented and diminished intervals have no explanation in the overtone series.

Some Anomalies of Intervallic Ratios

The intervals derived strictly from the overtone series are absolutely in tune; that is they do not *beat*. Beating will be discussed presently. However, perfectly in-tune intervals pose some problems in the tuning of fixed pitched instruments, such as the organ. As a tool to understanding these problems, the following procedure is of use: to add two intervals together, one multiplies their ratios. Thus a perfect fifth (3:2) and a perfect fourth (4:3) multiplied together give an octave (2:1)

$$3{:}2 \times 4{:}3 = 12{:}6 \text{ or } 2{:}1$$

Similarly, to subtract one interval from another, one divides the larger by the smaller.

An octave minus a perfect fourth gives a perfect fifth:

$$2{:}1 \div 4{:}3 = 6{:}4 \text{ or } 3{:}2$$

The Pythagorean Comma. If we move clockwise around the *circle of fifths* (the key circle) beginning with C and tuning each note precisely in tune with the one before, we, of course, ultimately arrive at B-sharp, *enharmonic* with the beginning C. (For a diagram of the circle of fifths see the Glossary,) But the note where we arrive is perceptibly sharper than the note with which we began. This can be expressed mathematically:

$$(\tfrac{3}{2})^{12} = {}^{531441}/_{4096} = 129.74+ \neq (\tfrac{2}{1})^{7} = 128$$

Here are the frequencies of pure intervals (perfect fifths and fourths) moving around the circle beginning with middle C (256 Hz). Instead of beginning low in the bass and ending up high in the treble, we move up a fifth and then down a fourth. Notice we end with B-sharp at 519 Hz, considerably sharper than 512 Hz (256 × 2).

| 256 | 384 | 288 | 432 | 324 | 486 | 365 | 546 | 410 | 615 | 461 | 692 | 519 |

Figure 8.6 Frequencies of Perfect Fifths and Fourths Around the Key Circle

This difference is called the *Pythagorean comma* after the same ancient Greek mathematician who gave us the Pythagorean theorem. The term "comma" in this sense refers to small differences in pitch arrived at by varying theoretical procedures. In tuning fixed pitch instruments, this comma must be distributed in some way as one progresses around the circle of fifths. There are a number of ways, called *temperaments*, to do this. While the subject is far too complex for this book, a brief introduction to it will be found beginning on page 126. Another anomaly, called the *syntonic comma*, concerns the relationship between major seconds (9:8) and the major third (5:4). If we add two major seconds (i.e., C to D and D to E) we should arrive at a major third (C to E). Again, the result is not the same as the major third derived from the overtone series.

$$9{:}8 \times 9{:}8 = 81{:}64 \neq 5{:}4 \text{ or } 80{:}64$$

The major third derived by adding together two perfectly in tune major seconds is perceptibly sharper than the major third of the overtone series. Again this must be reconciled by some means when tuning.

By adding three major thirds, we should arrive at an enharmonic octave: C to E plus E to G-sharp plus G-sharp to B-sharp (enharmonic with C). But again this does not happen simply because

$$5:4 \times 5:4 \times 5:4 = 125:64 \ (128:64 \text{ or } 2:1$$

The octave arrived at by adding three in-tune major thirds is considerably flatter than that derived from the overtone series. The difference is termed the *enharmonic diesis*.

Difference Tones, Resultant Tones, and Beats

Imagine that you are sitting behind another car at one of those stop lights which appears never to change. You and the driver ahead have on the right turn signals and you can see the flasher ahead and yours on the dashboard. By accident they are both flashing at the same speed. An observer too far away in see either light independently will simply see a single flashing light source greater than that of a single flasher. The cycles of the two lights are said to be in phase. Each supports the other.

But assume that the two lights are slightly out of phase. Observe Figure 8.7. It shows that light A is flashing every two seconds, but that B is flashing every 2.5 seconds. It begins with both lights in phase. They are reinforcing one another. B gradually moves away from A until it is completely out of phase at 5. The two waves tend to cancel one another out. They then move back into phase again at 10.

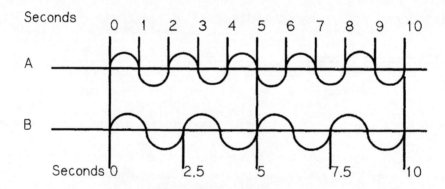

Figure 8.7 Two Waves In and Out of Phase

Now analyze what our distant viewer sees. Every ten seconds he sees the strongest light which then fades to a minimum at the five-second mark, then strengthens again to its maximum at the ten-second mark. The cycle now repeats. The combined lights are seen as waxing and waning every ten seconds. There is a resultant cycle of ten seconds' duration.

Now assume that we are no longer viewing flashing lights, but dealing with musical pitches, one at 150 Hz (represented in Figure 8.8 by wave A) and one at 100 Hz (represented by wave B). The length of waves is in inverse proportion to their frequency. Thus the wave length from 150 Hz will be two-thirds the length of the wave of 100 Hz. In the drawing wave A (150 Hz) is represented by two units and wave B (100 Hz) is represented by three units. The waves are in phase at point zero. Three and one half cycles of wave A are shown and two and one-third cycles are shown of wave B. The two waves sounding together will produce the interval of a perfect fifth (150: 100 = 3:2).

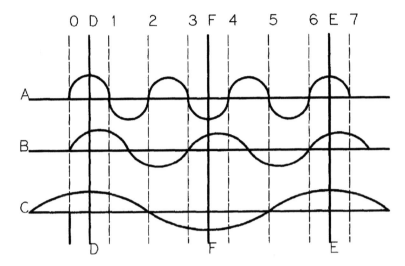

Figure 8.8 150 Hz Wave Superimposed on a 100Hz Wave and the Resultant

At points DD and EE, six units apart, waves A and B are reinforcing each other to the maximum degree. At half the distance between DD and EE (point FF), waves they are completely out of phase and at the nadir of their composite strength. The combined strengths of waves A and B from maximum at DD and EE and minimum at FF sets up a third oscillation represented by wave C. This wave proves to be six units in length (one-half that of wave B — three units). The resultant wave is then an octave lower than that of B and has a frequency of 50 Hz. (The actual form of the resultant wave in the figure above is more complex than shown. It is simplified for clarification.)

A *resultant* occurs when the frequency difference between two tones lies within the format of musical frequencies. Its frequency is derived from subtracting the smaller of its components from the larger. Such tones are often termed difference tones, a term which reflects their mathematical derivation. The resultant of two tones, one with a frequency of 500 Hz and the other with a frequency of 300 Hz, will have a resultant of 200 Hz. A resultant always has a frequency lower than either of its components. *Summation tones* are tones which are the sum of two sounding frequencies. Thus a summation tone of two frequencies 150 Hz and 250 Hz will have a summation frequency of 400 Hz. Summation tones are practically impossible to hear, belong to the arena of the physics lab, and have no practical musical value. The term *combination tones* refers to both difference and summation tones.

The resultant described in detail in Figure 8.8 and the explanatory text, which results in the ratio of 3:2, has a special function in organ building. Thirty-two foot stops, for all practical purposes the largest in the organ, are extremely costly to build and occupy excessive space. In situations where such stops are impractical and a 32' sound nonetheless is desirable, organ builders have resorted to resultant tones. There are two ways to accomplish this. In the first, the pipes of a 16' stop are wired so that when a stop tab or knob, generally marked *Resultant 32'*, is drawn, two pipes sound a perfect fifth apart. C and G sound together; C# and G# sound together, etc. The resultants will be an octave below the lower of a pair of pipes wired together. The result, however, is often unsuccessful, largely because all organs use some type of temperament, a fact that will not allow all fifths to be precisely perfect. A second and more successful method provides the pedal organ with a rank playing at 10⅔' pitch. This rank sounds the third partial of a thirty-two foot rank. When this rank is played along with the sixteen foot (the second partial of the 32' series) with which it is matched, the fifths will be pure and the resultant more satisfactory.

As two frequencies move closer and closer together and the difference between them becomes less than about ten cycles per second, we hear individual pulsations which are termed *beats*. As the two pitches are drawn nearer to one another, these beats, which represent the frequency difference between the two sounds, slow down and disappear. When they disappear the two frequencies are in tune with one another. No organ tuner could do his job without the phenomenon of beats. The absence of beats is really his best test that two pipes are in tune. The presence or absence of beats is also necessary in the setting of temperaments.

One classification of organ stops, the *celestes*, depends on intentional beating. A celeste stop is normally made of two ranks of pipes of string character placed next to one another on the chest. One rank is in tune. The second rank is intentionally sharpened by several beats. The resulting undulation is the characteristic quality of these stops.

The Organ and the Overtone Series

One way to view the organ is to regard it as a complex acoustic synthesizer. The organist is in control of numerous registers with varying timbres and pitches. From these he or she selects the particular stops to produce the desired sonority. From time to time a single stop may be selected, but the majority of times multiple stops are combined. While the organist may not be completely aware of it, the overtone series is critical to stop selection.

The core of most pipe organs is the principal chorus. A typical chorus consists of open flue pipes of the principal class. (See the next chapter.) Unless the instrument is a very large one, the basis of the chorus will be an 8' principal (i.e., one whose pitch is the same as that of the piano keyboard). Above it there will be principals at 4', 2⅔', 2', and a stop of multiple ranks termed a mixture. Mixture ranks cannot normally be sounded separately but act as a unit. The various ranks of the principal chorus relate to the overtone series as follows:

8'	1st partial (fundamental)
4'	2nd partial
2⅔' (or 3')	3rd partial
2'	4th partial
Mixture	Various ranks generally sounding multiples of the 1st and 3rd partials (2nd, 4th, 6th, 8th, 12th, etc.)

If the organ is a large one equipped with a full division of pedal stops, it is almost certain that 16' and not 8' registers will represent the fundamental of the division. The partials of that division would then be:

16'	1st partial (fundamental)
8'	2nd partial
5⅓' (or 6')	3rd partial
4'	4th partial
Mixture	Various ranks generally sounding multiples of the 1st and 3rd partials

From medieval times it was understood that ranks of unison and fifth sounding partials could reinforce the fundamental pitch. All overtones of unison or octave sounding ranks, no matter what pitch, have all the overtones contained in the fundamental series. For instance, all C's, no matter in what octave, have the same overtones. The overtone series of tones octaves apart contain no dissonances. This phenomenon is known as the *identity of the octave*.

Fifth sounding ranks, however, are somewhat more complicated. Compare the overtone structure of C with the first five overtones of G.

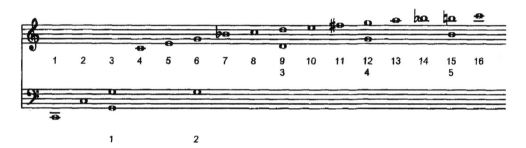

Figure 8.9 The Overtone Series on *C* Superimposed on that of *G*

Mild dissonances are formed when the third partial of the G series collides with the fourth and fifth overtones of the C series. Similarly the fifth partial of the G series collides with the seventh and eighth partial of the C series. These are mild collisions, and the ear easily accepts them.

The problem of dissonances becomes even more striking when we base a mixture rank based on the fifth partial (the major third sounding overtone) of the fundamental series. Figure 8.10 compares the upper portion of the C fundamental series with the e1 fundamental series.

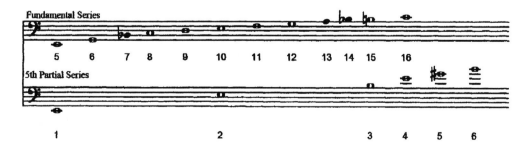

Figure 8.10 Portion of the *C* Overtone Series Superimposed on the e1 Series

The fifth partial of the C series is e, a third (or actually at tenth) above the fundamental. Its series has strong Bs which collide with all Cs. Its fifth partial (g-sharp) collides strongly with the eleventh, twelfth, and partials of the C series. The pungent overtones of third sounding ranks have had a mixed history in organ design. At times these ranks have been included in mixtures, but at other times they have been avoided or relegated to solo combinations such as the cornet (see below).

Ranks based on the seventh overtone, the out-of-tune minor seventh above the fundamental, are occasionally found in stop lists of very large organs. As one can imagine, their dissonant nature makes their use limited.

The amazing thing about synthetic registrations based on the overtone series is that when a rank is pulled, along with others in its series, the rank loses its individuality. Separate ranks in a combination based on the overtone series are no longer heard independently, but are heard as part of the corporate *Klang*. The cornet mentioned above is an excellent example. It is a common solo register made up of ranks sounding the fundamental and the next four partials (8', 4', 2⅔', 1⅗', and 2'). These ranks are often available as single stops, but are then combined in one of the most characteristic solo registers available at the organ. When this combination is used, the listener does not hear individual ranks, but hears a synthetic, complex sound at the fundamental pitch. In many complex registrations, the fundamental pitch may actually be weaker than any of its overtones. It is even possible in the physics lab (and occasionally in the proper acoustical environment at the organ) to demonstrate that, by the phenomenon of difference tones, the fundamental can be removed entirely, yet its pitch will still be heard.

Stop names, particularly in English and Italian organs, often reflect the origin of ranks in the overtone series. English organs often call the 2⅔' the *twelfth* (the 3rd partial), the 2' the *fifteenth* (the 4th partial), and the 1⅗' the *seventeenth* (the 5th partial). Numerical pitches are not normally given on stop knobs in these traditions.

The Acoustical Nature of Organ Pipes

The sounds of musical instruments are produced by coupling some means of excitement to some body which can be set into vibration. The sound of a piano depends upon a small felt hammer (the means of excitement) striking a metal string (the potential vibrating body). The microscopic projections on the horsehair of a violin bow excite a violin string into vibration. The vibrating lips of a trumpet player excite the air column of his horn into vibration. There are two distinct types of organ pipes characterized by their very different means of exciting columns of air into vibration: the labial or *flue* pipes and the *reed* pipes.

Labial or Flue Stops. Wind, when it hits a sharp surface, is deflected into eddies, which, if strong enough, can produce audible sounds. The phenomenon is often observed when high wind passes around the corner of a building and produces a whining sound. These eddies, sometimes known as *edge tones*, constitute the means of exciting a labial (flue) pipe to speak. The term "labial" means "of or pertaining to the lips," and in our context means an air flow across the mouth of a pipe. Obtain a recorder and study it. As you blow into it, the air is sharply divided as it moves forward from the *windway* across the sharp lip. This windway is a flue, a narrow channel through which air or gasses pass, hence the other name for this classification of pipes. Figure 8.11 is a drawing of a cross section of the upper portion of a recorder. It shows the mouthpiece, the windway, the lip with its eddies, and the topmost tone hole.

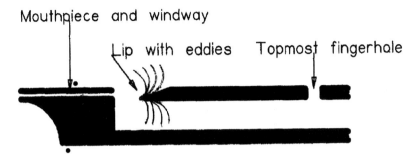

Figure 8.11 The Top Portion of a Recorder

Here is a drawing of a cross-section of a labial pipe. Its parts are labeled.

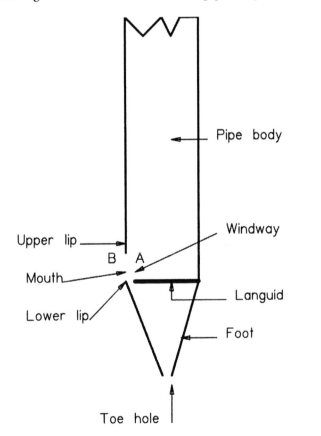

Figure 8.12 Cross Section of a Labial Pipe

When a pipe is winded through its toe hole, the wind passes through the windway as a sheet crossing the mouth. There is a momentary increase in pressure along the inside of the mouth (A). The reduced pressure on the other outside of the mouth (B) pulls the sheet in that direction. Reduced pressure is now on the A side and the procedure begins again. The wind sheet constantly oscillates from A to B. It is at this point that the body of the pipe comes into play. The mass of air contained in the body of the pipe dominates the rate of oscillation and hence determines the pitch of the pipe.

Now return to the recorder. If the instrument were severed just past the lip, one would have whistle in which the sound is largely the vibration of the oscillations alone. But in a recorder, as in a labial organ pipe, the force of the oscillations excites the column of air within the instrument. They literally knock the column of air into vibration. This column of air has sufficient mass to control the vibration of the oscillations which excite it. By lengthening or shortening the column, the mass of air in the pipe can be controlled and, as a result, various pitches produced. The shorter the column of air, the higher the pitch; the longer the column of air, the lower the pitch. Place your fingers over the holes of the recorder and blow into it. Carefully lift one finger at a time beginning with the lowest and a scale will result. What has happened is that the column of air is truncated at a point of the highest open hole. Each time a finger is lifted the length of the air column is shortened and the pitch rises. The length of the column is always the distance from the mouth of the pipe to the first open finger hole. The smaller the mass of air excited by the eddies, the higher the pitch; the larger the mass of air, the lower the pitch.

Before you put the recorder aside there is another phenomenon we need to explore. Cover all the holes again and blow gently. You will produce the lowest tone possible on that recorder. (On a soprano recorder that note will be c2.). Now blow somewhat harder and the pitch will move up approximately an octave. This is known as *overblowing*. Overblowing is critical to all wind instruments including the organ. Many times pipes, particularly those poorly voiced or with foreign matter in their mouths, will overblow. In these cases overblowing is a nuisance. There is, however, a class of pipes in which overblowing is intentional. *Harmonic flutes* are the most common, although there are other harmonic stops. Harmonic pipes are approximately twice as long as their nominal pitch demands. Each is pierced with a small hole, near its halfway point. These small drillings force the wind column to overblow. The fundamental of the pipe is essentially non-existent and its pitch is that of the first overtone. Harmonic flute stops are common on larger late nineteenth century organs and on many modern instruments.

Stopped and Open Pipes. There are two main classes of labial (flue) pipes: open and closed. Figure 8.13 on page 121 is a cross sectional drawing of an open, metal pipe. Its parts are labeled. The pipe is regarded as open since at the lower end it opens via the mouth and is open at the top. The *windway* or flue is formed by the lower lip and the horizontal *languid*, a thick piece of metal soldered at the juncture of the foot and body of the pipe.

Wind enters the pipe through the toe hole, passes as a jet though the windway, and forms eddies around the upper lip. The process is identical to that just described in the recorder. The eddies excite the air molecules in the pipe, and the length and volume of the pipe control the pitch and timbre of its sound.

A *node* is the point in a wave cycle in which there is momentarily no movement of air particles. An *antinode* is the point in the cycle of maximum compression or air molecules. In an open sounding pipe both ends of the pipe must form antinodes. (In Figures 8.14 and 8.15 the wave forms are shown simultaneously 180 degrees apart. Nodes are the points in which the waves intersect; antinodes are those points at which the waves contact the surface of the pipe.)

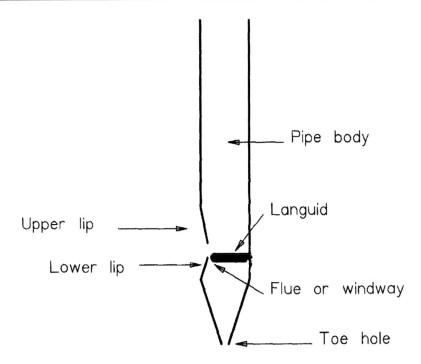

Figure 8.13 Cross Section of an Open Metal Pipe

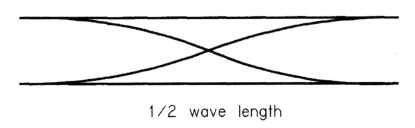

1/2 wave length

Figure 8.14 Fundamental Wave of an Open Pipe

The wave of the fundamental pitch of an open pipe is diagrammed as follows: Follow either line of the drawing and you will observe that within the pipe only one-half of a wave length is present. This means that the wave length of an open pipe is twice the actual length of that pipe. The lowest open pipe of an 8' rank has a wave length of approximately sixteen feet. The highest note of that same rank (assuming a sixty-one note keyboard) has a wave of approximately six inches in length. The lowest note of a 32' pipe, normally the largest used in organ building, has a wave length of some sixty-four feet.

But, as we have seen, no musical source is without overtone structure. Open pipes are capable of producing all overtones simply because it is possible to obtain antinodes at each end of the pipe for each partial of the fundamental wave. The diagrams below represent the first and second overtones (second and third partials) of an open pipe.

The first overtone (second partial), since its relation to the fundamental is 2:1, has a wave of one-half wave length (½ WL). The second overtone (third partial) has a relation to the fundamental of 3:1. Therefore its wave length is one-third wave length (⅓ WL). If we

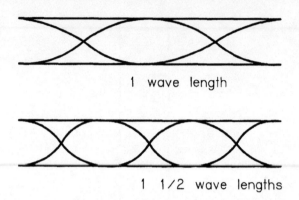

Figure 8.15 Second and Third Partials of an Open Pipe

continued the process, higher overtones would have ¼, ⅕, ⅙, etc., wave length ratios. Each of these can be diagrammed so that antinodes fall at both ends of the pipe. Hence, open pipes produce the overtone series without any omissions.

Many labial pipes are *stopped* at the top end, and these stopped pipes have a different acoustical structure. There must always be an node at the stopped end of these pipes. Fig-

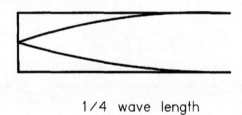

1/4 wave length

Figure 8.16 Fundamental Wave of a Stopped Pipe

ure 8.16 is a diagram of the fundamental of a stopped pipe.

Only one-fourth of the fundamental wave of a stopped pipe lies within the pipe itself. Therefore the wave length of a stopped pipe is approximately four times its nominal length. An eight foot stopped pipe has a wave length approximately thirty-two feet in length, or twice the length of an open pipe of comparable size. Thus a stopped pipe of four foot length sounds the same pitch as an open pipe of eight foot length (The lengths are approximate and differ from reality slightly.)

One particular advantage of stopped pipes is obvious: they are remarkable space savers. One obtains an eight-foot sound from a pipe four feet long. Particularly where space and money are major considerations, many organs have no open sixteen foot stop. The sixteen foot sound, almost mandatory in the pedal, is achieved by stopped pipes, the longest being only about eight feet in length. In small and tight swell boxes where ceiling height is low, builders often resort to stopped pipes four feet long to achieve an eight-foot pitch.

The overtone structure of stopped pipes differs from that of open pipes. The diagrams in Figure 8.17 on page 123 show the first two overtones possible with stopped pipes. Since it is necessary that the stopped end of the pipe be a node and that the open end an antinode, the next possibility lies at three-quarter wave length. The relationship between the fundamental (¼ WL) and this partial is 3:1. This, then, is the third partial (second over-

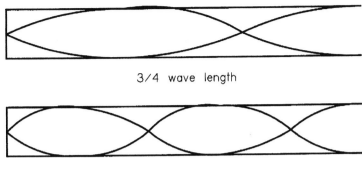

3/4 wave length

5/4 wave lengths

Figure 8.17 Wave Forms for the Third and Fifth Partials of a Stopped Pipe

tone). See the upper of the two diagrams. The next possibility lies at five-quarter wave length. The relationship with the fundamental, then, is 5:1 or the fifth partial (fourth overtone). See the lower drawing. This analysis can, of course, be carried further and will reveal that stopped pipes suppress even-numbered harmonics and stress the odd-numbered ones. The fifth sounding third partial is almost as prominent as the fundamental in some stopped pipes. In stops such as the *quintadena* or *quintaton* the voicer intentionally makes this twelfth as prominent as possible. This provides the stop with a piquant quality.

Before we leave the subject of stopped pipes, a word about nomenclature. When we say "an eight foot stop" we do not necessarily mean a stop in which the lowest pipe is approximately eight feet in length. What we really mean is a stop which has eight foot pitch or that pitch produced by an open pipe of that approximate length. A stop tab marked *Gedeckt 8'* (a stopped flute rank) will have a lowest pipe of approximately four foot in length.

Reed or Lingual Pipes. These pipes, far fewer in organs than flue pipes, produce their sounds in a very different way. The term *reed* does not mean a sliver of grass set in motion as in instruments such as the clarinet and oboe. The reeds in organ pipes are slivers of brass designed to vibrate in simple harmonic motion. The term "lingual" means "of or referring to the tongue" which, in turn, refers to the similarity of the organ reed to a tongue.

Reed pipes have two basic components: the elements housed within the boot, which fits in the toe hole on the chest and receives the wind, and the resonator, which fits into an opening in the top of the boot. The boot and its components are by far the more complicated, and we will begin here. These drawings represent a typical boot and its various parts.

Drawing A of Figure 8.18 (on page 124) shows the *boot* and its components with the boot *(1)* and the resonator *(G)* detached. *(A)* is the block carefully machined and made of lead. It supports the *resonator* above and the *shallot (S)* below. The block has a center hole which allows wind transmission from shallot to resonator. Also piercing the block is a tiny hole through which the tuning wire *(H)* projects. The *tongue (E)*, which is the actual reed, is slid into a small cavity at the point at which the shallot is attached to the block. The tongue is held in place by a tiny wedge of wood *(F)* forced between tongue, block, and shallot. The tuning wire, which has considerable spring tension, fits tightly against the tongue in such a manner that it can lengthen or shorten the length of the tongue allowed to vibrate.

Drawing B of Figure 8.18 shows the parts assembled in cross section.

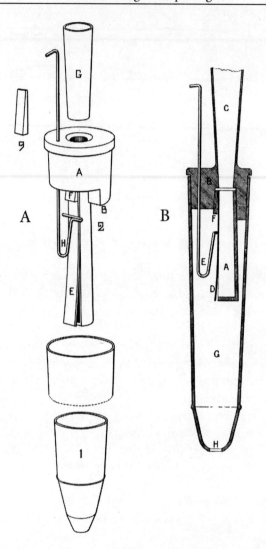

Figure 8.18 Reed Boot and Its Contents; A (Audsley II, 530), B (Audsley I, 397)

A	Shallot	E	Tuning wire
B	Block	F	Wooden wedge
C	Resonator	G	Boot
D	Tongue	H	Toe hole

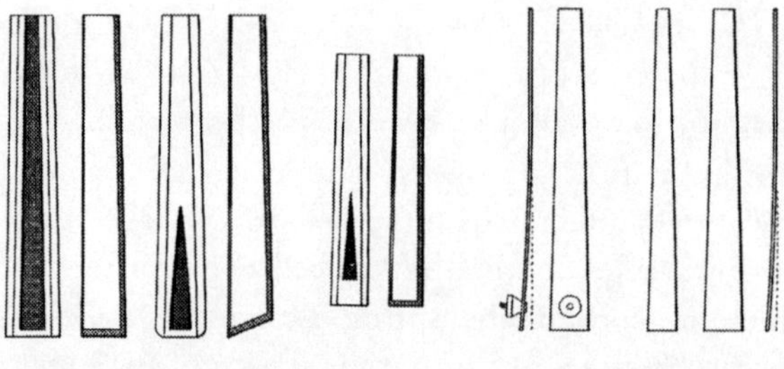

Figure 8.19 Various Shallots and Tongues (Audsley II, 590)

The drawings in Figure 8.19 show various shallots on the left and tongues on the right. Shallots are made of lengths of brass tubing, filed or ground smoothly on one side, and capped at the bottom end. As the drawings show, the area open to wind (in black) varies from one stop to the next and from voicer to voicer. The tongues are cut from thin brass sheeting and carefully and slightly curled. This curling prevents the tongue from completely closing the shallot at any time. In order to make larger tongues vibrate properly, they are sometimes weighted, as shown in the example on the right.

One might assume from these drawings that the components of the various pipes of a reed stop are identical. It is not so. The dimensions of all components must diminish in size as the stop progresses from bass to treble. As in all other elements of pipe making, there is little that can be done by manufacturing processes.

A reed stop works in the following manner: as wind is admitted through the toe of the boot, it enters the shallot through the thin opening between the tongue and the face of the shallot. This immediately causes a vacuum within the shallot, which pulls the tongue closer to the face. At a point slightly before full closure, the spring tension of the tongue pulls it in the opposite direction, and the cycle repeats at a frequency determined largely by the length of the tongue. If one places the boot and its components in a toe hole without the resonator it will sound when wind is applied to it. If the tuning wire is tapped down, the reed is effectively shortened and the pitch will rise. If the tuning wire is pushed upward, the pitch will lower. Without the resonator the resulting tones are generally raucous and unmusical.

When the resonator is inserted into the top of the block, an acoustical coupling takes place. The volume of air within the resonator largely controls the vibration of the reed, and, as the pipe is tuned by adjusting the tuning wire, the two come to something of a compromise at the pitch at which the pipe is intended to speak. This compromise is rather sensitive and sometimes almost ephemeral. Reeds, much more than flues, need frequent tuning. In the design of an organ, reeds should always be placed so they are easy to access.

In another sense the tuning of reeds is problematic. As wind instrument players will tell you, as temperature falls, their instruments go flat. When temperature rises, their instruments go sharp. The same is true of flue pipes. The cooler the temperature, the lower their pitch. The higher the temperature, the higher their pitch. There is also a minute change in the pitch of reed pipes, but it is in the opposite direction. Their pitch depends critically on the shape and mass of the tongues themselves. Since metals contract when they are cooled, tongues are shorter and stiffer when temperatures drop. Hence their pitch rises slightly. When heated their length and mass expands, and the pitch drops. When temperature rises, flues sharpen perceptibly and reeds flatten a bit. When temperatures drop, flues flatten and reeds sharpen. For this reason alone, it is important that the environment in which organs are placed should have carefully controlled temperature.

The marriage between the vibration of the reed and its excitement of the air in the resonator is not fully understood. One would assume, for instance, that the length of a resonator would be related to the wave length of its pitch (i.e., eight foot C should have a resonator of approximately eight feet in length, just as flue pipes do). This is not the case. The resonator of that note on a trumpet stop, one of the most frequently encountered reed stops, will be only about seven feet in length. Even so, this is termed a *full length resonator*.

Trumpets and their cousins, the oboes, have conical resonators. They tend to accentuate all the overtones of the spectrum, just as open flue pipes do. Crumhorns and clarinets have cylindrical resonators of approximately half their nominal length. They tend to emphasize only the odd-numbered overtones, just as stopped flue pipes do. We encounter precisely the same phenomenon in orchestral instruments. The oboe, bassoon, and the saxophone have conical bores and overblow at the octave. The orchestral clarinet and its family have cylindrical bores, and they overblow at the twelfth (third partial). Many other types of resonators exist, and their relationship to the vibration of the reeds is even more of a mystery. The next chapter will discuss some of these.

Temperament

We have already defined temperament as the slight modifications of pitch necessary to compensate for the Pythagorean comma. Serious problems of temperament occur only in *fixed pitch* musical instruments, particularly keyboard instruments. The vocalist, the wind player, and the violinist have the capacity to modify pitch instantaneously and with relative ease. Human hearing allows reasonable modifications of pitch before "out of tuneness" is perceived. Keyboard instruments, however, have no capacity for such liberties. Fixed pitched keyboard instruments are just that. Once they are tuned, they cannot be retuned quickly.

If an organ is new or has had its overall tuning degenerate, the organ tuner must first set the temperament (also known as setting the *bearing*). This is normally done on a single stop, most often the 4' principal on the great. Once the temperament is satisfactorily set, this stop will not be modified. It serves as the benchmark for the tuning of the remainder of the instrument. Review the discussion of the Pythagorean comma earlier in this chapter. Tuners normally set temperaments by moving around the key circle alternating perfect fifths with perfect fourths. If this is done consistently and all intervals are tuned precisely pure (i.e., they do not beat), we arrive, after twelve intervals, at a note obviously sharper than the note with which we began. This difference must somehow be dealt with, and the various means by which it is dealt with is the essence of temperament.

The subject *of temperament*, its history and practice, is far too broad a subject for a thorough discussion here. We can, however, provide a useful introduction. By far the most common compromise used in American organs is what is known as *equal temperament*. Here the tuner slightly flattens each fifth (or sharpens each fourth) by $\frac{1}{12}$ of the comma as he or she progresses around the key circle. No fifths are precisely pure. All are slightly flatted. From the practical standpoint, this is done two ways: by lifelong experience which indicates just how to temper each interval, or by electronic meters which can precisely break up the comma into twelve equal segments.

Since all temperaments are compromises, each has its virtues and each its vices. Equal temperament allows one to play in all keys equally well since one key is merely a transposition of another. Save for pitch, all keys are the same. One might assume this a virtue, but all keys are simply not, save for pitch, the same. C-sharp major and D-flat major are very different indeed, a difference that is certainly obvious to a singer or violinist and to a sensitive keyboardist as well.

In music, as in the other arts, tradition carries great power. Musical tradition indicates that flat keys are quieter and more subdued than are sharp keys. Playing a piece in D flat major is essentially different from trying the same piece in C sharp major. We cannot deny that on fixed pitch instruments using equal temperament the notes of these two keys are identical. In context, however, they are understood by the player very differently.

The other negative of equal temperament is that all intervals, except the octave, are out of tune. Our ears can accept this, and equal temperament has been the norm throughout the 19th and much of the twentieth centuries. It remains the temperament of choice of pianists, harpists, and many organ builders.

Challenging the unquestioned position of equal temperament in the organ world was a late twentieth century development. As part of the reappraisal and revival of older techniques in organ building, it was inevitable that tuning would become a concern. The leadership in revision of tuning practice certainly lay in the harpsichord world. Harpsichords simply do not sound well in equal temperament, and the ease with which they can be tuned allowed considerable experimentation. Connecting a temperament to the literature a harpsichord is required to play is a simple matter. The choice of a temperament for a new organ, however, involves far more.

There are numerous temperaments and new ones are still being proposed. To open the issue in a volume such as this is to open a Pandora's box. There is a classification of tunings, the *well tempered* ones, which on the one hand allows the performer to play in all keys and on the other allows some keys to sound more acceptable than others. As an example, we will describe a single one of these known as Kirnberger III. Kirnberger was an eighteenth century German theorist and a pupil of J.S. Bach.

We need also to review the *syntonic comma*. This comma represents the difference between the major third from the overtone series (5:4) and that derived from superimposing one major second atop the other (9:8 × 9:8 or 81:64). The syntonic comma, then, is 81 to 80. For practical purposes the size of both it and the Pythagorean comma are the same.

Tuning Kirnberger III is relatively simple. First, set C with a tuning fork. The comma will be apportioned among the four fifths beginning with C and moving clockwise around the key circle: C to G, G to D, D to A, and A to E. Each fifth is diminished by one fourth of the comma. One proceeds by tuning the major third from C to E until it does not beat. Then, by trial and error, slightly diminish each of the fifths listed above equally. Having essentially distributed the comma by the four fifths which have been tempered, begin with E and tune pure fifths clockwise around the circle to F-sharp. Then moving counterclockwise from C, tune perfect fifths until one arrives at D-flat. The remaining fifth, D-flat (or C-sharp) to F-sharp will be slightly flattened by $\frac{1}{12}$ of the Pythagorean comma. Once the temperament is set, all unisons and octaves are tuned directly from it. This temperament is shown diagrammatically in figure 8.20 on page 128. If you have had no experience with tuning and have access to a harpsichord, it would be helpful to try your hand at setting this temperament.

Central to well temperament is causing the major thirds of the tonic chords in the keys used most frequently to be as pure as possible. We have just observed that major thirds in Pythagorean tuning have the irrational ratio of 81:64. That is, they are noticeably sharper than the pure major third, 5 to 4. For instance, the Pythagorean major third above C = 256Hz has a frequency of 324 Hz as opposed to 320 Hz derived from the 5:4 pure ratio.

Now observe the major thirds derived from the temperament above:

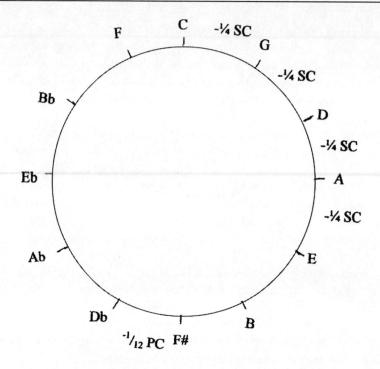

PC = Pythagorean Comma   **SC = Syntonic Comma**

Figure 8.20 Kirnberger III Temperament

Major third	*Compressed from Pythagorean by*
E flat to G	¼ SC
B flat to D	½ SC
F to A	¾ SC
C to E	1 SC (pure)
G to B	¾ SC
D to F-sharp	½ SC
A to C-sharp (D-flat)	¼ SC+ ½ PC

Notice how symmetrically the reductions progress beginning with E flat: ¼, ½, ¾, 1, ¾, ½, ¼. All other major thirds remain Pythagorean.

While before 1800 there were occasional explorations of keys with signatures greater than four sharps or four flats, these keys became common only in the nineteenth century. The purpose of well temperaments is to make the keys most commonly employed, those toward the top of key circle, sound as well as possible and yet allow the possibility for experimentation in more foreign keys. Bach's *Well Tempered Clavier* is the ultimate in such experimentation. The goal of well temperaments is not to make all keys sound equally well, but to make some keys sound as perfect as possible and to allow others to be acceptable. Remember Kirnberger III is only one of numerous well temperaments which have been employed, and others are still being proposed.

CHAPTER 9

Pipework

Materials and Fabrication

Organ pipes are made of wood and metal. We will deal with the latter first. The primary metal used in organ pipes is an alloy of tin and lead called pipe metal or *common metal*. Other materials, used less frequently, are zinc and copper. These two are readily available in sheets from which the pipes are cut. Pipe metal, however, must be cast by the pipe maker. A complete description of the art of making casting pipe metal and making organ pipes is available in Dom Bédos' great treatise (Chapters 6, 7, and 8 and Plates 64, 65, and 66). The essentials of the process, which have not materially changed over the centuries, are these:

1. The appropriate blend of metals as specified by the builder is placed in a cauldron and heated until the metals melt.

2. The molten metal is then poured out and spread evenly over a rigid table to form a thin sheet. See the drawing from Dom Bédos in Figure 9.1.

3. The sheet is then accurately scribed with the dimensions of each part of the pipes to be made. If these are labial pipes, these parts will consist of the body of the pipe and the foot. If reed pipes, it will be the resonators.

4. The lines which have been scribed are carefully cut by a razor sharp tool using a straight edge as a guide.

5. The metal that is to become the body of the pipe is then carefully rolled over a circular rod called a mandrel until its two edges are parallel and can be soldered.

6. The same is done with the conical feet and any portion of the pipe bodies which may be conical. Reed resonators are made in similar fashion.

7. The *languids* are poured into molds in preparation for soldering directly onto the pipe feet.

8. The bodies are now soldered to the feet.

9. The mouths are then cut in and soldered as specified by the builder.

It is necessary to stress that this is a simplistic explanation for a craft demanding the highest level of technical competence and experience. Remember that each pipe within a rank will have dimensions larger or smaller than all others in that rank and, hence, must be treated individually. This age old process is remarkably resistant to manufacturing techniques and is highly labor intensive.

The proportions of lead to tin in various pipe metals can vary from one in ten to ten

Figure 9.1 Casting Table (Dom Bédos, Plate 66)

in one. Tin is far more expensive than lead, and heavier proportions of tin are reserved for pipes which are visible, such as those which stand in the facade of an organ case. Lead is far more malleable than tin. Pipes with high content of lead can, particularly in heated situations, simply collapse. Feet can literally compress under the weight of a pipe. Particular care must be taken to support lead pipes to prevent these problems. Tin strengthens the alloy. The higher the tin to lead ratio is, the more secure the pipe. The most serious disadvantage of high tin content is cost. For this reason, pipes intended to be within the organ case or chamber, and therefore not visible, will have a higher proportion of lead.

Facade pipes are carefully planed or scraped with a sharp scraper. They are then burnished, a process which leaves them with a silver glow which is remarkably permanent. Other possibilities for facade pipes include painting, multi-colored stenciling and geometric embossing.

When copper is used for pipework, it is generally used for decorative purposes. It, too, is very expensive. It is often used for the resonators of reed pipes because of its stability. The cheapest of metals generally used in organ pipe making is zinc. Zinc is as stable as copper, but its major liability is simply that it is ugly. Its normal finish is an unappealing greenish gray. Where cost is a factor, zinc pipes are often found in profusion. Zinc is also difficult to cut and trim, and for this reason pipe voicers dislike it. Even when pipes are made primarily of zinc, their mouth sections and languids are often made of pipe metal to make voicing easier. While zinc is often used in order to cut cost, it has one other positive virtue. Where distortion of pipes with high content of lead is likely to occur and toes may collapse, these sections are often made of zinc. The same is true of the pipe feet and resonators of reeds.

As we have suggested above, the conical and cylindrical resonators of reed pipes are fabricated in the same manner as the pipe bodies of labial pipes. The toes of reeds are also made in a similar fashion. If the toes are made of pipe metal and not of zinc, that metal is thicker than usual. The shallots are constructed from pipes of brass filed and ground smooth on the surface that receives the tongue. The surface opening through the tube is then carefully cut according to the shape and dimension specified by the builder. The end of the tube is then closed by soldering a disc of brass onto the tube. The tongues are cut from sheet brass of appropriate thickness and then slightly bent upward. The tuning wires are bent from wire with appropriate thickness and spring tension to hold the tongue tightly to the shallot. The blocks are of lead and are fabricated by pouring the molten metal into suitable molds.

Some labial pipes have *ears* soldered to them on each side of the mouth. Figure 9.2 shows these ears *(A, B, C)*. While ears are more common than other types of hardware surrounding the mouth, string stops often have various additions, such as *beards*. The purpose of all these additions at the mouth of the pipe is to focus the wind sheet before it arrives at the upper lip.

Pipe ears have another function. On metal pipes which are cone tuned (see *tuning* below) or closed pipes which have had their caps permanently soldered into place, micro-adjustments to tuning are made by bending ears inward (to flatten the pipe) and outward (to sharpen the pipe).

The most common soft woods employed in pipe making are white pine, spruce, fir, and sugar pine. The most common hardwood is oak, but on occasions maple, cherry, and walnut have been used for special effects. All woods must be free of blemishes and knots. There is preference for quarter sawn wood. Quarter sawn wood has annual markings running essentially perpendicular to the face of the plank and not parallel to the face. Hence it is far less prone to warping. The techniques used to craft wood pipes is essentially that used in any other carefully done joinery. The parts are sawn, planed, and sanded, then joined by glue and occasional wood screws. Care must be taken that excess glue is not left inside a pipe, causing a potential node and poor speech. Figure 9.3 on page 132 is a drawing showing the components of a typical wooden labial pipe.

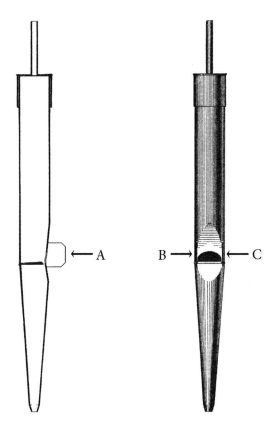

Figure 9.2 Labial Pipe with Ears (Audsley II, 537)

Number 1 shows a cross section of the pipe. The languid, windway, upper lip, mouth, and ears are shown. Number 2 shows the components assembled, and number 3 the components disassembled. These parts are:

A. the upper lip
B. the spine which strengthens gluing the lip to the body of the pipe
C. the pipe body
D. the optional ears

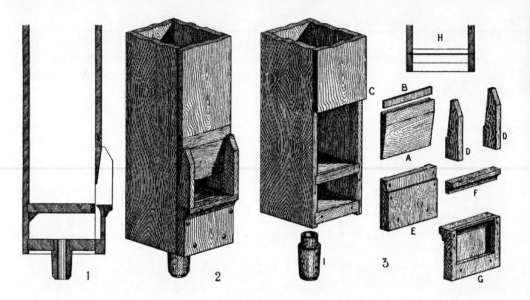

Figure 9.3 Wooden Labial Pipe and Its Components (Audsley II, 442)

E. the block which is screwed into the body
F. the optional beard
G. the block showing the recess for the windway

Figure 9.4 shows three types of mouths. *A* is the English type and the one most common in American organ building. *B* is a German variation, and *C* is the inverted form. Here the upper lip is reversed and the block lies on the outside of the pipe body.

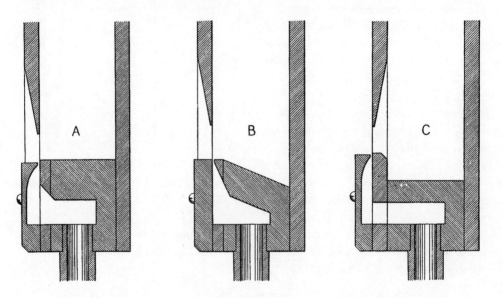

Figure 9.4 Three Types of Mouths of Wooden Labial Pipes (Audsley II, 440)

Most wood pipes are rectangular in cross section. One stop, the *flute triangulaire*, is triangular in cross section. Another oddity is the *Doppelflüte*, an open flute with two mouths. This doubles the wind sheet and gives the stop considerable power. The final oddity, which has recently reappeared on American organs, is the *Ludwigstön*, an invention of Ludwig, a pipemaker in the Holtkamp firm. It is a celeste stop contained in a single rank. Pipe bodies of the stop have a partition from the top of the pipe to the mouth, so that, in effect, there are two columns of air. These bodies are equipped with two mouths, one for each section of the pipe. Essentially, there are two pipes in one. One section is tuned slightly sharp to produce the celeste effect.

The use of wood is far less common in reed pipe making. Occasionally the resonators are constructed of wood. The boots of large reed pipes are often wooden. These are screwed directly to the chest and are drilled to receive the block.

Tuning Labial Pipes

There are basically two types of tuning of open, metal, labial pipes. The first, called *cone tuning*, constricts the open end of the pipe, causing it to flat, or flaring it, causing it to sharp. This type of tuning requires a set of specialized tools called tuning cones. One is shown in Figure 9.5.

Tuning cones are made in various sizes to fit various diameters of pipes. To flatten a pipe, the tuner taps downward using the hollowed end of the tool. To sharpen, the tuner taps down using the pointed end. Pipes which have been carefully cone tuned tend to remain in tune for lengthy periods of time.

The second method of tuning open pipes is called *slide tuning*. Affixed to the top of each pipe is a circular slide made of tin with a definite spring tension in the metal. Hence, the slide stays tightly around the pipe. By tapping the slide upward, the pipe is lengthened and thus flattened. By tapping downward the pipe is sharpened. The slides of large pipes often have springs around them to hold them tightly in place. Another method of tuning larger pipes is slotting. The metal is cut from the top of the pipe to produce a slot about an inch across and as long as needed. This metal is still attached to the pipe at the lower end of the slot. This metal is then rolled down. By rolling up more of the metal, the column of the pipe is effectively lengthened. By rolling the metal downward it is effectively shortened. For visual reasons, it is often necessary to make facade pipes considerably longer than their speaking lengths. These pipes may have extensive slotting opposite the facade face. Considerable portions of metal actually may be cut away. Figure 9.6 on page 134 shows two types of slotting. The one on the right is the more common.

Metal stopped pipes are generally tuned by moving their *stoppers*. These stoppers are similar to ordinary tin cans made to fit the outside

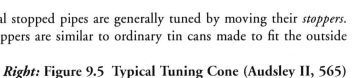

***Right:* Figure 9.5 Typical Tuning Cone (Audsley II, 565)**

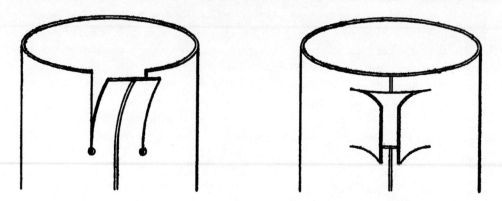

Figure 9.6 Tuning Slots on Open Metal Labial Pipes (Audsley II, 522)

diameters of each of the pipes. These stoppers are made of pipe metal and are lined on the inside with felt to prevent the leakage of air. Many antique organs and some modern instruments have the stoppers of metal pipes soldered in place. This practice is always associated with cone tuning of open pipes in which the builder expects little micro-tuning. When such tuning is necessary, it is effected by moving the pipe ears inward or outward.

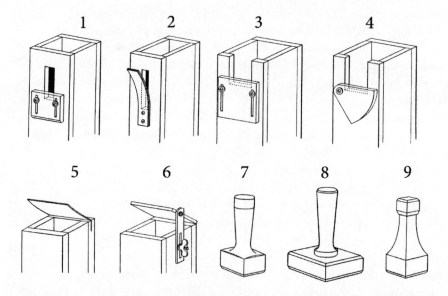

Figure 9.7 Various Means of Tuning Wooden Labial Pipes (Audsley II, 491–493)

Figure 9.7 shows six different means of tuning open labial pipes (1–6) and three different shapes for the stoppers of stopped wooden pipes (7–9). Numbers 1 through 4 show various methods of opening and closing tuning slots cut into the pipe bodies. Numbers 5 and 6 show the use of flaps which may be raised or lowered to effect pitch change. The flap of number 5 is made of pipe metal; that on the number 6 is of thin wood. The form of the stoppers is really immaterial. All stoppers are covered on their sides and bottoms with leather to resist the leakage of air.

The tuning of reeds is most frequently done by tapping their tuning wires. The pipe is sharpened by tapping downward, and thus reducing the vibrating length of the tongue. By tapping upward the length of the tongue in increased and the pipe is flattened. In the voicing of reed pipes designed to be tuned by manipulating the wire, the resonators are carefully tuned as they are to stay. A few reed stops are designed by their builders to be tuned by altering the resonators. These pipes will have slotting or other ways to modify the pipe. One should be certain when tuning reeds that he or she knows the builder's intent for each reed stop.

Mitering of Pipes

Observe orchestral wind instruments: the bassoon, bass clarinets, or any of the brass instruments. It is obvious that a column of air need not be straight in order to vibrate properly. Space limitations often make it necessary to shorten the height of large pipes in order to fit into such tight places as swell boxes. One way this can be done is by mitering. To miter is to join together two pieces whose ends are cut so that they represent the two angles formed by the bisection of an angle twice as large. Thus to miter a 90 degree angle, the mitered ends must be cut at 45 degrees. To miter a 135 degree angle, the parts must be cut at 67½ degrees.

Two prohibitions limit the *mitering of pipes*. First, there must be no miter of 90 degrees. In order to turn at 90 degree corner, one must make two miters, each bisecting a 135 degree angle (see B in the figure below). The second prohibition is that there may not be a miter at half the length of an open pipe. This point is the node of the first overtone. This prohibition is a problem only for open labial pipes. With stopped pipes no similar problem exists. The node of the first overtone lies outside the body of a stopped pipe.

Both metal and wooden pipes can be mitered. Drawings A, B, and C in Figure 9.8 show some common forms of mitering. D indicates how a pipe can be cut and its parts then soldered or glued together to form a miter. The drawing E is a schematic of a 360 degree composite miter one often finds in the basses of large reed pipes.

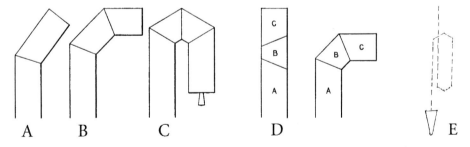

Figure 9.8 Types of Mitering (A, B, C, and D Audsley, II, 495)

Voicing

An extensive discussion of pipe voicing lies outside the limits of this volume. Voicing, in which the pipes are made to speak as the builder envisions, is a highly professional craft. Voicers must possess a concept of the ideal sound of each of the stops he or she voices. Beyond this, some of the factors controlled by the voicer of labial pipes are:

1. Wind pressure
2. Scale of the pipes
3. Size of the toe holes
4. Shape of the windway
5. Width of the mouth in relation to the diameter of the pipe
6. Height of the windway in relation of the width of the mouth *(cut-up)*
7. *Nicking* of the languid
8. Ears, beards, etc., attached to the pipe mouths
9. Type of tuning.

For reed pipes:

1. Wind pressure
2. Scale of the pipes
3. Size of the toe holes.
4. Shape of the shallot
5. Shape, thickness, and curvature of the tongues
6. Function of the tuning wires
7. Shape of the resonators
8. Tuning of the resonators.

Pipe Scale

From time to time we will mention *pipe scales*. The scale of a pipe relates to two things: first, the relationship of the diameter of the pipe to its length. An eight foot pipe five inches in diameter will have a larger scale than one four and a half inches in diameter. The second criterion in pipe scale is the point in a design in which the diameters of the pipes half. A simple way to think of this is a scale which actually is rarely used. If the diameter of the thirteenth pipe (i.e. the octave above pipe number one) is one half the diameter of that first pipe, that scale is defined as halving on the thirteenth pipe. In one sense, this scale is mathematically as it should be, since the octave ratio is 1:2. Organ builders more often prefer to increase the relative diameters of pipes as stops ascend. A common ratio is 1:2.82 (the square root of eight). This produces halving on the sixteenth pipe. Other scales go as high as halving on the twenty-fourth pipe. Everything being equal, the larger its scale, the louder a pipe will be, but the greater will be its suppression of upper harmonics. As one might expect, very broad scale pipes require higher wind pressure to make them speak properly.

Pipe Forms

It is essentially impossible to describe verbally the various sound qualities of specific organ stops. Words do not express sounds in ways specific enough to be of much help. The problem is exacerbated by the simple fact that the same stop made by two builders, and even two of the same stop made by the same builder, may, *in situ*, sound very different. For instance, we might say that an Italian principal sounds "fluty" but precisely what have we said? Does it sound more fluty than an orchestral flute or a Baroque flute? Does an organ trumpet on the great of a large organ in the front of a church sound just as the *en chamade* trumpet mounted at the end of the nave? For this reason this book will make no attempt to describe verbally the tone qualities of the various stops. This must be left to the individual experiences of the student, players, students, and lovers of the organ.

The variety of organ stops is practically endless, and organ builders, from time to time, insist on inventing new ones. The stops chosen for brief discussion below are those which one encounters most often on present day American organs. For more extensive dictionaries of organ stops see Audsley I, 505 and Williams/Owens, Appendix 2. Stops are grouped into four classifications: flutes, principals, strings, and reeds. The first to be discussed are the principal stops.

Principals

Principal pipes (Eng.: *Open Diapason*, Ger.: *Prinzipal* or *Praestant*, Fr.: *Montre*, Ital.: *Principale*) are the oldest in the organ. Indeed, until the later part of the fifteenth century, organs contained nothing but principal pipes. A principal pipe is an open pipe of moderate scale, normally made of metal, although wooden examples do exist. Principal pipes are made at all pitch levels from thirty-two foot to one foot. Principals are accorded special status in the majority of organ designs, since they are featured in the facade of almost all organ cases. The French term *montre* (meaning to display) originates in this special status. In Figure 9.9, on the left, is a drawing of a typical principal pipe. It has the more common form of mouth, the *bay leaf* or *Gothic* form. On the right is the more elegant *French mouth*, very often used in pipes in the facade.

There is no greater evidence for the assertion that the pipe organ is an acoustical synthesizer than in the composition of the *principal chorus (plenum*, Fr.: *plein jeu*). The principal chorus is the principal ensemble of the organ, and it fulfills for the instrument the similar function as does the string section of an orchestra. On a moderate size organ the principal chorus on the great manual will be based on an eight foot principal and will have above it ranks sounding at least five upper partials:

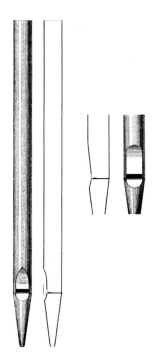

8'	fundamental
4'	2nd partial called most often the *Octave*
2⅔'	3rd partial often called the *Twelfth*
2'	4th partial often called *Superoctave, Fifteenth,* or *Doublette*
Mixture	Higher partials (*Mixtures* will be discussed below).

If the organ has a full complement of pedal principals, the fundamental will be a sixteen foot stop:

Figure 9.9 Typical Principal Pipe with Two Types of Mouths (Audsley, 519, 520)

16'	fundamental
8'	2nd partial again called *Octave*
5⅓'	3rd partial
4'	4th partial often called *Choral Bass*
Mixture	

In very large organs, the manual fundamental might be 16' with the following series: 16', 8', 5⅓', 4', 2⅔', 2' Mixture. The pedal fundamental may be a 32' principal with the following overtone series: 32', 16', 10⅔', 8', 4', Mixture.

Secondary manuals on all but the largest organs are unlikely to be equipped with a full principal chorus. The lowest sounding principal on these manuals is likely to be a 4', or even a 2'. Other classes of pipes assume the lower pitches. There is also a tendency in the design of a plenum to increase the scale of pipes as the pitches ascend. Hence a 4' principal will have a larger scale than the 8', the 2' a larger scale than the 4'. Increasing the scale in this manner gives a more incisive sound to the plenum.

Mixtures

A mixture is a multi-rank stop playing a combination of pitches which reinforce the overtone structure of the fundamental. Mixtures, which normally consist of principal pipes, have a long and distinguished place in the history of the organ. Indeed, the medieval organ, from which modern instruments developed, was nothing more than one huge mixture. Until the inventions of the spring chest and then the slider chest in the sixteenth century, it was impossible to separate one rank from another. This massive mixture was called the *Blockwerke*, and it spoke as a single unit. The invention of these two new chests made it possible to use portions of the *Blockwerke* and leave the remainder stopped.

Ranks in the *Blockwerke* sounded only the fundamental and fifth sounded pitches, and so it has been with the majority of *plenum* mixtures since. Mixtures in modern plena range from as few as two to as many as eight ranks, although on a medium size organ the great mixture is most likely to have four ranks. At a given pitch two of those ranks will sound some octave of the fundamental and two will sound some octave of a fifth sounding partial. Ranks in mixtures normally cannot be played independently. If a single note on a four rank mixture is played, four pipes will sound.

The lower the notes on the keyboard, the higher the harmonics selected for those notes in the mixture. It is impractical to carry a 1' stop to the top of a keyboard for the simple reason that the pipes become too short to have any real effect. They are too difficult to make, to voice, and to tune. So, then, the designer "breaks back" to larger pipes as the design of the mixture ascends the scale. The concept of breaking back is easiest seen in a small three rank mixture.

| C to e1 | 2 | 1⅓ | 1 |
| fl to g3 | 4 | 2⅔ | 2 |

The pitches used in this mixture are:

| 4' | Octave above the fundamental (the 8th) |
| 2⅔' | Octave and a fifth above the fundamental (the 12th) |

2'   Two octaves above the fundamental (the 15th)
1⅓'   Two octaves and a fifth above the fundamental (the 19th)
1'   Three octaves above the fundamental (the 22nd)

This mixture has a single break between e1 and f1. Each of its ranks drops an octave at that point. Figure 9.10 is a schematic of this mixture viewed from the front of the chest. The numbers at the base of the drawing show the register of the pipes (1 to 61 or C to c4) and those above show the pitch of the pipes within the mixture.

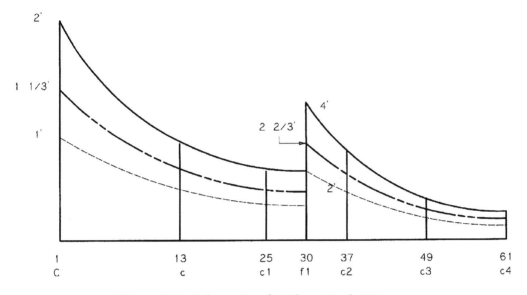

Figure 9.10 Schematic of a Three Rank Mixture

The larger the mixture the more complex its breaks. Below is the organization of the five rank *Bovenwerk* mixture on the Flentrop organ in the chapel of Duke University (from the *Dedication Brochure*. Used by permission).

C to E	1⅓	1	⅔	½	1
F to e	2	1⅓	1	⅔	½
f to e1	2⅔	2	1⅓	1	⅔
f1 to e2	4	2⅔	2 + 2	1⅓	1
f2 to g3	4	2⅔	2 + 2	1⅓	1⅓

In addition to the pitches in the three rank mixture above, this mixture uses

⅔'   Three octaves and a fifth above the fundamental (the 26th)
½'   Four octaves above the fundamental (the 29th)

Note also that the designer of this mixture wished the stress the 2' pitch in the upper register by requiring two pipes where we might expect only one.

Figure 9.11 on page 140 is a cross sectional drawing of the toe board of a four rank mixture. The drawing indicates the complex drillings which are necessary for such a toe-board. Wind enters via either a pipe valve in electric action or a slider in mechanical or electro-mechanical action. The wind is then dispersed to all the pipes for that note via the

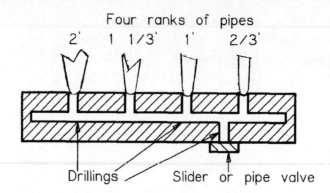

Figure 9.11 Cross Section of a Toe Board for a Four Rank Mixture

drillings. As pointed out above, it is impossible to separate one rank of a mixture from another, even for tuning.

In large organs one often finds two mixtures on the great, the first, called *grave*, with lower pitches, and the second, called *cymbal* or *scharf*, of higher pitches. This higher mixture is designed to give a cutting edge to the ensemble, and it is not designed to be used without the support of the deeper mixture below, of which it is really an extension.

Until this point we have discussed only mixtures in the plenum, and we have pointed out that they are composed of unison and fifth sounding ranks. From time to time, third sounding ranks, particular the 17th, have appeared in ensemble mixtures. These were common in the latter quarter of the nineteenth century in both English and American organs. Third sounding ranks, however, have never achieved long term acceptance in the plenum. Mixtures containing thirds were often incorrectly called *sesquialteras* simply because they contained third sounding ranks. Higher overtones of the series, other than octave and fifth sounding, have never found long term favor in plenum mixture design.

The proper use of the term *sesquialtera* refers to a specialized mixture used primarily, but not exclusively, for solo purposes. This mixture contains two ranks of large scale open pipes sounding the 12th (2⅔') and the 17th (1⅗'). Most often the stop is not carried to the bottom of the keyboard, but begins on tenor c, f, or c1 and goes to the top of the manual without breaking. It forms part of the *cornet* (see below) which is completed by the addition of flute ranks of 8', 4' and 2' pitches.

Flutes

Do not confuse two terms. All *flute* stops are *flues*, but not all flues are flutes. The term flute applies to a plethora of stops having in common with one another only that they are larger in scale and softer in tone than principal stops. While principal pipes have one form which may vary in scale, flue pipes have varied forms. Some are open pipes; some are closed pipes; and some of most the interesting are partially stopped pipes. The famous early Baroque composer and theorist Michael Praetorius, in his *Syntagma Musicum* (1615), gives an illustration of various flute pipes. The illustration, in Figure 9.12, is as current now as it was when it was first printed.

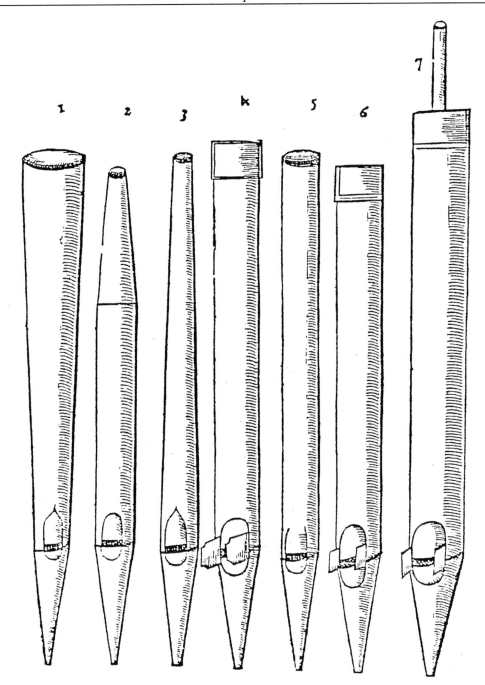

Figure 9.12 Various Flute Forms (Michael Praetorius, 1615)

Praetorius identifies the pipes as: (1) Dolcan 4', (2) Coppelflöte 4', (3) Flachflöte (flat flute) 4', (4) Klein bardeun (bourdon), (5) Offenflöte (open flute), (6) Gedact, and (7) Rohrflöte.

Below is an annotated listing of the most common flute stops likely to be encountered by American players. The naming of stops is fraught with problems. In the first place, there is the linguistic problem. American builders do not "bite the bullet" and use English terminology exclusively. Even a small organ console will show evidence of English, French, German, and even Spanish and Italian terms. Organ builders can be as chauvinistic as anyone else. Hence, the *Nachthorn* (Ger. Night horn) is called by French builders *cor de nuit*. Some builders seem to enjoy being idiosyncratic. One well known American firm has insisted on calling the most common of all flute stops, the gedeckt, a "copula." Finally, two stops with identical names, but made by different builders, may vary in construction and sound. Even two versions of a single stop built by the same builder may vary considerably in sound. No matter what the nomenclature, the best way to identify the qualities of various stops is simply by playing and listening to them carefully.

OPEN FLUTES

Bass flute: a large scale flute used in the pedal generally at 8' pitch.

Blockflöte (Eng. Recorder): an open flute of 4' or 2' pitch.

Clarabella: a large scale manual flute stop of strong and pleasant tone made of wood. To accommodate small spaces, its bases may be stopped pipes. Normal pitch is 8'.

Dolcan: an open flute pipe with conical shaped resonators. See the illustration above.

Doppel Flute: a powerful open flute with two mouths on opposite sides of its wooden body. Its normal pitch is 8'.

Harmonic flute: a flute of considerable power made either of metal or wood. From tenor f upward, the pipes are approximately twice their expected length. A small hole is pierced about half way up the body of these pipe to cause them to overblow at the octave.

Hohlflöte: (Ger. *hohl* = hollow). It is debatable whether the name refers to the fact that it is constructed of open (hollow) pipes or if it refers to the rather bland quality of the stop. It supports and fills out combinations particularly well, and for this reason is often chosen as the 8' flute on the great manual. It is normally made of wood although metal examples exist.

Melodia: an open flute stop made of wood. The lower octave is often consists of stopped pipes. The name indicates its sweet sound.

Nachthorn: The name is applied to both open and stopped flute pipes. In both cases it has a mild quality. It often appears at 4' pitch.

Nazard: 2⅔', *Doublette* 2', and *Tierce* 1⅗': These upper ranks of the cornet (see below) are normally open pipes of large scale.

STOPPED FLUTES

Gedeckt (from Ger. *decken*, to cover. Often misspelled *gedackt*.)*:* A fully stopped flute stop, normally of 16' or 8' pitch. It is probably the most common flute stop on American organs. It can be made of wood or metal. It is also known by the following names: bourdon, copula, stopped diapason, and in the bass by subbass, *soubasse*, and *Untersatz*.

Lieblichgedeckt: a small scale gedeckt of sweet sound

Quintedena: A small scale gedeckt voiced so that the third partial is more prominent than in most gedeckts. Also known as the quintaton, particularly at 16' pitch in the pedal.

PARTIALLY STOPPED FLUTES

A partially stopped flute is one which has some opening at the top of the pipe but otherwise is closed.

Koppelflöte (sometimes *Coppelflöte*). Its pipes are cylindrical through the first two-thirds of the resonator. At that point it tapers to an opening at the tip. The tone is very similar to the gedeckt, and the stop has the reputation of one which is easily blended with other pipes. Hence its name, "coupled flute." See Figure 9.12.

Rohrflöte (Ger. reed flute) or Chimney flute: The form of the pipe is similar to the gedeckt save for a single distinct characteristic: the metal version has a small chimney soldered to the center of the cap. The more common Rohrflutes have the chimney above the cap, but these can be contained within it. See Figure 9.13. Most examples are of metal but some are of wood. In this case, the handles of the stoppers are drilled through to effect the chimney. The function of the chimney is to bring out the third and fifth partials of the fundamental.

Spitzflöte (Ger. pointed flute): The form of the pipe is that of an inverted cone from the mouth of the pipe to its tip. The sound is something of a blend of flute and string tone. In this it is closely related to the *gemshorn*, which has a similar form.

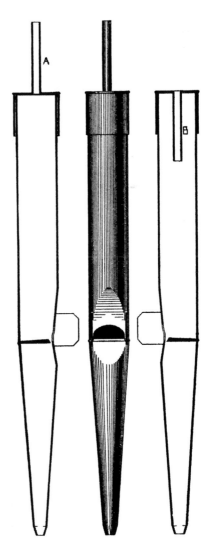

The Cornet

The *cornet* (pronounced *cor-nay*) is a compound solo stop made of flute pipes at 8', 4', 2⅔', 2', and 1⅗' pitches. It exists in two versions. The first of these, the *cornet séparé* or *cornet de récit*, was a critical element of antique French organs and is sometimes found in modern organs based on old French models. This cornet was a compound half-stop which began on middle c and ran to the top of the manual. It was normally mounted on its own chest high in the case above the pipes of the great manual. Its ranks could not be played independently. The 8' rank was stopped; the others were wide scale open flutes. The *cornet séparé* had its own manual keyboard.

Far more common on modern organs is a cornet made of five individual manual stops drawn most often from the positiv: gedeckt 8', flute 4', nazard 2⅔', flute 2', and tierce 1⅗'. On organs with mechanical stop action, the nazard and tierce are sometimes placed on the same draw knob. Pulling the

Figure 9.13 Forms of the *Rohrflöte* (Audsley II, 537)

knob to a halfway position actuates the nazard and pulling it all the way out actuates both stops.

Cornet, however, does have one other meaning in organ history. It also referred to a 2' reed stop in the pedal division of some northern European organs. The organ *cornet* has nothing whatsoever to do with the brass instrument spelled in the same way but pronounced *cor-net*.

Strings

String stops constitute the third large classification of labial pipes. String stops are always labial pipes of small scale. We have said that open flute pipes must be of wide scale and principal pipes of moderate scale. String stops are, then, of small scale. We have then:

      Wide scale: flutes   *Medium scale:* principals   *Narrow scale:* strings.

As the scale of pipes is reduced, the overtone structure becomes more complex. Hence open flute stops suppress all but the fundamental and perhaps the second partial. Principals tend to accentuate the lower partials, no more than the fundamental and the second and third partials. String stops accentuate partials up to the sixth and seventh. The violin family of the orchestra tends to have a similar complex harmonic sound. Hence, by analogy, organ pipes of the class are called, for better or worse, string stops.

In many string stops the second partial is as strong as or stronger than the fundamental. For this reason these pipes are often on the verge of overblowing at the octave. To counter this threat, pipe makers often place various hardware at the mouth of the pipe, the function of which is to restrain this overblowing. In Figure 9.14 are two examples. In the one on the left a small piece of pipe metal is soldered horizontally from one ear of the pipe to the other slightly below the mouth. In the second, a short dowel is placed in a similar position between the two ears. These are forms of the so-called *harmonic bridge*.

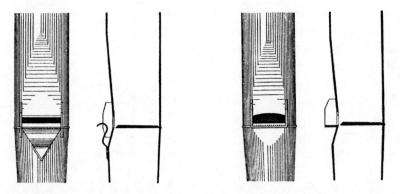

Figure 9.14 Harmonic Bridges for String Pipes (Audsley II, 552–555)

String stops are known by a multitude of names. Any stop having a name with a *viol-* prefix can safely be assumed to be a string. Other names are: salicionel, Erzähler, aeoline, gamba, fugara, and Geigen. String stops can vary in volume from the level of a small principal to the softest sound available from labial pipes (the aeoline). The same stop designation used by two builders may differ considerably in volume and in timbre. The scale of string pipes can vary from that of a small principal to the smallest scale pipes practical to fabricate. Again, the only way to get a good perspective on any stop is to play and listen carefully to it. One simply cannot rely on the stop designations alone, for they often are deceptive.

The string family has suffered as much as the flute family from attempts to imitate orchestral sounds. Such stops as the *concert violin* or the *viole d'orchestre*, which attempt to imitate the violin sound precisely, are ultimately doomed to failure for one simple reason. Members of the violin family all have a wide range of timbre, volume, and emotional flexibility. An organ stop has a single range of timbre and volume, and only limited ways to modify its emotional expression. It can only in a limited way imitate the orchestral strings.

Celeste Stops. A celeste stop is a combination of two ranks of pipes, one of which is tuned slightly sharper than the other. The most common celeste stops are strings (*voix celeste, viole celeste, unda maris,* etc.) although flute celestes are frequently found. The result of the mistuning of the two ranks is a soft and pleasant undulation. Most often the two stops both function when a single stop is drawn. Generally the rank which has not been sharpened will have its own stop knob or tab (for instance *viola* on one stop for the in-tune rank and *viola celesta* for both ranks). Hence, it would be impossible to play the sharpened rank alone.

There are two very useful stops which tend to bridge the gap between principals and strings. The *Geigenprinzipal* (*Ger. Geige = violin*) or, in English, *violin diapason*, is a large scale string stop, which, as its name indicates, has a pronounced principal quality. The dulciana, although it has in some examples a decided string tone, is really a small scale, soft principal. Both the violin diapason and the dulciana are frequent selections in small organs where their dual qualities of string and light principal are valuable.

Reeds

The structure of a reed pipe has already been discussed. See "Reed and Lingual Pipes" in Chapter 8 and particularly Figures 8.17 and 8.18. The shape of the shallot affects the tone of a reed by controlling the passage of wind that, in turn, controls the vibration of the tongue itself. There are basically two types of shallots, German and French. The former tends to limit the admission of wind and the second admits as free a flow of wind as the tube itself allows. The narrower and more covered German shallots produce a softer and more easily blended sound, and the open French shallots a louder and more powerful sound (see Donahue 9). Figure 8.18 in the previous chapter shows German shallots. The shape of French shallots is shown in Figure 9.15.

Below are brief discussions of some of the more common reed stops found on American organs. Reed pipes are identified by the shape of their resonators since the shallots and tongues are hidden within the boot.

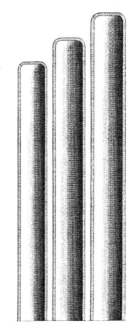

Figure 9.15 French Style Shallots (Dom Bédos, Plate 71)

Trumpet: The most common reed on American organs is certainly the trumpet, and it is a rare organ of any size which does not contain at least one. Stops tabs and knobs will show names in various languages and spellings: (trompet, trompette, trommet, tuba, etc.). When the stop occurs at 4' pitch, it is often called *clarion*. Sometimes the name is modified to designate some particular characteristic, for instance *tuba mirabilis* (splendid trumpet) or *tuba magna*. The bass orchestral instrument of the trumpet family is the trombone (Ger. *Posaune*), and these names often designate organ trumpets in the 16' range generally in the pedal division. In Figure 9.16 are pictured three common reeds found on American organs. A typical trumpet is on the left.

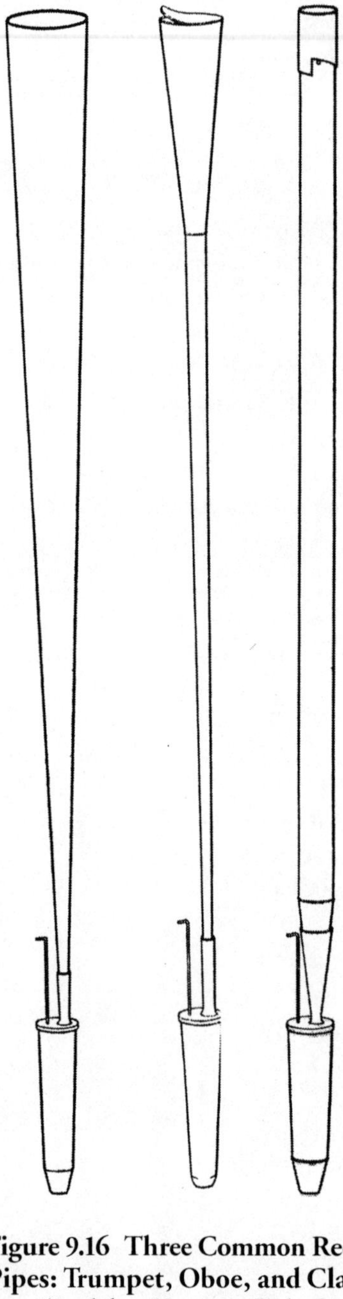

The resonators of members of the trumpet class are conical in shape and open at the top. Trumpets vary from one example to another in scale and in the size and shape of the shallots and tongues. Most of their resonators are of metal, but examples, particularly of larger pedal pipes, are sometimes made of wood. In cross section, wooden resonators are square and are inverted pyramids in length. Even the boots of such pipes may be wooden and are likely screwed into the chest. Trumpet resonators are characteristically full length (i.e. an 8' trumpet will have resonator approximately eight feet in length.)

Nothing is more critical to the response and quality of trumpet pipes than wind pressure. Large scale solo trumpets are more responsive when on pressures higher than that required for lingual pipes. For this reason they are often isolated on chests of their own. Not only are these trumpets more responsive, they are louder and more forceful. Wind pressures up to ten inches are common, and there are examples, which can only be described as barbaric, of pressures of 100 inches. In situations in which processions are common, such as churches with lengthy naves, there is often a high pressure trumpet which alone can balance the dynamic of the remainder of the organ. Some of these trumpets are likely to be harmonic. In a harmonic trumpet, the treble pipes are approximately twice the length one would normally expect. They are forced to overblow at the octave by the wind pressure provided them.

The sound of a reed pipe emanates largely from its open end. To enhance the effect of powerful reeds, there is a tradition of mounting trumpets, and less often other reed pipes, horizontally. *Horizontal trumpets (reeds)*, Spanish Trumpets (since their use appears to be Spanish in origin), or *trompette en chamade* are often mounted in front of the main case directly facing their intended listeners. (*Chamade* refers to a signal, normally from a field trumpet, used to announce to the enemy the readiness to parley.) Often there will be a battery of horizontal stops at various pitches. Horizontal trumpets have three advantages: they are visually impressive, their position sometimes makes them easier to tune, and vertical trumpets are prime candidates for falling dirt and trash. Horizontal positioning of the pipes reduces this threat. Unfortunately, their unique position causes them to be liable to bending.

It is impractical to make reed pipes of an 8' rank above g³. Therefore the extreme treble pipes of reed stops are

Figure 9.16 Three Common Reed Pipes: Trumpet, Oboe, and Clarinet (Audsley II, 598, 604, 608)

invariably open pipes of large scale. High up in the treble, the break between the reed and flue pipes can be made largely imperceptible. Obviously, on 4' reed stops more treble pipes must necessarily be flues.

Oboe (Fr: *hautbois*, Eng. *hautboy*): Almost as ubiquitous as trumpet stops are the organ oboes. These are not designed to imitate the orchestral oboe, but are organ voices in their own right. This reed is softer than the trumpet, but shares with it a reedy quality. The oboe is a very flexible stop. It blends well with ensembles of labial pipes and also can be a very effective solo voice. Its flexibility explains its frequency in smaller organs.

The resonators of the oboe are full length. They begin slightly conical for the first three-quarters of the pipe at which point they flare into bell shape (see Figure 9.16). Some oboes are partly covered as this illustration shows. Other examples are not.

Bassoon (Ger. *Fagott*, Ital. *Fagotto*, Fr. *Basson*): The bassoon is the bass of the orchestral oboe family. Stops of that name, although they are not intended normally to imitate the orchestral instrument, occur frequently, particularly at 16' pitch. The pipes of the stop are provided with full length and slightly conical resonators. The stop is considerably less powerful than the trumpets, and it takes up less room on the chest. For this reason, it is often used within swell boxes where a 16' reed voice is desired and where space is at a premium. In such situations half-length resonators may be used for the lower octave.

Crummhorn (Fr. *Cromorne*, Ger. *Krummhorn*, Eng. *Cremona*): Its origin probably was in imitation of the Renaissance ensemble woodwind instrument. As an organ stop, its standard form was found in the positiv of French seventeenth century organs, where it was the required reed. Crummhorns have half length resonators. These resonators are cylindrical if made of metal and rectangular, both in length and cross section, if made of wood.

Conical resonators, such as those used in trumpets, accentuate the entire harmonic spectrum. Cylindrical (or cubical) resonators emphasize the odd numbered partials just as stopped flutes do. The characteristic quality of the crummhorn depends largely on the prominence in its harmonic spectrum of the third and fifth partials (i.e. the nazard and the tierce.) The "cromornes" of the old French organs were more assertive than many on American organs today. As tastes changed in favor of milder reed tone, the stop morphed into its first cousin, the clarinet.

Clarinet: The orchestral clarinet was an invention of the early eighteenth century. Its primarily cylindrical bore acted as a stopped pipe sounding approximately an octave lower than its nominal length suggests and emphasizing the odd numbered partials. Organ builders no doubt observed the relationship between the sound of the orchestral clarinet and the existing crummhorn. By modifying the shallots and careful voicing, that stop's more assertive qualities were reduced. The organ clarinet was the result. See the right hand pipe of Figure 9.16. The clarinet became the reed stop of choice on the choir divisions of American organs. It is a particularly beautiful solo voice.

Vox humana: A group of organ stops called *regals* existed in profusion in the sixteenth and seventeenth centuries. Characteristic of these stops is that they have short resonators. One quarter and one-eight length were common. Many of these stops had unusual shaped resonators. Praetorius shows some of these, some with extremely bizarre shapes.

Regals, with a single exception, are rare on American organs (although they are frequently found in single stop instruments, also called regals, used by early music groups). The single exception which has survived in mainstream organ building is the *vox humana*. Just how the sound of this stop has been thought to mimic the human voice is something of a mystery.

The pipes of the vox humana are metal and have quarter length resonators. Superficially they look like truncated clarinet pipes. Since the resonators are so short, they can get buried in pipework where adjacent pipework can affect their proper speech. Hence they are very often have extremely long boots to lift the reed and shallot free of any impediments.

Imitative Orchestral Reeds: In the latter part of the nineteenth century and the first part of the 20th, one of the principal functions of the organ, particularly in cities and towns that lacked symphony orchestras, was to introduce the great symphonic works of Europe to American audiences. Inevitably this led to organ builders inventing stops that to some extent imitated the solo orchestral voices encountered in that literature. We have already touched on this trend in the discussion of string stops.

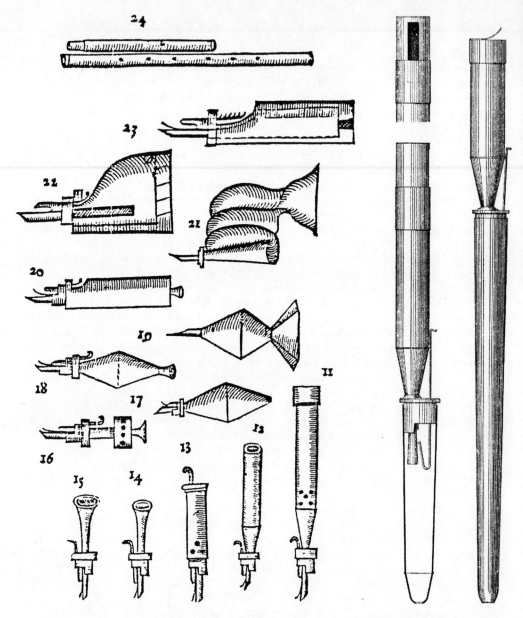

Figure 9.17 Regals (Praetorius: Syntagma Musicum, 1619)

Figure 9.18 Two Examples of the Vox Humana (Audsley II, 610)

As we have already suggested, all orchestral instruments have a wide range of color and expression which a single rank of pipes can hardly imitate with justice. The success of these stops lies less in the successful imitation than it lies in providing novel reed sounds to the organ palate.

The Racking of Pipes

Above the toe boards, pipes require support of some kind. For the majority of pipes, particularly those less than three feet in total length, this support is provided by *rack boards*. Each stop has its own rack board running the length of the chest from left to right. These are supported by rack pins placed so that they do not interfere with the pipes themselves and yet support the boards securely. The ends of the rack boards are normally screwed into solid wooden supports. Figure 9.20 shows the procedure. The end support is shown on the right. A is the rackboard, B the rack pins, C the pipes, D the toe boards, and E the end support.

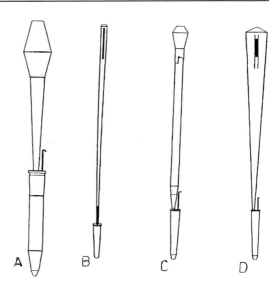

Figure 9.19 Four Imitative Orchestral Stops — A: English Horn, B: Orchestral Oboe, C: Basset Horn, D: French Horn

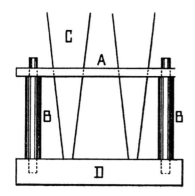
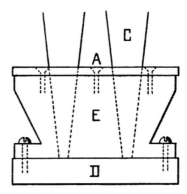

Figure 9.20 Cross Sections of a Rack Board (Audsley II, 225)

Rack boards must be carefully drilled to align perfectly with the toe holes below. The holes for the pipes themselves must be precisely drilled at the diameter of the pipes at the point at which they contact the toe board. The inside of these pipe holes are often faced with felt to reduce any vibration.

Pipes longer than about three feet, particularly those that are heavy and contain high lead content, must have more support. For this purpose frames are constructed to provide this extra support. As one might imagine, pipes longer that about eight feet require specialized support. All too often, heavy pipes may be inadequately supported. In pipes containing large portions of malleable lead, this problem can be particularly acute. It is not uncommon to find these pipes to have collapsed under their own weight. This is a particular problem in organ chambers with inadequate ventilation subject to high temperature.

Toy Stops

From time to time the conventional pipework of the organ has had added to it various devices producing other than truly winded sounds. These fall under the designation of toy stops. The *rossignol* (French for nightingale) consists of two labial pipes of high pitch inverted into a container of water. When these pipes are winded, the gurgling sound imitates the call of a bird. If the two pipes are a minor third apart, the stop is meant to imitate the cuckoo.

Four stops that are essentially bells are sometimes found on the organ. The most common of these is the *cymbelstern*. This consists of a set of high pitched bells, most often four, sometimes tuned but more often of random pitch, caused to sound by a rotating star wheel. The device, which has a long history, can be actuated electrically or pneumatically.

The others, the *glockenspiel*, the *tubular chimes*, and the organ *harp*, use small hammers, activated either electrically or pneumatically, striking metal tubes or bars. As in the piano, the hammers must return instantaneously or they will mute the vibrating medium. The glockenspiel is similar to its orchestral prototype and consists of small pitched metal bars chromatically arranged. The tubular chimes also are similar to the orchestral prototype and consist of relatively low pitched chromatic, metallic tubes.

The organ harp requires some comment. It is in no way similar to the orchestral harp, and just why it is named as it is is something of a mystery. The stop consists of metal bars of lower pitch than the glockenspiel. Each bar is placed above a rectangular wooden resonator tuned to amplify the pitch of the bar to which it is attached. The device belongs to the percussion family, not the string family.

CHAPTER 10

Achieving Optimal Sound Through
Location and Placement

The Organ and Its Room

Nothing is more critical to the success or failure of an organ than the room into which it is placed and the manner in which it is placed in that room. Excellent organs can be ruined by poor acoustics, and mediocre organs can sound well placed in reverberant rooms.

By far, the majority of organs built in the United States are destined for churches. The architectural considerations for organs built in concert halls and homes are not too different from those pertaining to church organs. The discussions which follow are directed to the organ in churches with the proviso that what is said also applies to organs in other situations.

Hopefully some readers of this book will be of non-organists who find themselves on building and organ committees of churches. These committees are often vested with decisions which the churches they serve must live with for a half-century or more. For this reason, information concerning the architectural positioning of organs cannot simply be presented in a fashion which accepts all as equal. The environment into which organs are placed is so critical and so unyielding that when that environment is in the planning stages, the decisions must be made with a maximum of knowledge and foresight. By "the organ" we mean, of course, the pipework as well as the playing desk (console). Here are the basic criteria:

- The organ must be in the room in which it is to sound.
- The organ should face the congregation it is to lead.
- The best situations for the placement of an organ lies along the center axis of the nave.
- High ceilings and large cubic volume of the building contribute to the success of an organ.
- As a corollary of the above, the organ should be situated above the level of the congregation. This, of course, suggests a balcony.
- Wall, ceiling, and floor surfaces should be constructed of hard materials.
- Sound absorbent materials should be held to a minimum.
- The organ should not be scattered about the church, and such adjuncts as antiphonal organs are suspect.

- The playing desk or console should be as close to the pipe work as possible.
- The organ should not be made to appear to be what it is not.

We will briefly discuss each of these.

The Organ Must Be in the Room in Which It Is to Sound. Were it not for many installations which violate this criterion, it might seems unnecessary to spell this out. No other musical instrument is routinely situated in a room detached from its listeners. Yet this is precisely the fate of hundreds of organs enclosed in organ *chambers.* Organ chambers, which will be discussed shortly, isolate the pipework and its components from the console and place them in an ante-room generally with minimum sound egress. It would seem obvious that no musical instrument could sound well given a situation fraught with such liabilities.

The Organ Should Face the Congregation It Is to Lead. Again this seems obvious. The organ may be sited either in front of the congregation or at its back. It may even be sited on side walls as long as its face is clearly in the direction of the congregation. Placing an organ in a deep transept in which it cannot directly face the people immediately diminishes the instrument's effectiveness.

The Best Situations for the Placement of an Organ Lie along the Center Axis of the Nave. This is really a corollary of facing the congregation. The historical position for the organ, certainly in Roman Catholic and Lutheran traditions, has been the west or rear gallery. This allows both height (see below) and direct egress of sound in the direction of the congregation. In pulpit centered congregations, the organ is often well placed directly against the east (front) wall with the choir immediately in front of the organ. In a few large English cathedrals one finds the organ mounted in the rood screen, which separates the nave from the choir. In such cases the organ opens in both directions, both to the nave and to the choir. This situation is an optimum one, both in terms of position and height.

High Ceilings and Large Cubic Volume of the Building Contribute to the Success of an Organ. Organ sound requires space in which to "bloom." Organ and choral music require spaces which are reverberate. An absolute minimum of two seconds of reverberation is required for organs to sound acceptably with higher reverberation most certainly desirable. The low ceilings of many churches wreak havoc with organ and choral sound. There is simply not space for the sound to develop and to surround the listener and singer with a warm musical environment. Other musical mediums do not necessarily require this lengthy reverberation, and some auditoriums have means by which reverberation can be partially controlled.

The Organ Should Be Situated Above the Level of the Congregation. Mounting the organ above the level of the congregation demands, of course, a high ceiling. The result is that the sound is directed into the spaciousness allowed by that ceiling. This allows the "bloom" to take place as it cannot in a dead acoustical environment. Congregational singing, which is certainly one of the major reasons that organs are in churches in the first place, requires an environment in which the average singer does not feel he is an island. The warmth of a well developed organ sound surrounds the singer in a way that cannot be replaced by other musical environments.

Wall, Ceiling, and Floor Surfaces Should Be Constructed of Hard Material. Soft materials with high sound absorption used in these surfaces work against acceptable reverberation. Carpeting and soft plaster are particularly injurious in this regard. Some architects seem to feel that the end all in creating an acceptable acoustical environment must be directed to clarity of speech. It is true that speech intelligibility is often a problem in rooms with long reverberation rates. However, this problem can be solved very easily by electronic means. What the organ demands cannot be so easily improved.

Sound Absorbent Materials Should Be Held to a Minimum. This, of course, is a corollary of that directly above. The reverberation of an empty room is greater than one filled with a congregation. People and the clothes they wear are highly sound absorbent. Any fabrics, such as altar hangings, curtains, and pew cushions, further provide absorbency. These should all be considered in figuring the total effective reverberation of a building. In regard to carpet, it is unnecessary to provide carpet underneath pews. If it is necessary at all, it should be used only in aisle areas.

The Organ Should Not Be Scattered About the Church, and Such Adjuncts as Antiphonal Organs Are Suspect. Some organs are disposed in a fashion that places one division at a significant horizontal distance from another. A cohesive sound from such instruments is almost impossible. While electrical circuits operate essentially instantaneously, sound travels relatively slowly (1100 feet/second). For instance, assume that an antiphonal organ is eighty feet from the main instrument. Sound from it arrives at the ear of the performer 1/14th of a second later than the finger motion which initiated it. This may appear to be slight indeed, but in practice it is enough to disrupt articulate playing (or, for that matter to win or lose athletic events). When organ pipes are displayed in the open (see below) they are often spread widely across horizontal space. A great division may be fifty or so feet away from a positive division and both some thirty feet from the console. These distances, again, disrupt articulate playing.

The Playing Desk or Console Should Be as Close to the Pipework as Possible. This, of course, is a corollary of the paragraph above. Electric action makes possible the situating of a console at almost any distance from the pipework. This capability should be exercised with extreme discretion. Even when consoles are moveable, they should be placed so that the organist can hear various divisions equally well. The closer the console is to the pipework the better.

Although mechanical action makes it impossible to place the console at great distance from the pipework, even a small distance can be a problem. In order to allow a player to simultaneously conduct a choir, mechanical consoles are often detached from the pipework and moved forward into the choir. In order to accomplish this, longer tracker runs are necessary. The longer those runs become the less responsive the mechanical action must become.

The Organ Should Not Be Made to Appear to Be What It Is Not. Good organ design takes into account both aural and visual elements. An organ, which inevitably will be a major component in the architecture of a church, should contribute to the visual beauty of the structure. The worst case scenario is the organ in chambers (see below). Placing the organ in an ante-room and covering its opening into the church with either an unimaginative grill or a facade made of false length pipes is the ultimate insult to the instrument. To treat the organ as one would treat a heating system is to doom the instrument to be unsuccessful.

Styles of Organ Placement

The Encased Organ. If one views the long history of the organ from the sixteenth century to the present, the majority of organs have been placed in freestanding cases. As we will see, it was fashionable for a relatively short time and primarily in the United States, for this procedure to be abandoned. It has now been resurrected by most better builders (see the Bibliography: Blanton, II). An organ case serves several functions:

- It supports the entire weight of pipes and chests.
- It defines the space occupied by the instrument.
- It focuses the sound in the direction of the listener.
- In some situations, but not all, it amplifies that sound.
- In some situations, but not all, it delineates the various divisions of the organ.
- It provides a visual, architectural, and artistic opportunity which in the finest examples rival the organ's musical qualities.

One needs to think of an organ case as a piece of elegant furniture. The external design of a piece of well made furniture generally describes the space defined by its function. We look at a bookcase and know without question that its function is to contain books. The same is true of a china cabinet, or a sofa. Even more to the point, the exterior of musical instruments, be it a piccolo or an entire symphony orchestra, has its external form. That form is determined by its function. Any knowledgeable person cannot confuse a guitar with a violin. That confusion is unlikely simply because each has its own defined space and form. For the greater part of its history, the organ had just such a recognizable form, and that form was articulated via its external case. One looked at an organ and knew it for what it was.

Not only does the organ case physically define its contents, it actually plays an important part in the production of the sound of an instrument. Symphony orchestras resist playing on open stages which direct sound poorly. Instead they generally play in sound shells, constructed on the stage floor, which direct and focus their sound in the direction of the audience. The organ case does precisely the same thing. A sound shell, however, can have only limited vertical effect. An organ case, however, can delineate sounds coming from divisions at several different heights. The sound from a division high up, an *Oberwerk*, is certainly different from that coming from a division directly above the playing desk, a *Brustwerk*.

Nowhere is the spatial relationship of two divisions of an organ more obvious than the placement of a smaller division directly behind the player. The addition of this second division (the German *Rückpositiv*, the French *positif-de-dos*, or the English *chair organ*) was most likely the earliest division added to the great organ. Since most organs were mounted in a gallery of some type, hanging another division over the rail behind the player was a natural addition. This traditional placement became almost mandatory in larger instruments in French and northern European traditions. Figure 10.1 on page 155 is a cross section of a portion of an organ from Dom Bédos' monumental treatise. It shows the *positif-de-dos* clearly.

The Dutch and northern German organ builders carried the spatial organization to its logical conclusion. In what has come to be known as the *Werkprinzip* (division principal), these seventeenth century builders gave each division of the organ its own enclosed case. These were then stacked one atop the other with the *Rückpositiv* remaining in its traditional place. The lower principal pipes of each division were displayed in the facade so that one could look at the entire case and visually understand what divisions it contained. Modern organs built on north–European tradition often follow the *Werkprinzip*.

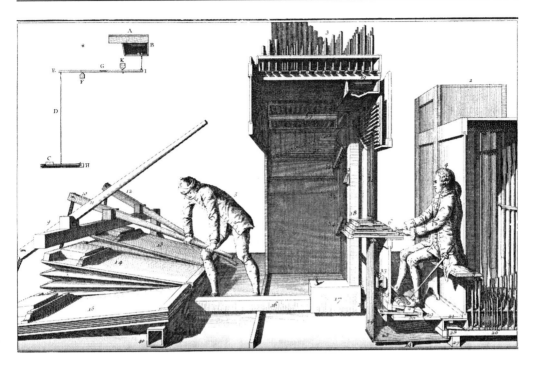

Figure 10.1 Cross Section of a Portion of an Organ (Dom Bédos, Plate 52)

In Figure 10.2 on page 156 the Flentrop organ in the rear of the Duke University Chapel, Durham, N.C., is a large mechanical action instrument built on the *Werkprinzip.* Its various divisions are labeled in the drawing. The facade pipes reveal that the *bovenwerk* and the *rugwerk* are based on 8' *prestants* and the pedal and *hoofdwerk* on 16' *prestants.* The echo displays no facade pipes, but is based on 4' pitch. In large mechanical action organs, it is characteristic to place the pedal pipes in towers generally at the sides of the manual chests. In other organs they are often placed in the rear of the manual divisions.

Organ cases reveal a wide variety of architectural styles which often mirror the style of the church in which they are placed. Figure 10.3 on page 157 shows two encased organs of differing styles. The one of the left is a large one manual organ. The decoration of the case, observed both in the crenellations and the finials, is derived from Gothic style. The facade pipes have the more elegant French mouths which have been gold leafed. The one on the right is in a contemporary building, and its case reflects that environment. It is a large two-manual organ with *Rückpositiv.*

Well designed organ cases actually amplify the sound of the instruments they contain much as piano and harpsichord soundboards do. For that reason they should be constructed of solid woods with thin panels supported by solid frames. *Pipe shades,* which fill the gaps between the tops of facade pipes and the ceiling of the case with carvings, have been asserted to have an effect on the sound. Their transparency would seem to make this debatable.

Finally, organ cases have been so strongly attached to mechanical action that some assume that the two must go together. There is nothing to preclude the combination of the traditional case with electric or electro-pneumatic action.

The Organ in Chambers. The advent of electric action, which, at least in the United States, almost completely displaced mechanical action (with or without pneumatic assists)

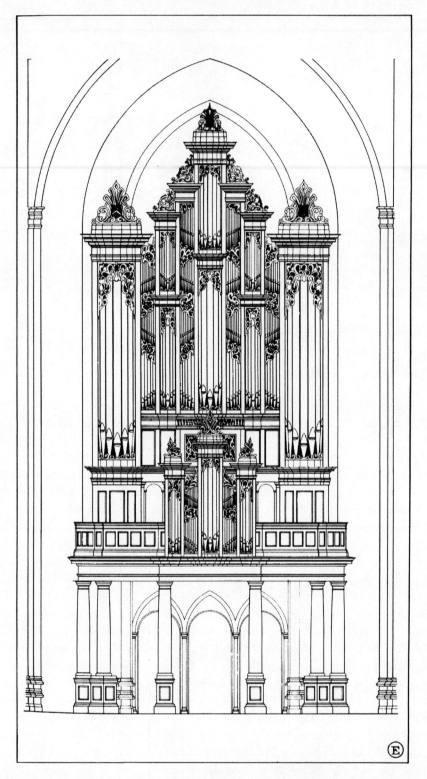

Figure 10.2 Flentrop Organ in the Rear of Duke University Chapel, Durham, North Carolina (copyright Duke University, used by permission)

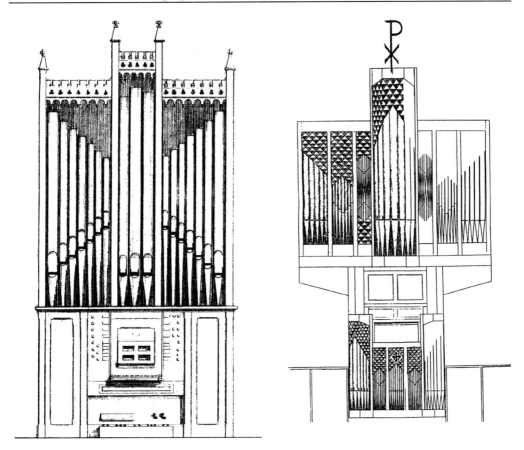

Figure 10.3 *Left*: J. Allen Farmer Organ at Saint Timothy's Episcopal Church, Winston Salem, North Carolina. *Right*: Brunzema Organ at Saint John's Episcopal Church, Charlotte, North Carolina.

was certainly an unmixed blessing. Electric action now allowed architects and organ builders freedom to do largely as they pleased with the placement of organs. This technological development was soon coupled with a theological one, the Oxford movement. The Oxford movement's neo-medieval orientation sought to make of the parish church a miniature Gothic cathedral. In the process, the musical establishment was moved from its traditional home in the west gallery into divided chancel pews in the east end of the church. The high altar now occupied the center of the east wall. The organ had no place to go, and so it was largely hidden.

The development in the Anglican communion of the divided chancel, the central altar and the hidden organ rapidly spread to the United States, where it became largely de rigueur in the design of Episcopal parish churches. Unfortunately, it was also adopted by Reformed, Methodists, and Lutheran communions. Even in the pulpit centered Baptist communion, the centrality of the visible baptistery occupied the center of the east wall. The organ became the orphan of the movement.

Organ pipework was now jammed into what were nothing more than large closets with openings into the chancel itself. The openings, which were rarely adequate to allow the organ sound to develop, were often covered with an unimaginative grill or equally unimaginative pipes. These facade pipes were rarely speaking ones and often were all of precisely of the same length and scale. There were even examples of the grill work being backed with drapery material, which in the course of time rapidly absorbed dirt particles. Sound could hardly penetrate the barrier. In order for the organ to have any presence in such a hostile environment, builders raised the wind pressure and increased the scale of the pipework. Pipes now did not speak in a normal and musical fashion. Dullness characterized their sound. The organ lost both its visual and its musical majesty. Electric action was, of course, a necessity.

Below are three possible plans for the organ in a divided chancel. The first has the organ on one side of the chancel with the grill work opening into the choir. In order for the organ sound to be heard in the congregation, its sound front must turn a 90 degree angle. The second is perhaps a bit better. Grill work opens both into the chancel and into the congregation. The third splits the organ into two chambers with some divisions on one side and some on the other.

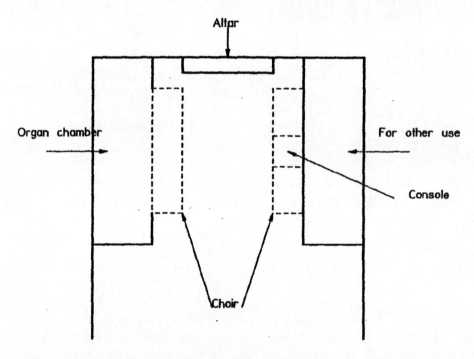

Figure 10.4A First of Three Plans for the Organ in a Divided Chancel

A modest effort was made in the 1950s to open portions of organs in chambers by cantilevering a portion of the pipework over each side of the chancel and above the back pews of the choir. This certainly helped a bit, but nonetheless, the organ in chambers violated so many of the criteria outlined in the first part of this chapter that such organs are generally unsuccessful compromises.

The Organ with Exposed Pipework. A reaction against the destruction of the historical organ began in the United States in the 1950s. At first builders took tentative steps to improve the organ in chambers. Grills and fake pipe facades began to disappear. Wind pres-

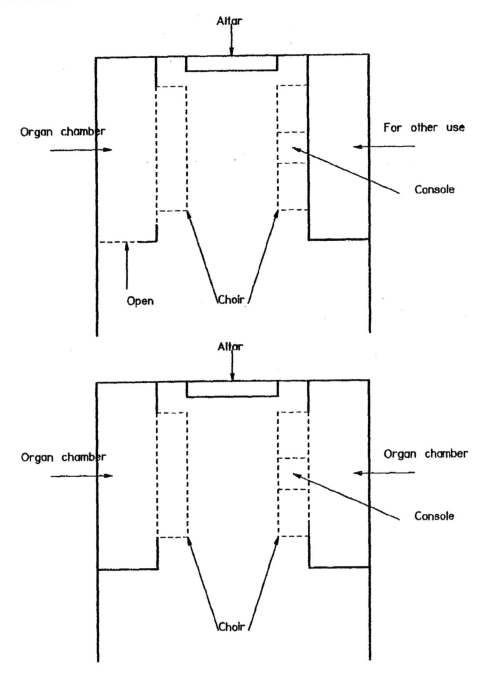

Figure 10.4B Second and Third of Three Plans for the Organ in a Divided Chancel

sures were reduced, more modest pipe scales followed, and stop lists began to imitate the historic instrument. We have just mentioned exposed cantilevered chests. The work of Walter Holtkamp, Sr., however, constituted the most extreme and creative reaction.

Holtkamp insisted that the room constituted the organ case, and consistently refused to place his instruments in rooms which worked to their disadvantage. Following the credo of Bauhaus designers that form followed function, Holtkamp brought the instrument into the open. He displayed unadorned pipework in pleasing designs which often left to open view such elements as working swell boxes. Figure 10.5 is a picture and a schematic of the pipework (not to scale) of the organ in the Chapel of Sweet Briar College, Sweet Briar, Virginia. Holtkamp died during the design process for this organ. The organ, then, is largely the work of his son, Walter Holtkamp, Jr. It is located in a spacious rear gallery.

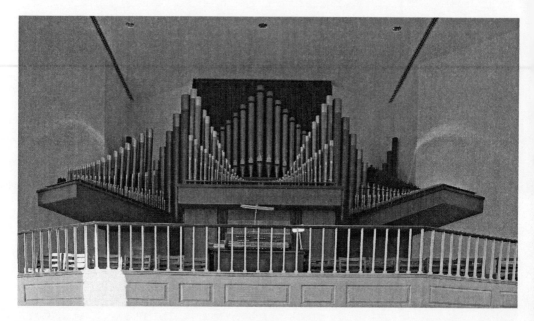

Figure 10.5 Holtkamp Organ at Sweet Briar College, Sweet Briar, Virginia (photograph by Michael Corbin, Lynchburg, Virginia)

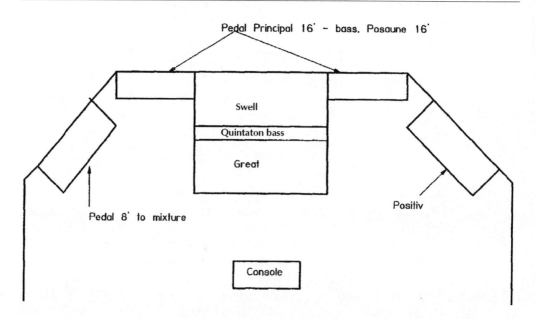

Figure 10.6 Schematic of the Same Organ

The great chest contains seven stops and the positiv also seven. The swell of seven stops is on two chests, one mounted above the other and both above the level of the great chest. The pedal chest on the left contains all ranks from 8' through the mixture. The room has a reverberation time approaching three seconds, and there is a means of damping the room if it is desirable. The ceiling is approximately thirty feet in height. Wall surfaces are hard plaster and wood. The floor is paved with granite and there are no carpets. Seat cushions provide some acoustical ballast. This organ and others similar to it represent the best of organs with exposed pipework.

CHAPTER 11

Can You or Should You
Fix It Yourself?

Caveat: Before you take any actions based on this chapter, consider that you may be on shaky legal grounds in regard both to the state of the instrument upon which you are working and your own personal safety. In the first place, the vast majority of organs are institutionally owned. You must assure yourself that the administration that owns the instrument you propose to service has expressed consent to you for your work. That consent must be in writing. Secondly, organ cases and chambers are dangerous places and a novice and an organ can be easily injured by carelessness and missteps. Undertaking repairs for which you are incapable can cause costly damage. The liability for your safety and the welfare of the organ must also be carefully spelled out in writing. Finally, many institutions have service contracts. Be certain you do not violate the terms of these contracts. Before you undertake to do any work on any organ, ensure that you have the blessings of the service personnel that are responsible for that organ. Preferably, that, too, should be in writing.

Nothing in the paragraph above or in any other passage in this book is intended or written to be used as legal advice or as a substitution for legal advice. For legal advice in these matters, as in all others, one should consult an attorney.

Introduction

You arrive for a Sunday service, turn the organ on, and nothing happens, or a single pipe continues to sound, or the combination action refuses to work, or one division of the organ is woefully sharp with another, or a coupler does not work, or a single necessary pipe is obviously out of tune, and, worst of all, panic sets in at just the wrong time. This chapter proposes to suggest some actions that can be safely taken by a resourceful and knowledgeable organist. It also proposes to suggest what one should not do unless equipped with considerable expertise and skill. The admonition from the medical world should be kept constantly in mind. *Do no harm.* If there is potential damage in what you propose to do, *simply do not take that action.* All organ technicians have horror stories of having to repair the repairs done by the organist. Don't contribute more.

Before you begin to do your own repair work, know your comfort level. If you are a person who is mechanically "all thumbs," admit it frankly. Do only the simple things. If, on the other hand, you are skilled, there are many things you can do. In order to aid persons in what their skill allows, each suggestion given in the discussion below will be rated as follows:

[*Class 1*] Actions which can be taken without fear of doing any damage, requiring no more expertise than flipping a circuit breaker.

[*Class 2*] Actions which require some special knowledge, although if done with forethought, can hardly cause damage.

[*Class 3*] Actions which are technically more sophisticated, may require some earlier assistance and instruction from professionals, and should be avoided if one is not certain of one's competence.

[*Class 4*] Actions which border on the skill of the trained professional.

[*Class 5*] Situations absolutely requiring the professional organ technician.

If you feel incompetent to deal with a matter simply *don't*. Leave the matter to the skilled professional. If possible, don't cause a technician to make a long trip early Sunday morning to your church to fix a simple and easily repaired problem. On the other hand, he or she does not want to arrive to fix a simple problem and find you have fallen into the pipework, are hospitalized, and an entire division of the organ is rendered useless.

Remember, too, that *the inside of an organ is an exceedingly dangerous place*. It has much in common with a construction site. Walk boards are often quite high and narrow. Ladders are often the means of moving from one place to another. Lighting is often poor. One often has to lean far over to fix a certain pipe. And, there are literally thousands of fragile and breakable parts, and a miscue can be devastating. *Whenever you are inside an organ case or chamber, be ultra cautious.* Both you and the instrument can suffer if you are not. Your own physical health can also be a factor. Stay out of organ spaces if you are overweight, have poor balance, or poor eyesight. One needs to have the agility of a monkey to work in this environment.

Preparation

It is an unfortunate truth that the close relationship between the musician and his instrument, a relationship that is taken for granted by most other musicians, is not shared by many organists and the organs they play. For instance, violinists and oboists are wedded to their instruments in a symbiotic way, and it would be unthinkable that a violinist could not replace a string or an oboist adjust a reed. A harpist or a harpsichordist can and must be able to tune, and tune they do before every performance and most practice sessions. To some degree, unmusical playing, endemic in the organ world, is explained by a simple fact that organists are not responsible for their own instruments. There is a gap between the player and his principal tool, a gap no good woodworker and most other musicians would countenance.

If you have managed to get to the final chapter of this book, it would seem obvious that you have an interest in the marvelous machine that is the pipe organ. Many excellent players first became fascinated with the organ as much for its mechanical complexity as for its musical potential. If you are willing to undertake some of your own maintenance, a part of your preparation is to develop such fascination.

Invest in a few good tools: a set of screwdrivers, a set of various kinds of pliers, perhaps an electric drill with the proper bits to drive and remove both slotted and Phillips screws, some tool for tuning (more about that later), a good pair of scissors, a small hammer and a small, soft bristled brush suitable for dusting the mouths of small pipes. If you have knowledge of simple electrical circuits, obtain an inexpensive voltmeter. Place these in a tool box and keep them together so that they are available at the moment. Do not lend these tools. The ones you have lent will be the very ones you will next immediately need.

Next you need to familiarize yourself with the organ for which you are responsible. Here is a list which outlines the basic information you should have at you fingertips:

(1) What type of action does the organ have?
(2) Where are its various divisions located?
(3) What type of stop action does the organ have and where are its components?
(4) What type of combination action does the organ have and where are its components?
(5) Information sufficient to locate any given pipe.
(6) The location of any access doors and just exactly how they are to be opened.
(7) How to turn on the lighting within the case or chambers.
(8) The location of the blower.
(9) The location of the rectifier if there is one.
(10) The location of any protective devices such as reset buttons or circuit breakers.
(11) Thermostatic controls for room heating and cooling.

Next, relate the material in this book and other similar sources to your own instrument. If the organ has mechanical action, most of its components are readily visible and easy to trace. With electric action the task is a bit more difficult. But, as best you can, trace the cable connections from the console to the chests. Learn where the banks of switches are located and how they can be accessed.

In preparation nothing is better than getting some professional advice, either from a professional tuner and maintenance person, the builder himself, or from an organ consultant. If you are lucky enough to be the organist of a new instrument, spend as many hours as possible observing the installation. As long as you do not make a pest of yourself, the installers are a ready source of information and they generally love to talk about their work. If new organs are being installed in your neighborhood, avail yourself of the opportunity to visit and observe. From time to time, organ guilds sponsor "organ crawls." Go on these. They are excellent opportunities to observe various instruments and make comparisons to that that you play. We are now prepared to address certain common problems and to suggest solutions, many of which can reasonably be corrected by the novice.

At the risk of being repetitive, before you begin any work inside an organ, make certain your legal status is clear and that you have permission from the owner of the organ to undertake tuning and repairs. If a clear legal relationship is not established, you very well could be held liable for any damage you cause to the organ, however unintentional. Organ technicians carry liability insurance of at least one million dollars to protect themselves against property and medical damage. The most effective method to avoid possible legal problems would be for you and the instrument owner to sign a waiver relieving you of all legal liability. See the opening caveat to this chapter.

The Main Switch Has Been Turned On but the Organ Does Not Play

1. [*Class 1*] The chances are very good that the problem is not directly related to the organ but to a general failure of the electrical supply. Note evidence of a more general power failure. If the console lights do not come on and you have reason to believe the blower is not working (two electrical components not directly related to one another), the chances are good that this is the problem. Check the circuit breaker which protects the organ's electrical supply. This is likely to be found in a panel box close by. Correct by simply resetting the breaker. If this does not rectify the problem and the circuit breaker again trips, call an electrician. Unless the problem has been found and corrected, do not continue to try to make the breaker hold.

2. [*Class 1*] In a completely mechanical organ, one with both mechanical key and stop actions, electrical supply relates only to the blower and console lights. If the organ is playable and the console lights are out, search the power supply for the lights only. If the console lights come on and the organ still does not play, it is almost certain that the blower is not functioning. Check the blower for its protective devices. If there is a thermal overload switch, check it. Perhaps the oil level of the bearings is low. Look for simple things. Remember that in the United States almost half of appliance service calls boil down to simple things such as line chords loose at the wall socket. Look for simple solutions, not complicated ones. More times than not, problems will have simple solutions..

3. [*Class 3*] If there is a general failure of the stop action, the key action, and the combination action, there are two possibilities: (1) the rectifier is not working or (2) these systems are controlled electronically and the system has failed. Both the rectifier and an electronic control system often have readily accessible fuses. Check to see if one is blown. Otherwise, the problem almost certainly lies beyond the capability of a novice. Call the service person.

A Pipe Speaks Poorly

Sudden poor speech in a pipe, either labial or reed, is most often caused by dirt, trash, or other foreign matter falling into the pipe. All sorts of things can fall into organ pipes. The author once had a hummingbird fall into a large reed pipe and die.

[*Class 2*] If the pipe is a labial pipe, first locate it. If it is possible to work on the pipe without removing it from the chest, do so. Lightly brush the mouth and windway to remove foreign matter, and then check to see if the problem is corrected. Do this gently. One organ tuner carried a bunch of turkey feathers which he used for this purpose. If it is necessary to remove the pipe in order to brush it, check its tuning when you return it to the chest. Particularly if the pipe is metal, do not handle it anymore than you can help and do not blow through it. Both heat the pipe and can alter the tuning. This is particularly true of small pipes.

[*Class 2*] If the pipe involved is stopped, check that its stopper has not slipped, a common occurrence. This is most likely to happen when the organ is situated in a hot and dry environment. If the stopper is obviously so loose that it will continue to slide downwards, remove the stopper. Cut a square of thin felt or thick paper slightly bigger than the base of the stopper, cut a miter at each corner, slip it around the stopper, and reinsert. Do not glue. Do not force your repair into the pipe. It should fit tightly but not so tight that the pipe might split. This is only a temporary repair to await a more professional treatment. Now tune the pipe.

[*Class 1*] If many stoppers are causing the same problem, alert the administration to an atmosphere dangerous to the organ. Low humidity (under 25 percent) is a disaster to all things wooden, the pipe organ particularly. Do not attempt to repair a more general problem. A single pipe is one thing; several are something else indeed. Await the technician.

[*Class 4*] If the pipe is a reed pipe, the situation is more complicated and sensitive. Before one undertakes to work on reeds without assistance, it is imperative to get an organ technician to go over the steps with you. Here is what one has to do:

(1) If the pipe is small enough, remove it. If it is too large to handle easily, slip the resonator from the boot. In larger reeds they are not generally soldered together. Set the resonator aside.

(2) Turn the pipe or boot upside down and shake lightly. Do the same to the resonator. Hopefully, this will dislodge any foreign matter. If trash comes out, replace the pipe, or boot and the resonator. Test that the problem is cleared up. Retune the pipe. If the resonators are large, great caution must be taken once you have lifted it off its supporting pins. There is now a danger of the resonator falling over and hitting neighboring pipework. Do not attempt to remove resonators taller than about six feet without assistance.

Steps 3, 4, and 5 below are hazardous and technicians themselves make mistakes at this point. One should never attempt these steps until you have had instruction from a technician and have his assurance that you are able to deal with the potential hazards.

(3) If step 2 fails, remove the boot to expose the shallot and reed. *With extreme care,* compress the tuning wire and pull it away from the reed. Carefully remove the wooded wedge holding the reed in place and remove the reed. *Remember, the last thing you want to do is to bend the reed even slightly.* Do not drop the wedge. It is easy to lose.

(4) The shallot should now be exposed. Clear out any debris it contains.

(5) Now, as carefully as you removed the wedge, reed, and tuning wire, replace them. Set the tuning wire as close to its original position as possible.

(6) Tune the pipe with its octave below. Remember the pitch of a reed pipe is largely determined by the length of the reed. You may find the pipe sounds far from its intended pitch. Do not be alarmed. It will come into tune. Again, exercise the care you would expect of a surgeon any time you deal with reed pipes.

A Pipe Ciphers

Certainly the most common problem encountered by organists is the *cipher*, the unwanted sounding of a pipe that will not stop.

[*Class 2*] The obvious and most temporary of solutions is simply to locate the errant pipe and temporarily remove it. To find the pipe can be exasperating if the sound seems to be coming from everywhere. You should be able, based on the material in this book, to find your way without trouble to the correct chest and rank. There are two simple ways to find the offending pipe: (1) Lick your finger and hold it just above the pipe tops. Do not touch them. Stop where your finger is chilled, and the pipe you are seeking is there, and (2) count from the top down (or the bottom up, if more convenient) at the keyboard. Do the same at the chest. You will have to take into account the type of chest you have: chromatic, V, W, N, etc.

[*Class 1*] However, if you are playing an electro-pneumatic organ with stop channel chests, there are other more permanent solutions which take even less time and do not require you to leave the console. The cause of a large proportion of ciphers is trash which wedges open the valve directly beneath the offending pipe. First turn off the organ and leave it off a few moments to allow the wind pressure to subside. Be certain the stop involved is on. Then turn the organ on again. Often this simple procedure will dislodge the trash without further ado. If this does not help, work the appropriate key rapidly up and down while the organ is on. The rapid on-off of the valve will often do the trick. If not, turn off all the stops and play with full forearms in a rapid staccato fashion.

[*Class 2*] If these procedures have failed, pull the pipe and let an assistant work the note. This should blow away the trash. Replace the pipe and retune it if necessary. Once the trash is dislodged by any of these procedures, the problem should not reoccur.

Multiple Ciphers on a Slider Chest

If you are playing an organ with slider chests, either mechanical or electro-mechanical, a single pipe ciphering is still possible but rare. More likely, all pipes mounted on that channel (i.e., the pipes for that particular note) will sound if their sliders are in the *on* position. Pull all stops mounted on the chest involved. If all stops sound the ciphering pitch, it is almost certain that the pallet for that note is not seating properly. Attempt to free the pallet.

[*Class 1*] First work the proper key up and down in hopes of freeing the pallet. *Do not use force.* If there is resistance, let the key alone. If this does not work, turn off the organ, let the wind pressure subside, turn the organ back on, and hope the problem disappears.

[*Class 3*] If the problem persists and you are playing a mechanical organ, you might trace the action for the note involved from keyboard to chest in hopes of spotting an obvious point of resistance. If you can easily clear the matter, you might do so but with extreme care.

[*Class 5*] In all other cases call the technician. On a mechanical action organ, if the cipher(s) above continue(s) and the key remains depressed when it is released, it is likely that the pallet spring is not functioning. This requires entering the chest, *something that should be undertaken only by a professional.* If this proves to be the case and the *bung*, the access cover to the interior of a mechanical chest, must be removed, it is instructive to observe the inner workings of a mechanical chest as the repair is effected.

Problems with the Stop Action

If the stop action is purely mechanical, there is little that can go wrong with it. The purpose of the stop action is so transparent and simple that once set by the builder, it is likely to remain trouble free for the life of the organ. The only problem which might occur is that of binding sliders. If sliders cease to move freely, do not attempt to force them. Breakage is likely if too much force is applied. This problem generally results from excessive high humidity causing the sliders to swell.

Players who are unacquainted with mechanical action are prone to draw or retire stops incompletely. As a result, the intonation of the stop involved is immediately changed. The novice often thinks there has been some type of mechanical failure, that, in fact, is not the case. If a player complains that an entire stop is out of tune, be certain this is not the simple explanation.

Electrified slider chests, if activated either by conventional low voltage circuits or controlled by an electronic unit, work the sliders by small electric motors. Many of these motors have adjustments which control the thrust and pull of the sliders.

[*Class* 3] Should one of these motors fail to operate, use the voltmeter to check that it is receiving its proper low voltage when the stop is activated. You will need an assistant here. To use the voltmeter to test for low voltage, set its function dial to DC with a range of about five to twenty volts. To test the voltage on the slider motor, hold the voltmeter's two probes on the two electrical contacts feeding the motor. The proper reading for low voltage organ circuits is from about 12 to 15 volts. Do not fear low voltage. Most persons cannot even feel this voltage and no one can suffer any ill effects from it. If the slider motor is not receiving current when an assistant works the stop and you are certain of your capability, you should check for the most obvious cause of the voltage failure. See the next paragraph.

Checking the Stop Knob or Tab Switches on Any Electric Stop Action

[*Class 4*] To check for failure of either stop tab or knob switches, first gain access to the working end of the stop knob or tablet (see Figure 4.15). Most of the time this access is easy, requiring the removal of a few screws and a panel or two. Stop controls are simple on-off switches. Check to make certain the low voltage feelers that the stop control crosses and effectively completes the circuit leading to the slider motor are in working order. (At some point, it might be a good idea to have your technician show you how to access not only stop controls but also manual and pedal key actions. This is knowledge you need to effect more complicated repairs, particularly ones dealing with bent or broken feelers.) If one or both of the feelers have become bent, use long nose pliers to bend them to their proper position. If one or both are broken, it is a matter for the professional to repair.

Adjusting a Slider

[*Class 4*] If it appears that a slider is traveling less or more than its appropriate distance and, as a result, it is obvious that the pipes of the rank it controls are not receiving proper wind, you might attempt to readjust the thrust of the motor. You will have to analyze the adjustment mechanism in order to reset it. This is not a repair one would be forced to make with any frequency. *Again, exercise care.* This is at the extreme of repairs which non-technicians should attempt.

Repairing a Combination Button (Piston) or Toe Stud

[*Class 3*] Combination buttons and toe studs sometimes stick in closed position. These are also simple on-off switches. When depressed a metal bar contacts the two feelers, completing a circuit (see Figure 7.8). A spring returns the switch to open position when the player releases it. If possible, remove the unit. Be careful not to break its wire leads. Check to make certain the return spring is working and there is no dirt or trash keeping the switch closed. Check the contacts to make certain these are in working order. Reinstall the unit. An aerosol type electrical contact cleaner available at any electronic supply store is helpful for this work.

Repairing a Sticking Key

[*Class 2*] One of the most common and annoying problems in all keyboard instruments, the organ included, is a key which does not properly rebound. While there may be other more complicated reasons for this, frequently the cause is excess humidity. Many, but not all, keyboards use pins which are oval in cross section as front guides. Very often if one removes the batten directly under a manual one can see these guide pins near the front end of the key. The wooden body of the key is slotted at the point at which it fits over the guide pin. This slot is frequently bushed with felt. The oval pins can be turned slightly to take up any slack which develops between felt and pin. (See Figure 3.8 and explanatory text.)

We are, however, addressing the opposite problem: excess friction between felt and pin. The most likely cause of this friction is swelling of the felt bushing due to absorption of moisture. While moving the key up and down, take it tightly in hand and move it to the right and then the left to compress the felt. This generally frees the key. If not, experiment with turning the oval guide pin to a position in which there is less friction between felt and pin. Be careful in these repairs. Too rough handling can break a key.

An Entire Manual Keyboard Does Not Play

[*Class 1*] This problem is unthinkable on a mechanical action organ and almost as unlikely on most electric action instruments. The most obvious cause can be traced to the *unison off* (see discussion in section Chapter 5), a device less and less common on most organs. First, be certain that the unison-off tab or knob has not been drawn and the device is unintentionally operative. This is most often the problem. Close the device.

[*Class 3*] If this fails and the unison-off appears to be still functioning, gain access to the working end of the stop tabs or knobs. Find the feelers for the unison-off device. The problem will most likely be that the circuit from one feeler to the other is open. Correct as you would any other tab or knob. Be certain that one of the feelers (the return feeler to ground) is properly grounded. Place your voltmeter on ohms. When you touch its two probes together, the meter should read zero. Now place one of the probes on one feeler. Place the other probe on the wire leading to the grounding busbar. If this procedure does not register zero, that feeler is not grounded. Try the other feeler the same way. If it, too, does not read zero, you have no ground. Trace the circuit and repair the ground.

A Sudden Change in Wind Pressure

[*Class 1*] Sudden changes in wind pressure are rare, and when they occur are almost always the result of either vandalism or carelessness. The flat surfaces on the top of an organ reservoir are attractive sites for someone to store heavy objects. Such objects, of course, raise the wind pressure. Keep reservoirs free of these objects. Sometimes builders expose the chord actuating the curtain valve. Foreign objects which impede functioning of that chord will cause a change of wind pressure. Remove these objects. If you are lucky enough to have an organ with an alternate manual wind supply, be certain that no foreign objects come near it. If these wind supplies have easy access, they are ready made attractions for vandals. Any other radical changes in wind pressure is a matter for the technician.

Tuning

[*Class 2*] Organists should acquire at least modest tuning skill. Here again, your organ technician will certainly give you instruction sufficient for you to keep your instrument playable from one scheduled visit to the next. In regard to labial pipes, your tuning skills should allow you to correct single pipes which go out of tune. For reed pipes it is necessary to be able to retune entire ranks with some frequency. A common table knife is the only tool one needs for tuning, although a very large screwdriver or chisel will do as well. If you wish to get more sophisticated, a flat metal bar about 18" long and about ½" wide with a small hook filed toward one end to catch and lift reed wires may be worth the trouble. Take into considerations these four things:

1. Do as little tuning as possible. Do not get in the habit of running into the organ to tune every little idiosyncrasy your ears catch. No organ is perfectly in tune and attempts to meet such a standard causes more harm than good.

2. *If your labial pipes are cone tuned, do not attempt to tune them.* More damage has been done to cone tuned organs by insensitive tuners than fire itself. You may brush the dirt away from a cone tuned pipe but do not attempt to retune it.

3. Do not handle metal pipes any more than necessary and do not get in the habit of blowing through them. Both actions heat pipes and make your immediate tuning of them invalid. Reed tongues, in particular, are vulnerable. They can rust when your warm breath condenses on their cold metal surfaces.

4. You will, of course, need an assistant to hold while you tune. The more knowledge the assistant has, the easier tuning will be.

In order to tune any pipe, one must have a benchmark, a pipe of either the same or the octave of the same pitch which one regards as in tune. When an organ is initially tuned or when a general tuning is undertaken, the tuner first sets the temperament (see Chapter 8). Generally this is done on the tenor c octave (c to cl) of the 4' principal on the great organ. This temperament is then transferred to all other divisions, and thus it becomes the standard for the entire organ. If the pipe or pipes you are tuning can be clearly heard against this standard, use it. However, when tuning softer pipes, there is a problem. Often the sound of the tuning stop swamps the softer stop or the louder stop draws the softer into tune with it, and so makes tuning impossible. If you are spot tuning soft pipes, simply tune them with the octave below on the same stop.

The tuning of labial pipes with tuning slides. Tuning is done by listening for the beats which are present when two pipes are out of tune with one another. (For a discussion of beats see Chapter 8). Practice in the following manner. Select two sounding pipes in tune with one another and of similar dynamic quality. With your tuning tool held flat against the side of one of the pipes, slowly tap down the tuning slider of one pipe and, as you do, listen for the beating. You are intentionally mistuning this pipe. As the pitch of the pipe progressively goes further out of tune (i.e., it sharpens), the beating will speed up. Now reverse the process. Bring the out-of-tune pipe into tune. As you tap upward, the beats will progressively slow until they disappear. When the beating is no longer audible, the two pipes are again in tune with one another. When they are absolutely without beats, the tones will "bloom." Next select two pipes that are an octave apart. Mistune the higher of them and then bring it back in tune.

Use your tuning tool gently. Tap lightly. Do not hit. Keep the flat side of the tuning tool against the pipe so that it comes readily into contact with the tuning slider. Remember that the same movement of a slider on a treble pipe makes a much greater difference in pitch than the same motion on a bass pipe.

When a labial pipe goes abruptly out of tune and it is slider tuned, it is almost certain that the slider has fallen or slid down. Sliders are made of metal with spring tension, and over time metal fatigue causes that tension to diminish. Remove the pipe. Remove the slider. Pinch it slightly to restore its tension and replace it on the pipe. Reset the pipe and retune. When many sliders begin to fail, it may be time to replace them all. Consult the technician.

At the risk of being repetitive, do not attempt to tune labial pipes which are cone tuned. Untold damage has occurred to pipework by novices trying to do so. Some technicians who have no tuning cones will mangle the ends of pipes attempting to tune them. Do not be a party to such vandalism. If a cone tuned pipe needs adjustment, carefully clean it. This will likely solve the problem.

The tuning of reed pipes. Much of the material above applies to the tuning of reeds. By their very nature, however, reed pipes go out of tune with much greater frequency than do flues. Indeed, labial (flue) pipes sharpen when the thermometer rises and flatten when it drops. For this reason, do not attempt to tune reeds if there has been a significant and sudden change in the room temperature. Tuning reeds should only take place when the normal temperature of the room has been stable for several hours. A conscientious organist will probably tune reeds before every important performance. The organ designer who places reed stops in inaccessible places should be boiled in oil.

Most reeds should be tuned by means of the tuning wire and not by altering any part of the resonator. A few, however, should be tuned by altering the resonator and not the tuning wire. *Before you tune reeds, check with the builder to make certain what his reeds require.* If your organ has some reeds which the builder recommends tuning by altering the resonator, it is better to leave this to the trained professional.

When appropriate to tune reeds by the tuning wire, tap downward on the wire to sharpen and tap upward to flatten. It is important to work carefully. A slight tap, particularly on a treble reed, can make a world of difference in pitch. For an 8' reed, tune the lower part of its register (up to about g1) with the tuning stop. Have the assistant withdraw the tuning stop, and tune the remainder of the trebles with pipes on the same stop an octave below. This is know as "tuning the stop with itself." Sometimes it is difficult, particularly in the bass register, to get the tuning tool into place to tap upward. This is where the hook filed into the tuning tool is of help. With it one can catch the tuning wire from above. For those reeds to be tuned by changing the resonators, consult the builder and follow his instructions.

Routine Maintenance

Just as any other complicated machine, pipe organs need routine maintenance. Nothing in this chapter is meant to suggest otherwise. Here are some guidelines:

- A routine maintenance contract with a competent technician calling for a minimum of one visit per year, but preferably for two, is required for any organ.
- The client and technician should agree, in general terms, when these routine visits are to occur. Do not expect a visit on December 20 so that your instrument will be in prime shape for Christmas. Remember other organists want the same thing, and before Christmas and Easter an organ technician always has more than he can deal with.
- The contract should specify the terms for emergency visits. Service on any Sunday morning at 9:30 should not be one of them.
- Keep a list of problems which have been encountered and need correction at the technician's next visit.
- Keep a log book of maintenance visits.
- Be certain that the hall is free and quiet during visits. Keep visitors away.
- Be certain that the normal temperature for the room is set the day before. Do not allow the temperature to be changed at night. That temperature should be the same as that at which the organ has been tuned in the past.
- Discuss any major work such as additions, complete retuning, re-leathering, and re-voicing, well in advance. Ask for written bids for such work.
- Be certain that the technician's bill is paid promptly. Nothing will assure you of further poor service than a bill unduly paid.
- Be kind to your technician. He needs to be one of your best friends.

Glossary

This glossary consists of terms that are *italicized* in the text.
Any of these terms that appear in a glossary entry are in **boldface**.

A order an order of pipe placement on the chest with the longest pipe in the middle and shorter pipes progressing downward, alternating from right to left. Sometimes known as the inverted V. See Figure 5.5.

action mechanical, pneumatic, electric, or electronic connections between the key and the chest and the stop control and the chest.

alternating current (abbreviated AC) an electrical current which reverses its direction in a continuously repetitive fashion. It is diagrammed as a sine wave. Commercial power in the United States alternates at the rate of 60 **hertz**. Alternating current is rarely used in organ building save to operate lights, blowers, and rectifiers.

amperage the amount of current within an electric circuit, as opposed to voltage, which is the force moving electrons through the circuit.

amplitude in any system of **simple harmonic motion**, the amount of displacement of a particle from the neutral position. In sound (and hence in music), the greater the amplitude the louder the sound.

antinode in a cyclical wave, the point at which there is no movement of particles. See **node**.

arcing the jumping of electrons across a gap. Arcing can cause corrosion at the point of the gap, and, in electrical organ circuits, malfunctioning contacts.

armature in an **electromagnet** (**solenoid**), the ferrous element drawn toward the core when current is applied to its coil. Armatures vary greatly in size and shape depending upon the use of the solenoid. For an example see Figure 4.9.

backfall an important component of mechanical action. It is essentially a first class lever normally mounted horizontally. Downward motion at one end produces upward motion at the other and visa-versa. See Figure 3.19.

backflow in duplexing in mechanical action, air flowing in the wrong direction, causing speech in both the borrowed and parent pipe.

balance rail a slat of wood running across a keyboard and under the keys. Generally it supports vertical pins which serve as the pivots for those keys that are first class levers. See Figure 3.8.

balanced swell pedal a swell pedal which remains fixed at the position to which it was last moved. All swell pedals in modern organs are balanced. Earlier swell pedals often required that the foot stay in contact with the pedal for it to remain in place or that some manner of latch down be available.

bar in a slider chest the partition which separates one groove from its neighbor.

Barker lever a device for providing pneumatic assistance to mechanical key action. The device and various modifications of it began to appear on organs in the mid-nineteenth century as pipe scales and wind pressure made traditional mechanical action unwieldy. See Figure 5.11.

bass flute a large scale flute in the pedal organ at either 16' or 8' pitch.

bassoon a reed stop at 16' pitch which is not necessarily imitative of its orchestral equivalent.

bay leaf mouth the most common form of mouth on labial pipes. It has a teardrop shape. Also called a Gothic mouth. See Figure 9.9.

beards small dowels or rods of pipe metal placed between the ears of some string stops to stabilize their pitch.

bearers thin pieces of wood slightly thicker than the sliders themselves placed between the table and the toe boards. Their function is to allow the sliders to move freely.

bearing the temperament set before a general tuning begins. It is normally set on the 4' principal of the great. It does not change and serves as the benchmark for all further tuning.

beats a succession of pulsations heard when two tones are out of tune with one another. The faster these pulsations are, the further the tones are out of tune. As the two tones are pulled into tune the beats gradually become slower until they disappear. At that point the tones are in tune. The phenomenon of beats is essential to tuning music instruments.

block the thick, circular component of a reed pipe, generally of metal, which supports the resonator and provides the drilling into which the **shallots**, **tongue**, and wedge are held. The block fits into the top of the **boot**. See Figure 8.18.

Blockflöte (Eng. Recorder) an open flute of either 4' or 2' pitch.

Blockwerke On the medieval organ all pipes were mounted on a single chest without stop action. Pipes were of the principal type in pitches from 16' to 1'. Pitches were both unison and fifth sounding. In essence, the *Blockwerke* constituted a gigantic mixture. One of the most significant mechanical developments of the early organ was splitting the *Blockwerke* into individual stops by the invention of both the spring and slider chests.

boot The lowest component of a reed pipe. It is placed in the **toe hole** and contains the **block**, the **shallot**, the **reed**, the **wedge**, and the tuning wire. It is generally made of metal but may be made of wood.

borrowing see **duplexing**

Bovenwerk Dutch equivalent of Ger. ***Oberwerk***.

Brustwerk a small division of an organ placed directly in front and slightly above the player. It often has doors which may be left open or closed.

bung a removable panel in the front of a mechanical chest which gives access to the mechanism, particularly to the pallets.

bus bar in an electric action organ, a heavy copper wire which returns all circuits to the negative pole of the power supply.

C-sharp side the right hand side of a V chest as viewed by the tuner.

C-side the left side of a V chest as viewed from the position intended for the tuner.

cam a projection on a rotating wheel which causes a mechanical action to take place when it is in a certain position. One use in mechanical organ action is to engage or disengage a **backfall**. See Figure 6.5.

capture system an electric **combination action** which literally holds (captures) a combination in readiness for its use by the performer. See figure 7.12 and surrounding text.

case the predominately wooden enclosure in which an organ is contained. Most often it is an elegant piece of furniture. Some cases reflect their contents rather precisely (see ***Werkprinzip***). Cases are characteristic of mechanical action organs but by no means are limited to them.

celeste a two rank string (or less often a flute) stop. One rank is intentionally sharpened to produce a wavering effect.

centrifugal blower a blower contained in a large circular steel case. Sometimes called a squirrel cage blower. These blowers are now activated by electric motors. See Figure 2.6.

chair organ the English name for the organ placed behind the performer. See ***Rückpositiv.***

chamber a room, generally off the larger room in which the organ is meant to sound, containing one of more divisions of an electric action organ.

channel the division within an organ chest. If the channels run from back to front there will be as many channels as there are notes on that chest. These chests are called **note** or **key channel chests.** If the channels run from left to right, there will be as many channels as there are stops on that chest. These are called **stop channel chests.**

check valve a valve allowing a liquid or a gas to pass in one direction but not the other. The simplest form is a **flap valve.** See Figure 2.5.

chest magnet a small **solenoid** and **armature** designed for the primary action of ventil chests. The chest magnet exhausts a channel that in turn allows a larger pneumatic to exhaust. See Figure 5.13.

chests boxes which support the pipes and contain the key and stop action actuating them. See Chapter 5.

chimney flute see ***Rohrflöte***

choir organ the third division on many organs (great — swell — choir). The term may actually be a corruption of **chair organ.**

choral bass the 4' principal on the pedal organ so-called since it often carries the chorale melody in choral preludes in trio style.

chromatic chest a chest in which the pipes are placed in order from the largest to the smallest. See Figure 5.2.

cipher the persistent and unwanted sounding of a pipe.

circle of fifths a theoretical circle of twelve segments each representing one of the semi-tones in the octave. The circle begins with C and progresses by the interval of the perfect fifth until it again arrives again at C. At some point in the circle it is necessary to make an enharmonic change (F sharp = G flat). Tuners, when setting a temperament, move from one point in the circle to the next.

clarabella a large scale wooden flute stop.

clarinet a reed stop designed to imitate the orchestral clarinet. It evolved from the earlier ***Krummhorn.***

clarion a trumpet stop generally at 4' pitch.

clavier another name for a manual **keyboard.**

combination a pre-set registration available to the player as he or she wills.

combination action the mechanism which makes setting, holding, and retrieving combinations possible.

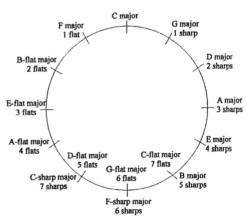

Circle of Keys Major Keys Only

C major
G major / 1 sharp
F major / 1 flat
D major / 2 sharps
B-flat major / 2 flats
A major / 3 sharps
E-flat major / 3 flats
E major / 4 sharps
A-flat major / 4 flats
D-flat major / 5 flats
C-flat major / 7 flats
B major / 5 sharps
C-sharp major / 7 sharps
G-flat major / 6 flats
F-sharp major / 6 sharps

combination tones tones which are produced not of physical vibration at their specific pitches but as a result of combining two related pitches. For, instance, a tone sounding 300 **hertz** and another sounding 200 hertz will produce a combination tone of 100 hertz. Such a tone is called a **resultant,** the most common and useful combination tone.

common metal the most frequent alloy used in pipe making. It is a combination of lead and tin in various proportions.

concert violin a string stop imitative of the orchestral violin.

concussion bellows small bellows attached directly to chests to absorb any unusual demand upon the wind system. Also known as Schwimmer or winker bellows.

cone tuning a method of tuning open **labial** pipes either by flaring (to sharpen) or narrowing (to flatten) the open end. Cone tuning is designed to be more or less permanent.

cone valve a type of valve shaped like a truncated cone fitting into an open hole. By moving the cone in and out of its hole, the valve can be opened or closed. See Figure 2.8.

console the portion of an organ containing at a minimum the stop and key controls actuated by the performer. It may contain much more mechanical linkages and electrical circuitry. Sometimes known as the playing desk.

contact block small wooden blocks attached most often to the underside of keys housing feelers which complete electric key circuits. See Figure 4.7 A and B.

contactor the moveable portion of a switch that, when activated, completes a circuit.

coupler a means by which the stops of one division of an organ may be played on another division. Couplers can couple at unison pitch, at the higher octave pitch (4' couplers) or at the lower octave pitch (16' couplers). There are also intramanual couplers allowing the stops within a single division to play either an octave higher or an octave lower.

crescendo pedal a large pedal directly above the pedal keyboard and to the right which brings on a predetermined order of stops from piano to double forte. Once set by the builder, the order of stops cannot be easily altered. The crescendo functions in a blind fashion (i.e., stop tabs or knobs do not move).

cuneiform bellows wedge shaped bellows. See **diagonal bellows**.

curtain valve a means of controlling the entrance of air from the blower. As the reservoir rises, it lifts a device similar to an inverted window shade. In so doing it restricts the air from the main wind duct in direct proportion to its use by the organ.

cut-up the relationship between the height of the mouth of a labial pipe to its width.

cycle for the purpose here, a single complete vibration. As diagrammed as a sine curve, a particle moves from the neutral point to the maximum amplitude on the positive side, returns to neutral, moves to the maximum amplitude on the minus side, and then returns to neutral. See Figure 8.1.

cymbal (Ger. *Zimbel*) a high pitched mixture in the plenum.

cymbelstern (Ger. *Zimbelstern*) a toy stop consisting of bells, normally four in number, actuated by a rotating wheel.

diagonal bellows a common form of bellows triangular in cross section. Also known as a **cunieform bellows**. See Figures 2.3 and 2.4.

diapason in American usage the term normally denotes an 8' principal. In English usage it refers to two stops the **stopped diapason** and the **open diapason.** These are often used together under the plural form, diapasons.

difference tone see **combination tones**

digital information the reduction of information to a series of ones and zeros which constitute the language of computers and other electronic devices.

diode a solid state device which allows current to flow in one direction but impedes it in the other.

direct action (also Direct Electric Action, trademark of the Wicks Organ Co.) a form of electric organ action in which each pipe has its own solenoid operated valve. These are directly wired to the key and stop action without intervening pneumatics or mechanics.

direct current (abbreviated DC) current that does not oscillate as does **alternating current.** Low voltage direct current is used in the vast majority of organ circuits. AC is normally used only for lighting, the blower, and the **rectifier**.

Direct Electric Action see **direct action**

divided chest a chest partitioned to allow for divided stops. The division normally takes place between b and c1 or c1 and c sharp1.

divided stop a stop divided so that its bass register can be played independently from its treble and its treble independently from its bass. See **divided chest**.

division a major section of an organ generally provided with its own manual and chest. A three manual organ will normally have four divisions three for the manuals and one for the pedal.

Dolcan an open flute stop with a slight conical flare from the mouth to the top of the pipe.

Doppelflüte a stopped flute with two mouths, one on each side of the wooden pipe.

doublette French name for a 2' principal.

drumstick coupler a form of mechanical coupler consisting of rods with rounded projections on one end. When activated by the stop knob, these projections are jammed between the keys of both manuals involved. See Figure 7.1.

duplexing the use of one stop native to a single manual on another manual or on the pedal. Also known as borrowing.

ears flap shaped projections of pipe metal soldered on the right and left of the mouths of pipes. These are used to focus the sound of the pipe and in some cases for tuning.

echo a small division of an organ sometimes completely encased or, in other situations, equipped with shutters.

edge tones the random sounds produced when wind passes around sharp impediments. Edge tones activate the air molecules in a labial pipe into vibration.

electric action an organ with electric connections for both the key and stop actions.

electromagnet a soft iron core surrounded by a coil of wire. When a current is induced in the coil it magnetizes the iron core. When the current ceases, the magnetism also ceases. **Solenoid** is another name for an electromagnet.

electro-mechanical action an organ action which in one way or another combines mechanical and electrical elements. The action normally used by the Austin Organ Company (see Chapter 5) is a good example.

electro-pneumatic an organ action that combines pneumatic and electrical elements.

en chamade a term denoting reeds mounted horizontally in front of an organ case.

enharmonic diesis the difference between an octave derived by superimposing three major thirds (5:4 × 5:4 × 5:4) and an octave derived from the overtone series (2:1).

equal temperament a temperament in which in each of the perfect fifths around the key circle is flattened by one-twelfth of the **Pythagorean comma**. Save for the pitch difference, all keys are equal.

exposed pipework pipework standing in the open within the room in which it is to sound without any surrounding chamber or case.

fan frame an assembly of **backfalls**, one for each note of a manual. These run from each manual key to its appropriate pull down on the chest. Since the distance between two pipes on the chest is much greater than the distance from one key to the next, the backfalls take the shape of a fan. The fan frame is used in lieu of a **roller board**. See Figure 3.22.

feeder bellows a bellows which is fed directly from the wind source which provides a stable wind supply to the entire wind system. Its pressure is higher than the secondary bellows it feeds.

feelers thin spring wires, often mounted in a wooden block, designed to carry an electric signal. In order to prevent corrosion due to **arcing**, these are most often made of silver. See Figure 4.7A.

fiber optic cable a cable made of exceedingly fine glass strands capable of carrying **digital information**. These are now at times used for connections between console and chest.

fifteenth English name for the 2' principal. The name derives from the fact that its pitch lies a fifteenth (double octave) above the fundamental.

fixed pitch instruments instruments such as the piano, harp, and organ over which the performer does not exercise immediate control of the tuning or pitch of a note.

flap valve a common form of **check valve**.

flexible winding a winding system which is intentionally designed to be slightly unstable. The player must be sensitive to this instability, and, when large demands are placed on the wind supply, modify his playing accordingly. He is said to be "playing the wind."

floating stop a stop which appears on more than a single manual. It essentially has no parent keyboard. A large, high pressure trumpet is a common floating stop and may be available on all manuals and the pedal.

flue pipe a pipe which produces its sound by coupling the **edge tones** with the body of the pipe. Also known as a **labial** pipe. Both names derive from the flue formed by the **languid** and the lip of the pipe. The majority of pipes on an organ of any size are flue pipes.

flute an entire family of organ pipes which, at least superficially, are similar in quality to flutes. The family has great diversity. The pipes are generally of wide scale. Some are stopped and others are open.

flute triangulaire an open, wooden flute stop with pipes which are triangular in cross section.

forzando a device which instantaneously actuates the majority of the stops of an organ. It is actuated either by a toe stud or **piston** and functions in a blind fashion (i.e., stop tabs or knobs do not move).

freestanding case essentially a piece of large furniture, sometimes ornately embellished, in which an entire organ (save sometimes the wind supply) is contained. Such cases require no other means of support.

French mouth a more elegant mouth than the **bay leaf mouth**. It is oval in shape. See Figure 9.9.

frequency the number of cycles per second (**hertz**) of a wave. The frequency of audible sound is normally regarded as approximately 20 to 20,000 Hz.

full length resonator a reed pipe with a resonator approximately as long as its nominal designation (i.e., an 8' reed will have a resonator approximately eight feet in length).

full organ another name for the **forzando**.

fundamental a sound generating an overtone series. The fundamental is the first **partial**.

gang switch a switch with multiple contacts designed to close multiple circuits with a single motion. There will normally be as many incoming circuits as there are outgoing ones.

Gedeckt (Ger. for covered) the most common designation for a stopped flute.

Geigen (Ger. for violin) a generic name for a string stop.

Gemshorn an open flute stop with a something of a string quality. Its pipes are tapered.

generator for the purpose of organ building, a device to produce **direct current** (DC) by revolving an armature within a coil of wire. These are often used in older organ installations and derive their power from the blower motor. Now DC current for organs is normally produced by **rectifiers**.

glockenspiel a toy stop consisting of tuned metal bars struck by hammers.

Gothic mouth another name for **bay leaf mouth**.

grave mixture a plenum mixture emphasizing lower pitches.

great the central division of an organ containing, among other stops, the principal chorus.

groove in a slider chest, the channel which runs from front to back under a single note. There are as many grooves as there are notes on the chest. One groove is separated from the next by a **bar**.

guide pins on a manual keyboard, the pins which keep the keys in alignment.

harmonic bridge a type of hardware placed across the mouths of string pipes in order to stabilize their sound.

harmonic flute an open flute of considerable power made either of wood or metal. From tenor f upward the pipes are approximately twice their expected length. A small hole is pierced about halfway up the body of the pipe to cause them to overblow at the octave.

harp a toy stop consisting of a row of tuned metal bars, each provided with a resonator tuned to its pitch. It is struck with hammers. There is no connection between the orchestral harp and this stop, which belongs to the percussion family.

hertz designation for a single cycle per second. Abbreviated Hz. 440 Hz equals 440 cycles per second or a '.

Hohlflöte (Ger. hollow flute) The term may refer either to the bland quality of the stop or the fact that it is made of open pipes. An 8' flute often used on the great organ. It has the capacity to blend well with other stops.

hoofdwerk Dutch for great organ.

horizontal reeds (reeds *en chamade*) These are reed pipes mounted horizontally generally in the front of the organ case. Since a large part of the sound of a reed pipe emanates from the end of the pipe, such reeds have a particularly strong presence.

identity of the octave the fact that the two tones of an octave have identical overtone series merely an octave apart. The two overtone series have no dissonant conflicts.

instrument a tool. A musical instrument is merely a musical tool.

inverted V chest a chest with the longest pipe in the center with C and C-sharp sides moving downward to the left and right. Sometimes knows as the A chest.

junction block a block at which two cables join. See Figure 4.12.

key one of the levers by which the performer plays the organ. Sets of keys designed to be played with the hands are called **manuals**; those designed to be played with the feet constitute the **pedalboard**.

key channel chest a chest in which the major divisions called channels run from the front of the chest to its back. Each key has its own channel. Also known as a **note channel chest**.

key circle see **circle of fifths**

key contact an electrical contact activating the circuit connecting that key with the key action of the chest.

keyboard one of the **manuals** or the **pedalboard**.

Klang the fundamental and its overtones of any musical sound.

Koppelflöte a partially stopped flute pipe. Its pipes are cylindrical for about two thirds of their length and then taper to a small hole at the top.

Krummhorn (Fr. cromorne) a cylindrical, half length reed imitative of the Renaissance instrument of the same name. It is the ancestor of the **clarinet** stop.

labial pipe a **flue pipe**.

languid the thick metal plate in a flue pipe separating the foot from the body of the pipe.

lever a bar to which are added three elements: the fulcrum about which it revolves, the force applied to it, and the weight which it moves. There are three classes of levers that depend upon the order of these elements on the bar. See Figure 3.1.

Lieblichgedeckt a small scaled stopped flute.

lingual pipe a reed pipe.

Ludwigstöne a unique flute stop in which a pipe is divided lengthwise into what are in essence two pipes. Each section is provided with its own mouth and sounds independently. One section is slightly sharpened to produce a **celeste** stop from a single rank.

machine stop a pre-set combination activated by a pedal generally bringing on the upper work on small antique organs.

manometer a simple tool for measuring wind pressure consisting of a glass tube bent in an S shape and partially filled with water. See Chapter 2.

manual a set of keys designed to be played with the hands. Also called clavier.

mechanical action an organ action in which the connections between key and chest, and stop knob and chest, function solely by means of mechanical linkages. Also known as tracker action.

mechanical pneumatic action an organ action in which mechanical and pneumatic elements are both used. See Figure 1.3.

melodia a wooden open flute stop of sweet sound. Its lowest octave is frequently made of stopped pipes.

mitered pipes pipes which have been angled in order to cut their overall height. See Chapter 9.

mixture a multi-rank stop playing a combination of pitches which reinforce the overtone structure of the fundamental. See Chapter 9.

module a unified component and, in organ design, generally an electronic component.

montre French term for the principal pipes in the facade of the great organ.

Nachthorn a mild flute stop generally at 4' pitch, sometimes made with open pipes and sometimes with stopped ones.

nazard (Fr.) an open flute pipe of 2⅔' pitch. A part of the cornet.

nicking a voicing technique whereby tiny grooves are cut into the face of the languid to control the transient sounds occurring at the beginning of pipe speech.

node in a cyclical wave, the point at which there is the maximum movement of particles. See anti-node.

note channel chest another name for key channel chest.

Oberwerk the upper case of a German organ built on the ***Werkprinzip***.

oboe a very common reed stop on American organs. It is similar to a small scale trumpet. The stop is not imitative, and hence is not the same stop as the orchestral oboe.

octave the 4' principal on the manual. Sometimes the 8' principal in the pedal is so designated.

octave coupler an intra-manual coupler playing notes an octave higher than the parent key.

offset chest a small chest set away from the main chest generally supporting a single stop or the bass pipes of a stop.

one-way valve see **check valve**

open diapason the English designation for an principal stop generally at 16' or 8' pitch.

open pipe a labial pipe that is open at the top, as opposed to a **stopped pipe**, which is closed. All principal, some flutes, and most string pipes are open.

overblown pipe a pipe which sounds its first overtone (second partial) rather than the fundamental. Overblowing in pipes may occur due to improper voicing or may be intentional in the case of some stops. See **harmonic flute**.

overtone series the predictable pattern of pitches that, to some degree or other, is present above a **fundamental** sounding pitch. The series is the basis for intervalic ratios for all perfect, major, and minor intervals. See Chapter 8 and Figure 8.3. Also see **partial**.

pallet in a slider chest, a rectangular, hinged, and spring loaded valve that is connected to a pull-down from the key action and that admits wind into a groove. The pallets are contained in the pallet box at the bottom of the chest. They can be accessed by opening the **bung**.

parallel wiring a series of electrical circuits so wired that each circuit receives equal voltage. This is the type of wiring present in organ circuitry. The antithesis to parallel wiring is **series wiring** in which each circuit receives only fractional voltage. Series wiring is never used in organ building. See Chapter 4.

partial a single element in the overtone series. The **fundamental** is the first partial, the first overtone is the second partial, the second overtone the third partial, etc. See Figure 8.3, where the partials are numbered.

pedal organ the division of the organ actuated by the pedal board. Many organs, some of large size, have only rudimentary pedal divisions. Others have very complete divisions.

pedalboard the keyboard designed to be played with the feet.

pipe metal see **common metal.**

pipe scale the relationship between the diameter of a pipe and its length.

pipe shades in an organ case, the ornamental carvings which fill out the space between the tops of the facade pipes and the ceiling of the case. A questionable assertion has been made that pipe shades affect the quality of the sound.

piston one of the buttons, attached either to the manuals or the pedalboard, that actuate the combination action.

pitman strictly speaking, the small, leaden valves in a **pitman chest**.

pitman chest a highly developed form of stop channel chest which has the advantage of almost instantaneous combination changes. See Chapter 5 and Figure 5.20.

playing desk another name for the **console**.

plenum the principal choruses of all manuals coupled together and to the pedal. Flute stops are sometimes added and even **tierce** sounding ranks are sometimes specified.

pneumatic small bellows designed to make very quick movements. They may be used as pipe valves or to actuate many other devices, such as key action.

pneumatic action a largely obsolete form of organ action in which the connection between key and pipe valve is operated by air pressure. Since these connections were made via small leaden tubing, the action is sometimes called tubular pneumatic action. See Figure 1.2 and accompanying text.

pneumatic assist a device for providing additional force to mechanical key action. See **Barker lever**.

Posaune (Ger. trombone) a 16' pedal reed stop of the trumpet class.

positif de dos French for **chair organ**.

positive organ an important secondary division on many American organs. Generally it does not stand in its traditional position behind the performer. If the great organ is based on an 8' principal, the positive will most likely be based on a 4' principal.

pouch another name for a small **pneumatic**.

prestant Although it originally referred to pipes in the facade, it now generally refers to the 4' principal on the great.

primary action the portion of an electro-pneumatic action which activates the pipe valves themselves. It depends upon small solenoids drawing little current that open passages that, in turn, deflate pipe pneumatics.

principal chorus all the principals on the great organ or, by extension the **plenum**.

pulldown the wire connecting the mechanical linkages from the key to the pallets of a slider chest.

Pythagorean comma the difference in pitch between the B sharp derived by moving around the key circle in perfect fifths and the C with which one began.

Quintadena or *Quintaton* a small scaled, stopped flute pipe voiced to emphasize the third partial.

rack boards boards, one for each stop, set about six inches above the toe board of a chest. These are carefully drilled to support the pipes at that height. The boards are set on rack-pins that fit into aligned holes drilled both into them and into the top boards.

rank a single staggered row of pipes running laterally across a chest. Pipes of a single rank belong to the same stop. Most stops have only a single rank. Mixtures, however, have multiple ranks. A thirty stop organ may thus have thirty-six ranks.

rectifier a device for converting AC current to DC and to step line voltage (220 v. or 110 v.) down to that used in organ circuits (c. 12 v.). Rectifiers, which are now more efficient and reliable than **generators**, now have replaced them in this function. Rectifiers are normally contained in steel boxes and set near the AC power source for the organ.

reed pipe organ pipes which produce their sound by coupling the vibration of a metal reed with a pipe serving as a resonator. They constitute one of the two principal classes of organ pipes, the other being flue pipes, also known as **labial** pipes.

regal reed pipes with unusually short resonators. One-quarter and one-eighth lengths are not unusual. In most American organs, the only regal one is likely to encounter is the ubiquitous vox humana.

relay a switching device by which a single circuit can activate numerous other circuits. See Figure 4.9.

reservoir a large bellows under pressure which supplies secondary bellows as the need arises.

resonator in a reed pipe, the portion above the boot. The resonator and the reed itself form an acoustical coupling, producing the right pitch and timbre. Resonators take all manner of shapes, each contributing to the quality of the stop.

resultant tone an acoustically produced tone whose frequency is determined by the subtraction of the frequencies of the two tones that produce it. For instance, two tones sounding 300Hz and 200Hz will have a resultant with a frequency of 100Hz. The phenomenon of resultant tones is used in acoustically producing 32' stops. See **combination tones**.

reversible switch a switch when activated the first time is on and when actuated again is off.

rheostat a device for regulating the strength of the current in a circuit by controlling the resistance in the circuit.

Rohrflöte (Eng. chimney flute) a partially stopped, wide scaled flute. If in metal, short tubes are soldered to the cap. If in wood, the chimneys are formed by drilling through the stopper handle. See figures 9.12 and 9.13.

roller board a large, monolithic board supporting rods that in mechanical action transfer motion laterally. Its purpose is to spread the action from narrow key width to the much larger chest width. See Figure 3.23.

rossignol a toy stop constructed of two inverted pipes of high pitch blowing into a container of water. It is designed to imitate the sound of birds.

rotary blower see **centrifugal blower**

Rückpositiv the division of an organ placed immediately behind the performer and often hung over a balcony rail. Eng. **chair organ**. See Figure 10.1.

rugwerk Dutch for *Rückpositiv*.

run the unwanted bleeding of air from one groove of a slider chest to its neighbor.

scale see **pipe scale**

scharf a high pitched **plenum** mixture.

series wiring a series of electrical circuits in which all elements consuming electrical power are along a continuous circuit, with each element receiving only fractional voltage.

sesquialtera a two rank solo mixture consisting of a 2⅔' (**nazard**) and a 1⅗' (**tierce**).

setterboard a simple and highly reliable type of combination action. The player sets his or her combinations by setting **toggle switches**. See Figure 7.11 and surrounding text.

seventeenth the tenth partial in the overtone series. It lies two octaves and a third above the fundamental.

shallot in a reed pipe, the modified tube affixed to the block against which the reed is placed. The reed vibrates against the flattened side of the shallot. See Figures 8.17 and 8.18.

short octave the modification of the order of keys of the lowest octave on many antique organs. The most common modification was the omission of C♯ and D♯. See Figure 3.7.

simple harmonic motion motion which is predictable and cyclical. A pendulum is an example.

sine curve for the purpose of this book, a graphic form of the wave of **simple harmonic motion**. There is first a movement to maximum displacement, second, a return to the neutral point, third, a move to minimum displacement, and finally a return to the neutral point. See Chapter 8 and Figure 8.1.

slide tuning a common method of tuning open flue pipes. Each pipe has affixed to its end a tight fitting, metal, circular slider. By moving it upwards, the pipe can be flattened; by moving it downwards the pipe can be sharpened.

slider in a slider chest, the drilled slats, generally of wood, that are activated by the stop action which moves them laterally. Sliders lie in recesses between the **table** and the **toe boards**. They are carefully drilled to match the drillings in the toe board. Each stop has its own slider.

slider chest See **slider**. The slider chest is characteristic of mechanical action, but may be used with other forms of action as well.

solenoid an **electromagnet**.

solid-state switching switching that is done electronically as opposed to that done electro-mechanically.

Spanish trumpets see **horizontal reeds**

spidering the shallow grooves cut around the drilling in the table of a slider chest to prevent **runs**. See Figure 5.10.

Spitzflöte (Ger. pointed flute) a partially stopped flute with pipes in the shape of inverted cones. The stop is similar to the *gemshorn*.

spring chest an early form of mechanical chest. It uses a complicated combination of small pallets, springs, and stickers in lieu of the slider mechanism. See Section 5.9 and Figure 5.16.

square a type of mechanical hardware in the shape of a right angle pivoted at its vertex. The purpose of a square is to turn motion by 90 degrees.

squirrel cage blower see **centrifugal blower**.

static pressure the wind pressure produced by the blower itself before it is stepped down for use in the various parts of the organ.

sticker a component of mechanical action made generally of wooded rods. This component is used only in compression (i.e., it is used in a pushing, not a pulling, motion).

stop a set of pipes of the same type and quality. More often than not a stop will contain one pipe per note of the keyboard to which it belongs. Some stops, however, do not run the entire length of a keyboard. Others, called **mixtures** or **celestes**, have more than one pipe per note. See **rank**.

stop channel chest a chest in which the main channels run lengthwise through the chest. Each stop has its own channel. When a stop is drawn, its channel is winded. If a stop is not drawn, the channel is remains at atmospheric pressure.

stop knob rounded projections attached to the rods which initiate the stop action. These are manipulated by the performer to change registrations.

stop tab another form of stop controls used in electric stop action. See Figure 4.15B.

stopped diapason English name for a *Gedeckt*.

stopped pipe one in which the top of the pipe is closed. Stopped pipes sound an octave lower than their actual length might suggest. Thus the pipe for the lowest note of a *Gedeckt* 8' is approximately four feet in length.

stopper that which closes the end of a stopped pipe. If the pipe is of wood, the stopper is also of wood. Stoppers are lined with leather or felt to achieve a tight fit inside the pipe. If the pipe is of metal, the stopper is a tight fitting can lined with felt slid over the end of the pipe. Stopped pipes are tuned by changing the position of their stoppers.

summation tone resultant tones which are the summation of the two frequencies that make them up. Hence a frequency of 200Hz and another of 100Hz will produce a summation tone of 300Hz. Summation tones are a matter for the physics lab. They have no use in music.

super coupler a coupler coupling notes an octave higher to their parent notes. It is also known as a 4' coupler.

superoctave the designation for a 2' principal generally on the great organ.

suspended action an extremely sensitive type of mechanical action involving the least possible number of connections between key and pallet. Actually, the key, which is a second class lever, literally hangs on the pallet and is returned by the pallet spring. See figures 3.6. and 3.26.

swell box in an optimal situation, the tight wooden box containing the swell division. At least one face of it is provided with shutters.

swell division a major division of an organ contained in a swell box or a swell chamber.

swell engine a device for actuating swell shutters. See Chapter 7.

swell pedal one of the large pedals directly above the pedal board used to operate the swell shutters.

switch a device for opening or closing one or more electric circuits. There are many types and sizes of electrical switches.

syntonic comma the difference between a major third derived from adding two in-tune major seconds (9:8 × 9:8) and the major third derived from the overtone series (5:4).

table in a slider chest the monolithic board which is glued to the bars which form the grooves. The table is drilled in the pattern of the pipes the chest will support. Its top surface is **spidered** to prevent runs. Immediately on top of the table are the sliders and the bearers. See Figures 5.6, 5.7, and 5.8.

temperament in setting the **bearing** in tuning, any of various systems to disperse the **Pythagorean comma**. See Chapter 8.

tierce French term for a stop sounding the fifth partial. The 1⅗' stop.

toe board the top board of a chest which directly supports the pipes.

toe holes the openings at the base of pipes through which wind is admitted. Their diameters can be altered in voicing.

toggle switch a two position switch. When moved in one direction the circuit it controls is on; when moved in the other direction the circuit is off.

tongue the actual reed in a reed pipe.

toy stop any of the many sounding additions to an organ which are not conventional winded pipes. Many are percussive: **glockenspiel**, drums, *Zimbelstern*, etc.

tracker thin strips, generally of wood, which span all lengthy distances in a mechanical action. These are used only in tension. They are so ubiquitous in **mechanical action** that it is often termed "tracker action."

transistor a solid state component which, for the purposes of organ building, can be used as a simple switch. See Chapter 4 and Figure 4.17.

tremblant à vent perdu (Fr. tremulant with lost wind) a type of tremulant in which small puffs of wind are periodically exhausted into atmosphere. See Figure 2.12. and surrounding text.

tremblant doux (Fr. gentle tremulant) a tremulant which places a slight wavering impediment in the wind line. See Figure 2.11.

tremulant a device to produce a slight waver or trembling in the wind.

trumpet one of the most common reed stops. It normally has full length, conical resonators.

tuba (Latin for trumpet) a designation for a trumpet stop, often for a 16' one in the pedal.

tuba mirabilis, *tuba magna* designations for a trumpet stop of large scale and high wind pressure.

tubular chimes a toy stop consisting of tuned bells in the form of pipes struck by hammers.

tubular pneumatic action see **pneumatic action**

tuning wire on a reed pipe, the wire entering the top of the **block**. By tapping it down, one sharpens the pipe. By lifting it one flattens the pipe.

turbine see **centrifugal blower**

twelfth a 2⅔' (sometimes improperly labeled 3') stop sounding the third partial.

unda maris a soft **celeste** stop.

under expression a division of the organ contained behind swell shutters.

unification the derivation of two or more stops from a single rank of pipes.

unison off a device, usually associated with octave couplers, which negates the unison sounding pitches of a manual. If the unison off is pulled without other couplers, the manual becomes mute.

unit chest a direct action chest normally supporting a number of stops depending on unification. See Chapter 5.

unit organ an organ depending almost entirely on **unification**. See Chapter 6.

Universal Wind Chest the idiosyncratic wind chest used exclusively by the Austin Organ Company. It depends on a combination of electric and mechanical elements. See Chapter 5.

V order a chest in which the two longest pipes are at the left and right ends. The pipes descend in whole tones to the shortest pipes in the middle of the chest. See Figure 5.4.

ventil a large valve admitting air into a section of a chest. Some ventils admit air into a significant portion of a division, such as a section containing the reeds and mixtures. Others admit air into a single stop channel.

ventil chest a chest in which each stop channel is provided with its own ventil.

viole celeste a common two rank **celeste** stop of string pipes.

viole d'orchestre a string stop imitative of the orchestral violin.

violin diapason a small scale **principal** pipe with a string quality. Since it so versatile, it is often used as the 8' principal on a secondary manual.

voicing the art of making organ pipes speak appropriately. See Chapter 9.

voix celeste see *viole celeste*

voltage the force pushing electrons through a circuit, as opposed to **amperage**, which is the actual amount of current flowing through the circuit.

vox humana the only stop of the **regal** class found with any frequency on American organs. See Figure 9.18 and surrounding text.

well temperament a class of **temperaments** in which all keys are not equally satisfactory but all are useable. The Kirnberger temperament described in the text is an example. See Chapter 8.

Werkprinzip a form of organ design in which each division is placed in its own case. One division is generally behind the performer, the *Rückpositiv*, and the others are stacked one atop another. Each division has its own facade pipes which are a clear indication of the function of that division. Pedal pipes are normally placed in towers on the sides of the stacked cases. This type of organ was characteristic of north Germany in the seventeenth century.

whipple tree swell engine a form of **swell engine** actuated by exhausting multiple small pneumatics one at a time. See Figure 7.18 and accompanying text.

windway the path wind takes entering a **flue** pipe, particularly the slit between the lip of the pipe and the **languid**.

winker bellows see **concussion bellows**

Zimbelstern a **toy stop** consisting of four or more small bells actuated by a rotating hammer.

Bibliography

Amerongen, C. van (translator). *The Way Things Work*. 2 vols. New York: Simon and Schuster, 1967 and 1971.

Audsley, George Ashdown. *The Art of Organ Building*. 2 vols., 1905. Reprint, New York: Dover Publications, 1965. (Abbreviated in the text as *Audsley I* and *Audsley II*.)

_____. *The Organ of the Twentieth Century*. 1919. Reprint, New York: Dover Publications, 1970. (Abbreviated in the text as *Audsley III*.)

Barnes: William Harrison. *The Contemporary American Organ*. 8th ed. Glen Rock, N.J.: J. Fischer and Bro., 1964.

Bédos de Celles, Dom François. *The Organ Builder*. 2 vols. Translated by Charles Ferguson. Raleigh, N.C.: Sunbury Press, 1977. (Abbreviated in the text *Dom Bédos*.)

Blanton, Joseph Edwin. *The Organ in Church Design*. Albany, Texas: Venture Press, 1957.

_____. *The Revival of the Organ Case*. Albany, Texas: Venture Press, 1965.

Bonavia, Hunt. *The Organ Reed*. New York: J. Fischer, 1950.

Donahue, Thomas. *The Modern Classical Organ*. Jefferson, N.C.: McFarland & Company, 1991.

Douglass, Fenner. *The Language of the Classical French Organ*. New Haven: Yale University Press, 1969.

Fesperman, John. *Two Essays on Organ Design*. Raleigh, N.C.: Sunbury Press, 1975.

Holtdt, Ingrid, and others. *Roskilde Domkirkes Orgel (Concert Program)*. Roskilde, Denmark, 1991.

Jorgensen, Owen. *The Equal-Beating Temperaments*. Raleigh, N.C.: Sunbury Press, 1981.

Klotz, Hans. *The Organ Handbook*. Saint Louis: Concordia Publishing House, 1969.

Lewis, Walter, and Thomas Lewis. *Modern Organ Building*. London: William Reeves Bookseller, 1939.

Peterson Electro Musical Products, Inc. *Organ Control Systems*. www.Petersonemp.com, 2000.

Randel, Don Michael, editor. *The Harvard Dictionary of Music*, 4th ed. Cambridge, Mass.: Belknap Press of Harvard University Press, 2003.

Soderland, Sandra. *A Guide to the Pipe Organ*. Colfax, N.C.: Wayne Leupold Editions, 1994.

Whitworth, Reginald. *The Electric Organ*. 3rd ed. London: Musical Opinion Ltd., 1948.

Williams, Peter, and Barbara Owen. *The Organ, The New Grove Musical Instruments Series*. New York: W.W. Norton, 1988.

Winter, Helmut, editor. *Die Schnitger-Orgel in Cappel*. Hamburg, Germany: Verlag Karl Dieter Wagner, 1977.

Wright, Michael, and M.N. Patel, editors. *How Things Work Today*. New York: Crown Publishers, 2000.

Index

189